Calm Mind, Perfect Ease

Venerable Hsin Ting

Buddha's Light Publications, Los Angeles

By Venerable Hsin Ting
Edited by Venerable Miao Hsi and Mark Ragsdale
Cover design by Wilson Yau
Book design by Mark Ragsdale
Translated by Fo Guang Shan International Translation Center

Published by Buddha's Light Publications, USA Corp.
3139 S. Hacienda Blvd.
Hacienda Heights, CA 91745, U.S.A.
Tel: (626) 961-9876 Fax: (626) 961-4321
E-mail: info@blpusacorp.com
Website: www.blpusacorp.com

Originally published as xinding zizai（心定自在）by Mega Idea Co Ltd., 2016.

ISBN: 978-1-944271-40-4
Library of Congress Control Number: 2019945029

Table of Contents

Acknowledgement

We would like to take this opportunity to thank the many people who contributed to this project of Buddha's Light Publications. We especially appreciate the efforts of Venerable Tzu Jung, President of Buddha's Light Publications. Special thanks to Fo Guang Shan International Translation Center's Executive Director, Venerable Yi Chao, for her invaluable advice and assistance. We would also like to thank Venerable Hui Dong, Abbot of Hsi Lai Temple, for his support and leadership.

We would also like to thank Fo Guang Shan International Translation Center for the translation, Wilson Yau for the cover design, and Venerable Miao Hsi along with Mark Ragsdale for editing and book design. Our appreciation also goes to everyone who has supported this project from conception to completion.

Resolving Worries from the Perspective of Dharma

Venerable Huei-kai

The Most Venerable Hsin Ting is an elder Dharma brother who I respect deeply. It can be said that in the current Buddhist world, he is the rare monastic who surpasses the decathlon of a Dharma teacher. From speaking the Dharma, Buddhist chanting, Water and Land Dharma Service or Yogacara Ceremony, Dharma service liturgy, administration of Dharma functions, writing books, composing lyrics, calligraphy, temple construction, to social education etc. all of which he is an expert in, a true master in both letter and the sword. People like myself are left in the dust in comparison.

In addition, his states of compassion, endurance, tolerance, gentleness, acceptance, and non-differentiating are such that people like me have no comparison. Anyone asking him for anything, he'd never say no. A well-known "Mr. Nice Guy," he has the heart and mind of a bodhisattva. Though he has a wealth of experience and seniority, he never put on airs and instead, is always very amiable and personable.

While he has been busy year round with Dharma service administration, the Most Venerable Hsin Ting never forgets to practice. He delves deep into the sutras and has a very thorough realization and understanding of "dependent origination and nature of emptiness." He has deep practice of the "right view of dependent origination" within *The Connected Discourses,* while actively actualizing it in his daily living.

This book, *Calm Mind, Perfect Ease* consists of his cultivation insights of many years which combines meditation and emotion management in eleven chapters. The book focuses on explaining the various issues of the body and mind of modern people, employing the "right view of dependent origination" within *The Connected Discourses* as the medicine for treating different kinds of worries arising from the body and mind and attaining the state of calm mind and perfect ease.

The key to cultivation in Buddhism is no other than the three learnings of precept, concentration, and wisdom; and the three wisdoms of hearing, contemplation, and practice. The actual application of practice is none other than the three karmas of body, speech, and mind and the six sense bases of eyes, ears, nose, tongue, body, and mind. In the book, the Most Venerable Hsin Ting provides easy to understand instructions on how to apply the meanings within *The Connected Discourses* in our everyday living; how to purify the mind and reduce stress, how to cultivate mindfulness, how to apply efforts on precept, concentration, and wisdom as well as hearing, contemplation, and practice; how to transform our three karmas and six sense bases; how to reduce worries to depart from suffering to gain happiness; and how to cease emotions of anxiety. All of which are lessons in life which modern people urgently need to learn and practice.

I thank the Most Venerable Hsin Ting for sharing his precious insights and experience with all of us. May I offer my blessings to all readers for gaining benefits within the Dharma, and at the same time, allow their body and mind to settle, through precept, concentration, and wisdom; as well as hearing, contemplation, and practice!

Venerable Huei-kai is the Vice Abbot of Fo Guang Shan Buddhist Order, professor of Life-and-Death Study, and Vice President of Nanhua University, Taiwan

Press the Stop Button, then Even the Fastest Blowing Fan will Stop

Venerable Hsin Ting

In 2005, I wrote the book, *Meditation and Wisdom* based on the cultivation in the meditation hall; readers found the content very practical and later the English translation of the book was made available. The book was recognized in 2015 by the Jenkins Group Living Now Book Award as the Gold Medal winner of Best Book in Meditation and Relaxation.

In other words, whether it is people in the East or the West, they have always been greatly interested in Buddhism, taking it very seriously. Many bestsellers in recent years have selected perspectives and made elaborations with emphasis on daily living. For instance, *The Secret* expounds on mental strength; *Power of Mindfulness* focuses on the Noble Eightfold Path; *The Diamond Cutter* is based upon the emptiness principles for strategy making; *The Five People You Meet in Heaven* talks about the phenomenon of transmigration; *Full Catastrophe Living* clearly explains the importance of"right thought" as practice in the preface.

The Buddha was born in the world, he further renounced, attained enlightenment, and taught in the world; all the Dharma the Buddha spoke to people are teachings beneficial for a life of happiness. In my humble opinion, the happiest matter in life is having no attachments or obstacles in the mind. Hence, whether it is people who learn Buddhism or those who do not, they need to learn to manage their emotions and learn the principle of causality, believing that all phenomena in the world arise due to relevant conditions. This is the condition for my writing a follow-up book after *Meditation and Wisdom: Calm Mind, Perfect Ease ~ Lessons on Emotion Management in Combination with Meditation.*

I believe that the practice of meditation is the only method for managing emotions well. Through long-term psychological adjusting, and subduing to calm the mind; to focus the mind or to settle the mind for reaching single-mindedness with no confusion. Once our mind is not turning and changing in following external states and no longer influenced by what is happening externally, then we can influence what is around us and its atmosphere, further progressing to attain harmony in any inter-personal relationship.

However, how do we practice meditation? The Buddha told us we should contemplate our inhalation and exhalation, which is called *ānāpānasmṛti*, or practice of breath-counting. Looking after our breaths is indeed the simplest method of practice. Every day, just make use of ten to fifteen minutes; keep a pure mind and focus our consciousness through breathing, then we will immediately feel our body and mind getting lighter and relaxed. Over time, our cells will gradually transform and the body can sustain the state of ease.

It is worthy to mention that I use many *suttas* from the *Connected Discourses* in this book because I feel that this discourse has unique features relevant to the human world. It emphasizes cultivation based on practical issues of one's self and personal body and mind. They do not discuss mystique and do not depart from actual living.

In the past, people in general categorize the *Āgamas* as "Small Vehicle" Buddhism with self-liberation as the goal of practice. Actually, Small Vehicle Buddhism is the foundation of Mahayana Buddhism. After all, the cultivation methods of these *arhats* are the Law of Causality, principle of Dependent Origination, the Four Noble Truths, and the Noble Eightfold Path. The biggest difference is these *arhats*, on reaching the state of no further learning and realizing *nirvāṇa*, are unlike bodhisattvas who through their own vows and initiatives, or due to the blessings of buddhas with mindful protection and exhortation in extensively practicing the bodhisattva way. That is to say, bodhisattvas must have the foundation of an *arhat* and also know how to subdue one's body and mind through meditation. It is said in the *Mahaprajñā Sutra:* "Bodhisattvas mahasattvas cultivate *prajñāpāramitā,* having no attachments to all dharmas, can then enhance giving, pure precepts, tolerance, diligence, concentration, and *prajñā.*" Such is the principle.

Moreover, the "no attachments" of *arhats* is the eighth stage of bodhisattva path; within this stage there are not any thoughts. From here, it is the self-initiation of compassionate vows in extensively practicing all benevolent matters and universally benefitting all beings. We can say that it is only by following the teachings of the Buddha for *arhats*, which are the Noble Eightfold Path, the Three Dharma Seals, and Dependent Origination in order to reach this stage (eighth level). Therefore, arhat and bodhisattva have a close converging point, it is the key of discussion for the latter half of this book.

As for what is "great compassionate mind?" In the *Diamond Sutra section 3, The Heart of the Mahayana,* the Buddha said to Suhbuti, "Of all sentient beings, be they born of eggs, wombs, moisture, or transformation, or whether they have form, or no form, or whether they are able to perceive, or do not perceive, or are neither able to perceive nor not perceive, I cause them to enter *nirvāṇa* without remainder, liberating them." The meaning of which is regardless of what type of beings, I will think of all ways to help them accomplish Buddhahood, this is the most thorough vow of great compassion.

So how do we do that? Basically, we should practice the "three goodness and four givings:" do good deeds, speak good words, and think good thoughts; give others confidence, give others joy, give others hope, and give others convenience. In progressing further, it is to pray anytime, anywhere for all beings in the universe to be safe and at peace, free from fear or natural calamities; every thought in the mind is for the sake of sentient beings.

Emotion management is a lesson modern people must learn. Practicing meditation allows the mind and spirit to be calm; then furthering practice to cultivate our body, speech, and mind in order to eradicate worries and truly attain joy and happiness. People have worries is due the six sense organs of eyes, ears, nose, tongue, body, and mind frequently pursuing what can be seen, heard, felt, and known, giving rise to thoughts. Then tainted attachments that are unable to let go arise; the possessive cravings due to greed, anger, and delusion mire people deeply within, with no way to free themselves.

An electric fan turning at high speed, once the stop button is pressed, then no matter how fast the speed it is turning, the fan will slowly reduce speed till finally stops without moving. Emotions or worries are similar, if we know how to employ the wisdom within the mind to observe the nominal forms due to the combination of various causes and conditions, then we are able to "subdue the tiger and tame the dragon," transforming worries into happiness.

This book can only be completed with the support of many volunteers taking time to proofread with great care, for that I am most grateful. I would also like to thank Mega Idea Co Ltd., for their generosity in publishing the Chinese original and their professional planning. Finally, my blessings to all the readers: Have a calm mind and perfect ease, and be happy every day!

Chapter One
Purify the Mind and Reduce Stress: It All Begins with Breath-Counting

In the past, people often emphasized the results of their IQ testing scores; students with high IQ are generally seeking the best schools to attend and when seeking employment, only the best businesses could warrant promising futures. Eventually, people recognized that individuals with high IQ may not necessarily bring harmony to interpersonal affairs, hence many tragedies came about again and again; a few examples include committing homicide due to failed romances, suicide via carbon monoxide poisoning, or domestic violence. Upon further examination of the reasons behind this, all point toward people's inability to manage their own emotions and to reduce stress in a timely manner. In the end, they failed themselves.

Meditation: A Practice Strengthening Emotional Wisdom

In recent years, people have refocused on the importance of EQ or emotional quotient. This term EQ was first proposed by psychologist Peter Salovey and was meant to be an indicator to which degree people are able to control their emotions. Unlike IQ, individuals can improve their EQ through guidance.

From the Buddhist perspective, I think, cultivating meditative concentration is the most direct method. Through a long period of calming the mind, concentrating attention, and maintaining awareness we will no longer be influenced by external circumstances and our mind will not revolve around changing states. Buddhism does not hold a license on meditation and neither do monastics for that matter. Meditation is something that everyone can learn. Especially for people in a fast-paced, modern life, meditation might be even more necessary for mental and physical relaxation. The state of Chan is not lofty or out of reach, nor is it as magical or mystical as novels portray it to be. All it takes is a gentle attitude, cordial expression, and a non-wavering mind; you then have the definitive condition to cultivate Chan and meditative concentration.

Take more deep breaths to extinguish the fire of anger of the mind

Some people rarely follow the instructions of others because they are overly egotistical. These people are easily angered, ill-tempered, and often found scowling. Consequently, nobody dares to communicate, consult, or report to them. I once saw a minibus pass a full-sized bus, only to have the bus driver pull up next to the minibus and launch into an angry tirade against the driver. Is that necessary? As love and emotion take place in our daily lives; if there is neither emotional relief nor proper control, we will become as unstable as a ticking time bomb.

Once a young American drove to an intersection and saw an elderly woman who was preparing to cross the street. He stopped his car and courteously allowed her to pass before crossing the intersection. However, the elderly lady, being quite advanced in age was staggering slowly; the young driver lost his patience and rolled down his window barking, "Hey, grandma, could you hurry it up a bit?" In return, the elderly lady hollered back, "Youngster, haven't you heard the saying that 'from cradle to grave each step takes you one step closer to death?' What are you in such a hurry for, young man?"

Perhaps you might refute that by saying, "I just could not control myself!" When this happens, you may take a few deep breaths and make sure that your energy does not rise to the neck, head, forehead, or face areas; this is how you keep your composure. Instead, hold your energy at the lower abdomen so you maintain a cordial demeanor; this is how you sustain kindness. In Chinese, not getting angry is called *bù sheng qì*, meaning not giving rise to energy, and maintaining one's demeanor is called *chén de zhù qì*, as holding energy. See? If you conduct yourself in this manner, you will not get carried away by your emotions.

Attachments to Love Easily Bring about Depression

Perhaps you wonder, "How are emotions generated?" In fact, emotions are facets of love; joy, anger, sorrow, and pleasure. These are also known as desires or dreams which spark the pursuit of happiness, but it is also the source of suffering and sadness. For example, it is fun to play with a puppy, but if the puppy falls ill, there is sadness and when the puppy eventually dies, many pet owners shed a considerable amount of tears over the loss. Therefore, happiness and suffering are deeply rooted in desire; both are especially intertwined with love.

Love is resilient and tenacious; something that cannot be severed. I once read a report that a married couple had divorced and after a short while, the wife wanted to reconcile and get back together with the husband; unfortunately, the husband had decided to move on and no longer had the interest in starting over. The wife even went so far as to conspire with the daughter, filing a missing person's report in order to track him down. Eventually, the police were able to track him down, yet when the husband came to the police station, he expressed his resentment toward the relentless pursuit by the wife. The police also later learned of the truth regarding their family dynamics. There is a saying in Chinese which likens love to when the lotus root is broken, its clinging silk remains. This is used to describe how love is resilient, hard to let go of, and hard to sever.

Anxious at times about gains and losses, giving rise to resentments

Once emotions change, anxiety about gains and losses quickly follows. This applies to all phenomena seen, heard, smelled, tasted, or touched; whatever is in accordance with desire, delight, praise, and joy arise. Once acquired, one will guard the object of desire tightly and become afraid of its change or disappearance. Once lost, one will feel pain and sorrow, and for those living under this condition, emotions change constantly. The outward symptoms may be somewhat severe, or violent, or leave us elated, and at times grief-stricken, even putting us on the verge of a nervous breakdown.

Aside from the various facets of emotions of joy, anger, sorrow, pleasure, distress, suffering, and excitement, there are also some retaliatory forms of emotion. There was once a young storekeeper who installed a sound system in his store and put out very loud music. The owner of the neighboring store in the coffin-making business, came by to persuade him to lower the volume of his music. Not only did the young storekeeper not heed the request, he ended up raising the volume. Out of recourse, the coffin store owner decided also to install his own sound system. Given his line of work, he felt that he would counter the young storekeeper's antics with specially selected ballads like "Right Here Waiting," "Someday Soon," and "When Will I See You Again." This is a joke of course, but I am sure that you have come across similar situations where two parties fall into retaliatory emotional states.

Often thinking of this and that and cannot quiet down

Another kind of emotion is the tendency towards depression. Once there was an old man who bought himself a two-story house. He lived on the bottom floor and rented out the upper floor. One day a young man came to talk with him about renting the upper floor. The old man told him, "I won't charge you much for rent, but I have one condition; you must not be loud. I dislike having a lot of noise in the house." The young man nodded his head, promised he would not be noisy, and consented to the rental agreement. Everything was going well until one day the young man went out to his friend's birthday party. He got back quite late at night, and went to his room to get some rest. Exhausted, he flopped down on his bed, and was too tired to even move. He sloppily kicked off his shoes hitting something and made a loud thud. The next day before dawn, the old man came knocking on his door. The young man sleepily answered, "Yes? What is it?" The old man replied, "We agreed early on that while staying here, you wouldn't be noisy. Why did I hear loud thudding sounds late last night? You startled me awake and then I couldn't get back to sleep." The young man answered, "I'm sorry. Last night I was too tired to remove my shoes by hand, so I kicked them off instead. I guess the shoes must have hit the floor and made a loud noise. I promise it won't happen again." The landlord admonished, "Right, you must not ever do that again."

Some time passed and again the young man came home late at night. He went to his room to rest. Without thinking, he fell into his old habit and kicked off one shoe. Thud! He quickly snapped out of it and remembered that he might wake the old man downstairs. He then bent his other leg up and gently removed the remaining shoe with his hands. The next day, the old man stood outside his door again knocking away. The young man opened the door and immediately apologized by saying, "Sir, I'm so sorry. Last night I mindlessly kicked off one shoe which made a really loud noise, so I was really careful to gently remove the other shoe with my hands." The old man answered, "There are two shoes in a pair; after I heard the first thud, I kept waiting for you to kick off the other shoe!" This points out that a phrase, a sound, or an incident is enough to cause agitation or anger to arise in a person. Emotions are quite powerful indeed. Wouldn't you agree?

Here is another such story: Once there was a young man who had recently married. He came home from work, and as soon as he got through the door, his wife bombarded him with a series of questions and complaints, "Why are you getting back so late? I don't know who was on the upper floors watering plants; now our balcony is all wet..." She noticed that he had yet to respond, so she kept going, "Hey! Are you dead? Did you hear what I said?" She continued, "The refrigerator is still making the buzzing sound, didn't you call the repairman a few days ago to come fix it? Go help me tidy up the balcony." Later that night, the young man lied in bed sleeplessly and thought to himself, "I heard my mother-in-law is irksome just like my wife, and if my wife and I later have a daughter she could very well turn out to be nagging as well. If that happens, how will I ever get any peace?" If this emotion continues to embroil for a long period, the young man will eventually either seek a divorce or become depressed.

Emotions can have a direct impact on physical health. Fury damages the liver, nervousness damages the intestines and stomach, and repressing emotion may cause high blood pressure, physiological irregularity and other abnormalities. These situations are especially well known to experienced Chinese doctors. Therefore, I often say, purifying the mind is the first step towards better health!

Five Contemplations to Resolve Emotional Issues

Whether it is attachments to love or the ensuing depression, worries, anxiety, or frustration can be resolved through the practice of meditation. Through the process of meditation, different countermeasures can be used in accordance with the array of circumstances.

1. People that get angry easily, with their minds rooted in hatred

Counter anger by contemplating loving-kindness and compassion to expand our mental capacity. To cultivate loving-kindness and compassion, we must love ourselves and make the following four wishes: "May I be free from hostility, may I be free from hatred, may I be free from obstacles and conflicts, and may I be able to dwell in happiness wherever I go." After we cultivate and gain strength, we should impart blessings upon three groups of people:

i.) Contemplate on the person whom you respect the most, and should be someone of the same gender and still alive. For example, they could be your teachers or parents to whom your heart will naturally give rise to reverence and love. Next, you should extend the four wishes to them as blessings and share your loving-kindness.

ii.) Contemplate the acquaintances with whom you have a shallow karmic affinity. For example, they could be your neighbors or someone with no conflict of interests. Bless them in the same manner with the four wishes and extend your loving-kindness.

iii.) Contemplate your enemy. They could be someone you wish not to see or even prefer to avoid due to unpleasant encounters in the past. Here too, you should extend the four wishes to them as blessings and share your loving-kindness.

Compassion and loving-kindness is the ability to be empathetic, uphold the five precepts, and respect others. Everything in the world exists in a state of mutual dependence. Along with mutual respect and tolerance, we should also strive to break through our own limitations by sharing unconditional loving-kindness and extending great compassion to all, collectively and in totality; lastly, the evoking of one's own unlimited mental power in creating a life of happiness.

2. People who are not able to distinguish right from wrong, with their mind confused and rooted in ignorance.

Contemplate on causes and conditions to understand the truth behind phenomena for proper discernment. Śākyamuni Buddha attained enlightenment within meditative concentration by contemplating with right thought the transmigrating process of life. With right thought Buddha was able to undertsand dependent origination of life and discovered the law of cause and effect; the common law governing all phenomena in the universe.

If you are able to understand the truths of all phenomena for its dependent origination and empty nature, you then realize the profundity of how myriad conditions come together; in this way, you will be able to transform ignorance into wisdom. Aside from this, one may contemplate with right thought: all conditioned phenomena are impermanent to tame desire for power; and all phenomena are without an independent self to rid attachment of the five sensual desires. However, in order to be able to use these methods successfully, we must first understand the law of dependent origination.

3. People who suffer for love and broken-heartedness, with their mind entangled in the lusts of men and women

Counter improper sexual temptation by contemplation of impurities: Contemplate the bluing, bruised appearance of a corpse, then it becomes bloated, swollen, rotten, maggots-hatching, ruptured, and fluid-leaking; later there is only bones remaining, tendons splitting, and even bones separating... try to contemplate this again and again. When a man looks upon a woman, he might begin to think about a slim physique, amicable smile, fine hair, and her crisp sweet voice. He may begin to think about her daily and the more he thinks of her, the more he comes to like her. The more he thinks of her, the more he wishes to see her every day, and she grew upon him. This is called the attachment of love, and it is the key for conditions that lead to transmigration. This strong, powerful attachment will propel us endlessly back into the womb, lifetime after lifetime.

If we wish to be free from the attachment of love, then we ought to think of her shortcomings, her impurities. Think if she has died or burned in a fire where her body is charred, her fair complexion and blushed skin burned to black. As such, fear and a sense of repulsion will arise.

If we wish to enter into the Buddhist path, we ought to consider doing the opposite of what is done in the secular world. There, people pursue sensual pleasure, which is just a nominal form. The Dharma teaches us to seek what is true, empty in nature, serene, at ease and happy. In order to leave the greed-ridden nature of our worldly state of mind far behind, we must contemplate the body's impurities, decay, and shortcomings. If we contemplate as such, our lust naturally subsides and attachment to love weakens.

4. People who are egotistical, conceited, and complacent, with their mind rooted in arrogance

Counter mental attachments by the contemplation on differentiating fields also expressed as the contemplation on skillful means, and the contemplation on the eighteen compositional fields of cognition. Contemplate yourself and the external fields as conditioned upon and made of elements such as earth, water, fire, wind, space, and consciousness. Since our body and external fields are not yours nor mine, why should there be any arrogance?

5. People who are burdened with physical infirmities and obstacles, with their mind mired in karmic obstructions

Strengthen one's power in self-healing by the contemplation of Buddha.

Four methods of the contemplation of Buddha are:

i) Recitation of the Buddha's name: Known as invoking the Buddha's name, and also making prostrations to Buddha.

ii.) Contemplation of Buddha: With no iconography to rely on, we may follow the sixteen visualizations from *The Contemplation of Infinite Life Sūtra* to mentally visualize the resultant reward of Amitābha Buddha; the wonders of the Pure Land.

iii.) Visualization of the statue of Buddha: Before beginning this practice, observe a statue of Amitābha Buddha. Then vividly imagine the compassionate countenance of this great Buddha, and continue until you are able to visualize Amitābha Buddha's entire body. When successful, Amitābha Buddha will manifest upfront and bestow you with illumination, empowerment, blessings, and teachings. This state of meditative concentration is known as visualization *samādhi*.

iv.) Reciting the Buddha's name with contemplation of the truth: Understanding of dependent origination, in other words, understand that Amitābha Buddha's physical attributes arose through dependent origination and have no inherent nature. Even the Pure Land itself arose through dependent origination and has no inherent nature. Whether it is: reciting the Buddha's name, visualization of the Buddha, accomplishing the buddha of "mind is buddha, mind becomes buddha" during visualization or the reward body of Amitābha Buddha, all of which arises from causes and conditions, having no inherent nature. Therefore, being able to observe dependent origination on contemplation of the Buddha's reward body or his manifestation body, we can connect with the truth, and the contemplation of Buddha and truth.

Mt. Lu Venerable Master Hui Yuan's Attainment through Visualization

Among the four methods related to Buddha-recitation; reciting the Buddha's name allows the mind to concentrate to a certain level, but it does not allow us to enter into meditative concentration. This is because the state of meditative concentration is beyond sound as a phenomenon; even if we recite silently, the phenomenon of the Buddha's name keeps appearing in our mind. The First Patriarch of Chinese Pure Land Buddhism, Venerable Master Hui Yuan had attainment through his practice of visualization of Buddha; such that the pure and auspicious image of Amitabha Buddha came to mind clearly whether his eyes were open or closed. This is the foundation of the Dharma method of the field of the mind.

Foundation of Meditative Concentration
Ānāpānasmṛti
Contemplation of Counting the Breath

Among the previously described five methods of contemplation, the fifth method is often taken in place of the fourth method, the contemplation of differentiating realms. If adding on contemplation of counting the breath, these five methods are known as the "five contemplations," often referred to as ceasing or stopping, the purpose of which is to cease or stop distracting thoughts and delusions. These are the keys for starting the practice of cessation and contemplation.

The counting of breath is known in Sanskrit as *ānāpānasmṛti*. *Āna* refers to inhalation and *apāna*, exhalation. This is one of the most common and fundamental methods for achieving meditative concentration in Buddhism. In my own experience, counting of breath is the foundation for cultivating meditative concentration. Aside from being able to treat mental clutter, it is also as effective as *qìgōng* in increasing physical health. Especially for people suffering from sleep disorders, they should practice the counting method diligently. Furthermore, practicing of the breath-counting method will gradually guide the breathing to become deeper and longer, this can improve metabolism, promote bodily circulation, lower our blood pressure, or even repair stomach ulcers.

The following is a simple explanation of a few methods:

The first method: Simply looking after the breath

In the *Connected Discourses*, Buddha instructed; find a quiet location, sit upright, and focus on the tip of the nose. Because the emotions are different, the speed, force, length, and depth of breathing also differ. Consequently, when focusing on the breath, one observes the breath diligently and attentively; may be long inhalation, short exhalation; short inhalation, short exhalation; short inhalation, long exhalation; or long inhalation, long exhalation; look after it very carefully. Mindfulness of breathing starts at the beginning of inhalation all the way until it ends; when exhaling, also maintain focus on that exhalation until it ends.

With regards to posture, one should lift the chest and keep the back and spine aligned. If you are able to sit in full-lotus posture, then it is best to do so; but if not, there is no harm in using half-lotus. Sitting in a chair with legs hanging downward is also fine, as long as the mind is stabilized. The tip of the tongue should rest on the roof of your mouth, and lips should be closed. Breathe naturally and do not make any special effort to stick out or tuck in your abdomen.

If you sit in half-lotus position, you should switch your legs to be different in the morning and evening sittings. For example, if in the morning, you had your right leg on top of your left leg; in the evening, you should have your left leg on top of your right leg. In the long run, this will help prevent slanted posture. If you are meditating for the whole day, you may alternate your leg positions in between sittings. It is best to keep your eyes completely closed, but if you practice a meditation involving the setting sun or water-gazing as your object of meditation, you may open your eyes slightly or keep them closed in accordance with your own habit of practice.

Some people who are not in good shape might experience tightness in their chests or weak breathing. Nonetheless, these people must be patient, and continue on. If one feels stifling, stuffy, and tight in the chest area, make effort to recite silently Buddha's name or the luminous six-syllable mantra: *oṃ maṇi padme hūṃ*, this will strengthen your inhalations and exhalations. When the breath becomes natural, set aside recitation of Buddha's name or the mantra and focus on the breath. For those not familiar with recitation, there is no harm in turning on recordings of Buddhist chanting; then again, when the breath becomes natural, turn off the recording. Do note that the strength of your breathing will change in accordance with your own focused intentions.

The second method: Counting breaths

When counting breaths, count either inhalations or exhalations. When counting inhalations, for the entire sitting, only count inhalations. Similarly, when counting exhalations, only count exhalations during the entire sitting. Do not switch between the methods within one sitting session; also, do not count "breathe in as one, breathe out as two, breathe in as three, breathe out as four..." In other words, only count either inhalations or exhalations, do not count both.

When counting inhalations, focus on the tip of your nose. Breathe in and count "one;" although exhalations are not being counted, you should pay attention throughout the entire length of your breath up until your exhalation has finished. Focus diligently and do not relax your focus. When you inhale again, count "two," and skip counting exhalation. When you inhale again, count "three," and so on until you reach "ten." At that point, start again and count your breaths from one to ten, and keep repeating the process in this manner.

Once you are able to stay focused, you will find out that your breaths are growing longer and longer, stronger and stronger; even making some sounds. This happens because throughout the day, your sensory nervous system, such as your eyes, ears, mouth, and body are in so much contact with external surroundings; therefore, your mind's attention is scattered accordingly. Once you fall asleep, aside from your nose, all other sense organs quiet down; breathing continues in full strength, focused on the nose area. Breathing naturally becomes stronger, and you could even start snoring! Please note that during one round of breath-counting from one to ten, should you lose count of your breaths because of wandering thoughts or worries, you must not guess what number you left off on; instead, you must start over again.

Do not consider breath-counting as simple; we all breathe every day, who doesn't, why is it so troublesome? Sakyamuni Buddha described this method and contemplation of impurities as the "sweet nectar gate." Sweet nectar is the ambrosia of immortality; while these methods sound simple, they are not easy to practice.

Unless you are able to completely let go and can return to looking after your breath right away once distracting thoughts arise, you will not be able to accomplish the practice of "looking after your breath." Do not be overly ambitious at first and take a step-by-step approach. If you are yet able to contemplate emptiness here and now, it is better to take the practical approach of starting to observe breathing.

Breathing Directly Affects Our Physiology and Psychology

The reason for emphasizing counting the breath is that breathing is the bridge between physiology and psychology. When our minds give rise to emotions such as happiness, anger, sorrow, pleasure, greed, hatred, or ignorance; why then would facial expressions, speech, and physiology undergo change? This is because the internal energy activates first. A clearest example is when one becomes angry, our internal energy rises to the neck, face, and then to the top of the head; there is a Chinese expression, "The face reddens and the neck swells." For this reason, those with high blood pressure and the elderly are not suited to rage and fury because internal energy and the blood travel alongside one another. When we breathe, oxygen is processed by our lungs, delivered to our hearts, and then carried along by our blood to the rest of our bodies. Being overtaken by rage can be likened to a properly functioning garden hose that is suddenly severed from its shut-off valve after being run over by a car. Especially for an elderly person, having expanded vascular tissues, blockages, or fragile blood vessels in the head being particularly thin might find that a sudden momentary eruption could even lead to a cerebral hemorrhage or stroke.

While in a fury, without exercising restraint to calm down, this anger will grow stronger and stronger; you might even start flailing about wildly, shaking with rage, or gnashing your teeth. All these are due to changes in the internal energy. When greed arises and especially when deluded thoughts of sexual lust arise, the internal energies move toward the more sensitive areas of the body; eventually, bodily fluids secrete. This is the same principle that brought about the universe into existence: First there was gas, then there were liquids, and lastly, material forms were able to solidify. The process of a child being born also occurs in this manner.

In ancient times, Wu Zixu is said to have had his hair go completely gray overnight due to severe distress. A number of years ago in mainland China, there was an artist who was arrested due to issues in tax filing; over the course of one night, his hair also turned gray completely. Other physiological symptoms associated with unstable emotional states may lead to loss of appetite, insomnia, or diarrhea; these are all closely related to internal energy. Therefore, maintaining balance of internal energy is extremely important.

Why is it said that internal energy is a bridge between the mind and body? Perhaps you all have heard that Buddhism and Indian philosophy delineate materiality within the universe into four great elements - earth, water, fire, and wind. Any material form whether animal, plant, or mineral, is made up of these elements. Their characteristics are as follows: earth has a stabilizing nature, water has a cohesive nature, fire has a ripening and transforming nature, and wind has a light and active nature. The four elements of the body can only be driven by internal energy. When air is breathed into the lungs and the heart, it has been transformed into an energized state, it is refined and not visible to the naked eye. As with acupuncture, once a needle is inserted into a nerve point, then there will be an experience of the flowing of internal energy.

Practicing *qìgōng* or receiving acupuncture are methods of treating illnesses. Similarly, counting the breath also has healing effects. It is especially effective in combating depression, bipolar disorders, and insomnia. It further aids in the maintenance of abundant energy; that is why it is said that power requires internal energy and also why the word for strength in Chinese, *lìqì*, is made up of the character for strength, *lì*, and also the character for internal energy, *qì*. However, for Buddhists, the key point is to cultivate a state of mindfulness until reaching the stage of meditative concentration. The emphasis is not for the practice or cultivation of internal energy.

The four stages of the breath: bellowing winds, broken panting, low-pitched breathing, and internalized breathing

Perhaps some people might ask, given that Buddha instructed us to stay mindful with our breathing, should our exhalation be long and inhalations short; or perhaps inhalations long and exhalations short? Or either both are short or both are long?

There is not one single answer that fits all. As the quality of everyone's physique are different, physiology and physical health are likewise different. However, based on the experiences of patriarchs and virtuous practitioners throughout history, there are roughly several levels. In the beginning stage, if we focus solely on breathing, inhalations and exhalations both become longer and longer; inhalations might be long, rough, and even noisy. This is quite similar to sleeping; the eyes are not engaged in seeing, the ears not listening, the mouth neither eating nor speaking, and the body not doing anything at all. All the strength of the breath is focused at the tip of the nose; therefore, inhalations become quite noisy, rumbling on like a train or motorcycle.

Due to the sound of breathing, this stage is called bellowing winds. People have different physiques; those with a suitable physique will find their breathing to be smooth. Nonetheless, not everyone will experience this bellowing effect. Although most people who practice diligently will likely have experienced this at some point.

The second stage is called broken panting. This is not the sort of panting experienced while racing or jogging. A better simile would be the sort of panting experienced by children who have been crying for a while until they've used up their energy. When they finally see their mothers and feel a sense of relief, their words are held back throughout the search for breath. Some adults also experience this phenomenon after wailing and crying.

Especially for those who have married or are older, the interference of emotions and sensual desires causes the body to grow somewhat weaker and some acupuncture points on the body may even be blocked. At times inhalations are quite long and coarse; these are signs of blockages being opened up. This is somewhat similar to using a plunger to unclog blockages; after a few plunges, the pipes sputter and then flow clearly. Therefore, after long, coarse breathing, the body can clean away the waste, and because of this, the body needs more internal energy; when the energy cannot be replenished all at once, the phenomenon of broken panting occurs.

Those with a relatively healthy physique generally do not experience these phenomena, however, it is natural to experience hiccups, belching, and passing gas. After a deep-tissue or shiatsu massage, a person might also find themselves hiccupping, or even their bowel movements changing such as the stool being darker, indicating that impurities are being released. As a result, this stage of broken panting will gradually improve your physique.

The third stage is the entry into low-pitched breathing. Since the physique has improved, the breaths become longer and longer; however, we still hear the sound of breathing. Unlike the first stage, the sound of breathing can only be heard by ourselves while others near will not be able to hear it.

After some time, one will enter the fourth stage which is called internalized breathing. At this point, breathing is rather subtle; faint and drawn out, seemingly undetectable. It appears to be just moving around the *dantien*, the abdominal area. In ancient times, this was called "turtle breathing" or "embryonic breathing." If you look at a turtle's mouth, it is usually closed tightly, preserving its breath, therefore they have a remarkable longevity.

If you are able to regularly take care of your breathing, you may not necessarily gain the full benefits of practicing *qìgōng*, yet you will experience some of the effects that improve your physical health. Some people seek training in *qìgōng* to heighten the experiences associated with sexual lust. In fact this misperception will actually increase the rate of physical decline. The essential goal and the reason for practicing and looking after the breath is to enter deep into meditative concentration.

Make contemplation of breath-counting into a habit

The cultivation of meditative concentration begins with observing the breath through patience. This is not a matter for just a day or two, in other words, one ought to cultivate it into a habit. For example, once you board an airplane, instead of reading the newspaper or chatting with other passengers, you may decide to observe your breath. Even if your practice gives way to sleeping while on the airplane, it would still be good. When sitting in the car with no passengers around to talk with, you may focus the breath while attentively watching the road. When this becomes a good habit, then we can be focused everywhere we go, and we are able to open or close our mind as we wish, at will.

Improve Spiritual DNA Through the Mind

Modern people take meditation as part of their self-relaxation practice and find peace and strength for their spirit from within. However, why is there so much suffering and worry in the world to the point that people can hardly breathe. It is because we often unknowingly become attached to our body and mind as the self. We become bound to the image of the self, unable to release ourselves from it!

When our sensory system; the five consciousnesses of the eye, ear, nose, tongue, and body come into contact with the external physical world, on the arising of the feelings of suffering, joy, sorrow, and happiness, each of us will have different behaviors and reactions. That is the sixth consciousness of differentiation. If we keep grasping strongly, not letting go till death, it is the function of the seventh consciousness. Practitioners are able to control the seventh consciousness so that even while dreaming they can clearly distinguish it as a dream and their emotions will not follow the states within the dream. The eighth consciousness is similar to our memory, *ālaya-vijñāna*, I call it spiritual DNA. This is what Buddhism taught about the eight consciousnesses.

Each day, our inner passions develop into behaviors. No

matter whether these behaviors are in the forms of verbal, physical, bodily or mental actions, all become memory that is energized. In brief, according to its quality, superior or inferior, wholesome or unwholesome, moral or immoral, it guides us into the next existence as heavenly beings, humans, animals, or ghosts. In other words, spiritual DNA known in Mahāyāna Buddhism as the eighth consciousness will shape every aspect of rebirth.

If we wish to have quality spiritual DNA, the easiest way is to always have a kind mind and often perform wholesome actions. Since all behaviors arise from the mind, through wisdom and meditative concentration, we should recognize that all matters in the world are impermanent, we will be able to control our emotions and desires, subduing our mind. The Buddha often taught us that our fate is controlled by ourselves and our future lives are also managed by us. We have absolutely no right to complain or blame others.

Our body and mind are composed of the five aggregates

Nonetheless, the mind of sentient beings is extremely stubborn, frequently forming attachments to all sorts of conditions, always giving rise to ignorance, and consequently the mind is quite difficult to train and discipline. In fascicle number 267 in the *Connected Discourses*, there is a clear explanation of consciousness of the self within each and every single one of us, and we deeply love our body and mind (form, feelings, perception, mental formation, and consciousness).

> Thus have I heard:
> One time the Buddha was residing at Anāthapiṇḍada's Park in Jeta's Grove near Śrāvastī.
>
> At that time the World-Honored One addressed the *bhikṣus*: "Sentient beings spend a long time cycling through lifetimes in *saṃsāra* which is itself without beginning. They do not understand how suffering originates and are thereby impeded by ignorance and bound by craving. *Bhikṣus*, this is just like the case of a dog tied to a post with rope. The object binding the dog has not been severed, so

the dog just revolves around the post. Whether the dog stands or lies, it cannot separate itself from the post. In the same way, foolish sentient beings who, with regard to their physical forms, are unable to separate themselves from lust, craving, longing and thirsts, transmigrating in physical forms; they revolve around their physical forms, whether standing or lying they cannot separate themselves from their physical forms. The same for feeling, perception, mental formation, and consciousness, they revolve around feeling, perception, mental formation, and consciousness, whether standing or lying they cannot separate from consciousness.

Bhikṣus, thoroughly contemplate and examine your mind. Why is that so? Because your mind has been defiled by desire, anger, and delusion for a long period of time. *Bhikṣus*, due to agitation of mind, sentient beings are thereby agitated; due to pureness of mind, sentient beings are thereby purified. *Bhikṣus*, I have never seen such a multicolored physical form as the multicolored bird, and yet the mind is even more multifaceted. Why is that so? Due to the multifaceted mind of the animal, its physical form is multicolored.

Therefore, *bhikṣus*, thoroughly contemplate and examine your mind. *Bhikṣus*, your mind has been defiled by desire, anger, and delusion for a long period of time. It should be known that due to agitation of mind, sentient beings are thereby agitated; due to pureness of mind, sentient beings are thereby purified. *Bhikṣus*, you should know! Have you ever seen the multicolors of the bird known as a 'caraṇa?'"

The *bhikṣus* answered: "Yes, we have seen it, World-Honored One."

The Buddha addressed the *bhikṣus*: "Just as the caraṇa is multicolored and intricate, I say that the mind is also multifaceted and intricate in the much the same manner. Why is that so? Due to the multifaceted nature of the caraṇa's mind, its form is multicolored. Therefore, you should thoroughly contemplate and examine your mind because of repeated defilements by various forms of desire, anger, and delusion for a long period of time. Due to agitation of mind, sentient beings are thereby agitated; due to pureness of mind, sentient beings are thereby purified. This is just like how after a master painter or his protégé prepares both a blank canvas and fully mixed paint palette, he can then paint whatever images he wishes to paint.

Bhikṣus, foolish sentient beings do not understand the reality of physical form: the origin, cessation, craving, danger, and relinquishing for the physical form. Due to their not understanding the physical form, they delight and become attached to it; due to their delight and attachment to the physical form they give rise to future rebirths of the physical form. Such foolish beings do not understand the reality of feeling, perception, mental formation, and consciousness: the origin, cessation, craving, danger, and relinquishing of consciousness. Due to their not understanding consciousness, they delight and become attached to it; due to their delight and attachment to consciousness they give rise to future rebirths of consciousness. They will thereby give rise to future physical form, feeling, perception, mental formation, and consciousness; as such they will not be liberated from physical form, not be liberated from feeling, perception, mental formation, and consciousness. I say that they will not be liberated from birth, ageing, sickness, death, sorrow, affliction, and suffering.

There are noble disciples who often hear the Dharma and can understand the reality of physical form: the origin, cessation, craving, danger, and relinquishing of the physical form. Due to their understanding of the physical form, they do not delight or become attached in it; due to their not delighting or attached to the physical form they do not give rise to future rebirths of the physical form. They understand the reality of feeling, perception, mental formation, and consciousness: the origin, cessation, craving, danger, and relinquishing of consciousness. Due to their understanding of consciousness, they do not delight or become attached to consciousness; due to their not delighting or becoming attached to it, they do not give rise to future rebirths of consciousness. Due to their not delighting or becoming attached to physical form, feeling, perception, mental formation, and consciousness, they are liberated from physical form, they are liberated from feeling, perception, mental formation, and consciousness. I say they are thereby liberated from birth, ageing, sickness, death, worries, sorrow, and suffering."

After the World-Honored One had spoken the *sutta*, the *Bhikṣus* were delighted to hear the words of the Buddha and faithfully received this teaching and practice!

~From Fascicle 267 in the *Connected Discourses*

This *sutta* explains that once the body and mind cannot separate from lust, love, longing, and thirsts (craving), we are subject to endless transmigration with *saṃsāra.* It does not matter whether we are born as a human or animal, all day long we go round and round for the sake of our own life. This is just like the dog which has been tied to a post with a rope, and cannot escape from the post.

In this situation, the World-Honored One taught his disciples to contemplate carefully and to closely observe their minds. Given that our minds have been under these influences for a long time, our minds are muddled and clouded by greed, anger, and ignorance. Therefore, it is said that when the mind is in a state of agitation, sentient beings experience suffering; when the mind is in a state of purity, sentient beings experience clarity (liberation). Interestingly, the World-Honored One continued his explanation by employing the "bird with colorful plumage," the "caraṇa," and the "painter," to describe the complicated minds of people.

The World-Honored One said, "Disciples, there is a kind of bird whose colorful plumage displays a wide variety of hues which cover its entire body. Because its mind is multifaceted, its plumage is multicolored. But you know? Our minds are even more complicated than that bird."

The World-Honored One further stressed the importance of observing the mind by stating, "Therefore, disciples, you should carefully contemplate your mind. For a long time, our mind has been defiled by greed, anger, and ignorance. Have you ever seen a caraṇa, the bird with the multicolored plumage?"

The *bhikṣus* answered, "Yes, we have seen it, World-Honored One!"

The World-Honored One said, "Just as the caraṇa has multicolored plumage, I'd say that the caraṇa's mind is also this way. Why do I say so? Because the caraṇa's multifaceted mind is the condition that causes its multicolored appearance. Therefore, you should carefully contemplate and examine your own mind. For a long time, our mind has been defiled by attachments to greed, anger, and ignorance. So when the mind is agitated, sentient beings are agitated; when the mind is pure, sentient beings are pure. This is just like how after preparing a blank canvas and palette of paints, a master painter or his protégé is able to paint whatever images he wishes to paint."

At the end of the *sutta*, the Buddha reminded all his disciples that they should realize with wisdom the five aspects of arising, cessation, craving, affliction and renunciation and of the five aggregates as they really are. As such, then they would not have attachment of the physical body, and be free from the shackles of feeling, perception, mental formations, and consciousness. At the same time, they are also able to be liberated from birth, aging, sickness, death, anxiety, sorrow, affliction, and suffering.

After reading similes above, it is not hard to fathom that the verse, "The mind is like a master painter who is able to paint all kinds of subjects" in the *Flower Adornment Sūtra* originally came from this *sutta*. Additionally, we often recite the verse, "If one wishes to know all the buddhas of the three time periods, one should observe the nature of the dharma realm. Everything is produced through mind alone;" this also is an extension from this same *sutta*. Also in the *Vimalakirti Sutra*, there is the following Buddhist philosophy: "Bodhisattvas who wish to purify their lands should purify their minds; when the mind is pure, the Buddha Land is pure." Similarly, this originates from sacred teachings of Early Buddhism.

The origin of suffering is our attachment to self

To understand Buddhism, we need to understand the law of dependent origination. Neither the material nor the spiritual realms could exist outside of dependent origination. Understand that all phenomena in the world arise based on causes and supporting conditions; they in turn mutually rely on and support one another to come into existence. Therefore, they have no self-nature and their essence is empty. Furthermore, since the world is impermanent, we can transform delusion into enlightenment, mundane into noble, and defilement into purity, everything is full of hope. Since the world has no self-nature, we know we should be grateful for the myriad conditions which enable success; thereby, learn the value of teamwork and adopt an attitude of deep humility, actualizing the Dharma in an active manner.

One day the Buddha asked a disciple, "If a leaf fell from a tree, how would that make you feel?"

The disciple replied, "I would have no feeling at all!"

Buddha asked further, "What if your *kāṣāya* was torn?"

Without hesitation, the disciple answered, "I would feel anguished!"

The Buddha asked back, "How is it that you feel nothing when a leaf falls from a tree but if your *kāṣāya* was torn, that would cause you to feel anguished?"

"Because the *kāṣāya* is mine." The disciple answered frankly.

This is the cause of suffering. The suffering in our lives comes from attachment to the self and the belief that it is permanent and truly exists. This belief then turns into deep attachment toward I, mine, and all things endeared to me, not letting go. Since we are yet to renounce these attachments, we pursue further; hence, love and clinging lead to the substance of "becoming," and leading us to be reborn endlessly. This way, we are born then pass away; after passing away, we are reborn again. The cycle of rebirth continues without respite.

All phenomena and matter in the world all come to be through the accumulation of myriad causes and conditions. Furthermore, all phenomena and matters undergo constant changes. If we are able to use *prajñā*-wisdom and reflect on all causes, conditions, and effects in our lives as we encounter them, then we will naturally be able to "realize that the five aggregates are empty." As we let go, not taking account, we are no longer carried along by advances and setbacks of the external environment and creating anxiety for the body and mind due to emotional fluctuations. As such, we are able to "overcome all suffering." In this way, we can completely resolve the suffering and worries of life. Otherwise, if we blindly chase after the temporary, unreal happiness offered by the external environment, we are just temporarily numbing ourselves but unable to actually resolve the fundamental problem.

Chapter Two
To Calm the Mind, First Understand the World and the All

All phenomena in the world are within the bounds of causes, conditions, and effects; for when there are causes paired with the appropriate supporting conditions, the effects are bound to manifest. For instance, a piece of cloth is the cause, it takes supporting conditions such as scissors, thread, needle, and tailoring work in order to sew it into a piece of clothing, the effect. In other words, all necessities for living as well as our emotions and states are connected with causes, conditions, and effects.

Whether our minds are at peace or worried, there are also causes, conditions, and effects. Once a mother asked me, "After people pass away, is it better to be cremated or buried?" I said, "Cremation is better." She responded immediately, "I fear it'd be painful!" I said, "You see, all that is burnt rises upwards, and so be able to reach heaven. The liquids from burials will seep into the dirt, and there are bugs growing in the earth. So which do you think is better, cremation or burial?" She nodded her head and said, "I understand, my mind is more at ease now."

Consequently, effects will differ in accordance with different ways of thinking. For example, pounding on a table will have a nice sound when you strike it out of appreciation while remarking "Wow! What a beautiful table." On the other hand, if you pound on a table while cursing at someone, the sound of your pounding will be rough and jarring. In learning Buddhism, the most important aspect is the cultivation of right view and right understanding. Being able to understand the reality of the world, we will not be arrogant when things go our way and not sad when we lose. Dependent origination as taught by the Buddha is neither mind-only nor materialism-only, but instead, it is through the connection between body and mind and cognition of the mind and external surrounding in understanding all phenomena.

The World is Dangerous, Fragile, and Perishable

In observing the effects in this lifetime, we should know that these are born from the causes and conditions of the past. Therefore, when we face setbacks we should not blame others, but should reflect and change ourselves. Buddhism's life philosophy is: On thoroughly understanding the reality of the world, we actively improve ourselves, for helping others.

What is the reality of the world? The Buddha explained as follows:

The effect of the interaction of the body and mind

Thus have I heard:
One time the Buddha was residing at Anāthapiṇḍada's Park in Jeta's Grove near Śrāvastī.

At that time, a *bhikṣu* named Samṛddhi went to visit the Buddha. He prostrated before the Buddha's feet and then sat to one side. He asked the Buddha, "World-Honored One, what is that which is called the world?"

The Buddha replied to Samṛddhi, "What is called eye, form, eye consciousness, and eye contact; eye contact gives rise to feeling due to conditions: internal feelings of suffering, pleasure, or neither suffering nor pleasure. Same applies to ear, nose, tongue, body, mind, dharma, mental consciousness and mental contact; mental contact gives rise to feeling due to conditions: feelings of suffering, pleasure, or neither suffering nor pleasure. This is what is called the world. Why is that so? When the six sense bases arising culminates then the relevant contacts arising also culminate. As such, this is the origin of massive culmination of suffering.

"Samṛddhi! If there were no eyes, no form, and no eye consciousness, and no eye contact; hence, no feeling arises due to conditions of eye contact; therefore, no internal feeling of suffering, pleasure, or neither suffering nor pleasure. With no ear, no nose, no tongue, no body, no mind, no mental objects, no dharma, no mind consciousness, and no mental contact; hence, no feeling arises due to conditions; therefore, no internal feeling of suffering, pleasure, or neither suffering nor pleasure. Thereby, there is no world and likewise no designation of world. Why is that so? When the six sense bases have been extinguished, contact is then extinguished, as such, the origin of massive culmination of suffering is extinguished."

After the World-Honored One had said these words, the *bhikṣus* were delighted to hear the words of the Buddha and faithfully received this teaching and practice.

~From Fascicle 230 in the *Connected Discourses*

The main teaching of this *sutta* is: Once while the Buddha was residing at Anāthapiṇḍada's Park in Jeta's Grove near Śrāvastī, a *bhikṣu* named Samṛddhi asked the World-Honored One, "What is the world?" The Buddha replied, "When the eye responds to (a condition) visible object, eye-consciousness arises. When eye, form, and consciousness are engaged to give rise to what is called contact. With eye contact as condition, feelings come to be, including suffering, pleasure or no suffering nor pleasure. As the ear cognizes sound, nose cognizes scent, tongue cognizes taste, body cognizes tactile objects, and consciousness cognizes mental objects, these processes lead to arising of the respective consciousness; ear consciousness, nose consciousness, tongue consciousness, body consciousness, and mind consciousness, resulting in feelings of suffering, pleasure, or neither suffering nor pleasure. This is what is called the world. Why is that? It is because of the arising of the six internal sense bases, the relevant contacts arise eventually leading to birth, aging, sickness, death, anxiety, sorrow, agitation, and suffering, this is simply the origin of massive culmination of suffering"

In other words, when objects of our liking appear, feelings of elation and pleasure tend to follow. If our mind develops attachment toward desirable objects, the six perceptions, six volitional formations, and six cravings will follow. If our mind becomes more and more attached, we will inevitably be unable to get our minds off the desirable objects, we will tend to think of them over and over again; this stage is known as "craving." With the power of craving, these thoughts become stronger; such thoughts will lead to strong attachments and they will naturally lead to physical and verbal actions; this emerges as behavior. In Mind-only studies it is known as manifest functioning, the stage known as "clinging." When action is taken, it leads to the driving force for beings into their next rebirth.

This driving force is known as the link of "becoming" in the Twelve Links of Dependent Origination. In karmic theory it is known as "unmanifested karma." In Mind-only studies, it is permeated into the eighth consciousness, the *ālaya-vijñāna*, to become habitual tendency. In modern language, it has become our memory. Depending on the strength and types of memories, it will lead us into our next existence. Consequently, birth, aging, sickness, death, anxiety, sorrow, agitation, and suffering – this is simply the origin of massive culmination of suffering. The helplessness of it is that this could only be endured and there is no escape from it. This is the reality of the world; that is why it is often stated that "the world is full of suffering," "the world is an ocean of suffering," and "the world truly is suffering; through and through!"

From the arising of this, that arises; and from the ceasing of this, that ceases. Hence, ignorance ceases and mental formation ceases; mental formation ceases and consciousness ceases... leading to the cessation of birth, aging, sickness, death, anxiety, sorrow, agitation, and suffering, this is simply the cessation of the origin of massive culmination of suffering. In other words, all the suffering in the world and even the cycle of rebirth (*saṃsāra*) can be unbound and resolved. Therefore, the Buddha addressed Samṛddhi and further explained the transmigration and cessation gate of cause and effect, the Dharma method of liberation from life and death.

So when the Buddha explained about the world, it was from the rising of the world through the six sense bases and then onto its cessation. Clearly, through right thought of the Noble Eightfold Path, the Buddha contemplated deeply the cycle of rebirth, life and death, and the transmigration and cessation stages of life and death. It should be noted that where mentioned in the *sutta,* "...

no eyes, no sight, no eye consciousness," we must contemplate the emptiness of six senses, six objects, internal and external, and all phenomena through the nature of emptiness of *prajñā*-wisdom.

Interestingly, here we can see traces of how teachings from sacred texts in Early Buddhism developed into *Mahayana Perfection of Great Wisdom Sutra.* This is especially true of what is said in the *Heart Sūtra* reading: "Thus, in emptiness, there are no form, feeling, perception, mental formation, or consciousness. No eye, ear, nose, tongue, body, or mind; no form, sound, scent, taste, touch or dharmas; no eye consciousness nor mind consciousness; no ignorance nor the extinction of ignorance; even unto no aging and death nor the extinction of no aging and death." This also serves as evidence that Mahāyāna sutras cannot be separated from the origins in the sacred *suttas* of Early Buddhism. Mahāyāna sutras just simply emphasize again the teaching that "all forms are empty in their essence!"

When the Buddha explained about the world, he certainly did not explain it from the perspective of metaphysics, but instead referred to the encounter of the physical world by the optic nerves of the physiological systems; leading to the arising of mental states, a three-in-one approach, namely "contact." Immediately after contact, is the arising of feeling; once feeling arises, we chase after desirable objects and when that pursuit is fruitless, we become nervous or angry. When the pursuit is fruitful, we protect that which has been gained, and if it is taken away, we become angry. Therefore, anger arises from greed, and if greed is absent, there will be no anger. Additionally, individuals with strong egos are more likely to fall into anger. For example, they will tend to think, "I want such and such," "you should listen to me," and "how dare you not listen to me?" Therefore, much suffering and worries ensue and there is no way our state of mind will be happy.

If we were to properly manage our emotions, we ought to contemplate the empty nature of all phenomena and not overly assert our ego. It is best to just take things easy. Let whatever may come, come; let whatever may go, go. Originally, there was no thing!

Emptiness is Not an Abstract Existence Detached from Actual Phenomena

Emptiness in Buddhism is different from "nothingness" in English. A cup is something you can say is characterized by emptiness because it is of different porcelain made from suitable clay; clay is combined with water in order to be shaped into a cup and lastly, it needs to go into a kiln to be heated at over one thousand degrees to take its current form. If we look at it with a high precision instrument, it is just atoms, electrons, protons, molecules, and quantum in a floating state. You would discover that there is no cup whatsoever! Everything in the world is like this; what we see and the true nature of that phenomenon are not the same.

The nature of form is fragile and decaying

Thus have I heard:
One time the Buddha was residing at Anāthapiṇḍada's Park in Jeta's Grove near Śrāvastī.

At that time, a *bhikṣu* named Samṛddhi went to visit the Buddha. He prostrated before the Buddha's feet and then sat to one side. He asked the Buddha, "World-Honored One, what is that which is called the 'world?"

The Buddha told Samṛddhi, "What is known as the world is fragile and decaying. Why do I say it is fragile and decaying? Samṛddhi! The eyes are a fragile and decaying phenomenon. Where there are form, eye consciousness, and visual contact; visual contact gives rise to feelings due to the conditions: internal feeling of suffering, pleasure, or neither suffering nor pleasure. All of these are likewise fragile and decaying. Ears, nose, tongue, body, and consciousness are also the same. The phenomenon which is said to be fragile and decaying, that is what is called the world."

After the World-Honored One had said these words, Bhikṣu Samṛddhi was delighted to hear the words of the Buddha and faithfully received this teaching and practice.

~From Fascicle 231 in the *Connected Discourses*

In this *sutta*, Bhikṣu Samṛddhi asked, "What exactly is the world?" The Buddha replied, "That which is fragile and decaying is called the world. Why is that so? Because the sensory organ of the eyes is a fragile and decaying phenomenon; when eyes, form, and eye consciousness come together, resulting in contact. Through the causes and conditions of visual contact, feeling arises, including feelings of suffering, pleasure, or neither suffering nor pleasure. All of these phenomena are also fragile and decaying. The same applies to the ear, nose, tongue, body, and mind. That is why the world is a fragile and decaying phenomenon."

All phenomena arise relying on causes and supported by conditions

The world is not only a phenomenon which is fragile and decaying, but also empty in nature. The Buddha spoke about this in the following:

> Thus have I heard:
> One time the Buddha was residing at Anāthapiṇḍada's Park in Jeta's Grove near Śrāvastī.
>
> At that time, a *bhikṣu* named Samṛddhi went to visit the Buddha. He prostrated before the Buddha's feet and then sat to one side. He asked the Buddha, "World-Honored One, the world is said to be empty but why is it said to be empty?"
>
> The Buddha told Samṛddhi, "Eyes are empty: a phenomenon empty of permanence, eternity, unchanging, and also empty of the self. What is the reason for this? This is the way of nature. When form, eye consciousness, and visual contact; visual contact gives rise to feelings due to the conditions; the feeling of suffering, pleasure, or neither suffering nor pleasure. These are also empty: a phenomenon empty of permanence, eternity, unchanging, and also empty of the self. What is the reason for this? This is the way of nature. Ears, nose, tongue, body, and mind are also this way. That is called the empty world."
>
> After the World-Honored One had said these words, Bhikṣu Samṛddhi was delighted to hear the words of the Buddha and faithfully received this teaching and practice.
>
> ~From Fascicle 232 in the *Connected Discourses*

Bhikṣu Samṛddhi asked further, "What is it meant by the world is empty?" The Buddha taught: "Eyes are empty: a phenomenon empty of permanence, eternity, unchanging, and also empty of the self. What is the reason for this? This is the way of nature." This passage explains how eyes are not the self and not of the self. The Buddhist notion of self" is something that eternally resides, is real, completely free, and also its own master. However, eyes are impermanent, subject to near-sightedness, and ailments such as presbyopia, cataracts, and glaucoma; all these bring much inconvenience to life. Where could one find a self which is fully real, eternal, completely free, and joyous? Lastly, the Buddha emphasized that the ears, nose, tongue, body, and mind are also this way and therefore, it is said that "the world is empty, all phenomena of arising and ceasing are not real."

When the Buddha referred to the world as being empty, here it is based upon the six sense organs interacting with the six sense objects and thereby the arising of the six consciousnesses, the six contacts, and the six feelings; all are empty in nature of permanence and eternity. The Buddha explained that "all phenomena are empty."

"This is the way of nature" means that the nature of all phenomena is as such. The extension of this phrase is related to what is said in the *Heart Sūtra:* "Form is not different from emptiness, emptiness is not different from form. Form is emptiness, emptiness is form."

Right observation of the cessation of the world as it really is

The Buddha spoke of the truth as: "this exists, thereby that exists; this arises, thereby that arises; this does not exist and thereby that does not exist; this ceases and thereby that ceases." It is only through contemplation of Dependent Origination, the Three Dharma Seals, the Four Noble Truths, and the Noble Eightfold Path that we can understand the empty nature and dependent origination of the universe; the truth of all phenomena arising from the coming together of causes and conditions.

Thus have I heard:
One time the Buddha was residing at Anāthapiṇḍada's Park in Jeta's Grove near Śrāvastī.

At that time, the World-Honored One addressed the *bhiksus*: "Now I will speak about the world, the cause of the world, the cessation of the world, and the path to the cessation of the world. Listen carefully and contemplate well!

"What is that which is called the world? It can be called the six internal sense bases. And which six are they? The internal sense base of eye, that of ears, that of nose, that of tongue, that of body, and that of mind.

What is that which is called the cause of the world? The arising of desire, joy, and greed; these causes accumulate.

What is that which is called the cessation of the world? The cessation of the world occurs when the accumulated causes, the simultaneous coming desire, joy, and greed, are all eliminated without remainder, abandoned, terminated, exhausted, left behind, annihilated, ceased, and extinguished.

What is that which is called the path leading to the cessation of the world? That is the Noble Eightfold Path of right view, right intention, right speech, right action, right livelihood, right skillful means, right mindfulness, and right meditative concentration."

After the World-Honored One had said these words, the *bhiksus* were delighted to hear the words of the Buddha and faithfully received this teaching and practice.

~From Fascicle 233 in the *Connected Discourses*

The Buddha said, "What is the world? It is the six internal sense bases; eyes, ears, nose, tongue, body, and mind, this is the Noble Truth of Suffering." What is that which is called the cause of the world? It is the arising of all desire, pleasure, and greed for the future; accompanied by craving and the bondage of greed, unable to extricate ourselves. What is that which is called the cessation of the world? The cessation of the world is when the arising of all love, pleasure, and greed for the future are eliminated, abandoned, and extinguished. "What is the 'path leading to the cessation of the world?' It is the method to extinguish the bondage of greed and desire in the world. It is the Noble Eightfold Path – right view, right intention, right speech, right action, right livelihood, right effort, right mindfulness, and right concentration."

In this *sutta*, the Buddha further explained how we should examine the cause of the world and the cessation of the world and to contemplate the law of Dependent Origination according to the Four Noble Truths – suffering, the cause of suffering, the cessation of suffering, and the path leading to the cessation of suffering.

I. The Noble Truth of Suffering: The six internal sense bases (six sense organs) take the respective six external sense bases (the six dusts) as objects. They initiate the arising of the six consciousnesses, the six contacts, and the six feelings, resulting in suffering and pleasure.

II. The Noble Truth of the Cause of Suffering: The six internal sense bases take the respective six external sense bases as objects; together, initiate desire, joy, and greed, leading to craving, clinging, and becoming.

III. The Noble Truth of the Cessation of Suffering: The complete elimination without remainder of desire, joy, and greed which arise when the six internal sense bases engage with the six external sense bases.

IV. The Noble Truth of the Path Leading to the Cessation of Suffering: To end the desire, joy, and greed which arise when the six internal sense bases engage with the six external sense objects; we need to observe the world of the six senses toward the respective six sense objects with right view and right thought as fragile, decaying, impermanent, and empty in nature (the way of nature). Then in day to day life, we actualize right speech, right action, and right livelihood, uphold the precepts, and practice right mindfulness (four bases of mindfulness) and right meditative concentration. As such, we can overcome habitual tendencies, eradicate worries, and realize *nirvāṇa.* The Buddha kept reminding us to complete our practice of the Noble Eightfold Path in accordance with the Four Noble Truths in order to gain liberation from the world.

The twelve sense bases are the all, all existence

From the above, the world referred to in the *Connected Discourses* is based on the body and mind which are filled with impermanence, suffering, changes, fragility, and decay. Moreover, the Buddha also mentioned terms such as the all, all existence, and all *dharmas.* They also referred to the world and are defined by the twelve sense bases.

The all of the world is contact of the physical body and material objects

> Thus have I heard:
> One time the Buddha was residing at Anāthapiṇḍada's Park in Jeta's Grove near Śrāvastī.
>
> At that time, Brāhmin Jāṇussoṇi went to visit the Buddha, after they greeted each other with a half bow, he sat to one side. He asked the Buddha: "Gautama! What is that which is called the all?"
>
> The Buddha replied to the *brāhmin*, "The all is the twelve sense bases: the eyes with physical forms, the ears with sound, the nose with scent, the tongue with taste, the body with tactile objects, and the mind with cognition; these are what are called the all. If anyone was to say, 'The all as spoken by Śramaṇa Gautama, I now abandon and stand for a different understanding of the all.' If someone asked him further about this, he would not know how to answer and would thereby increase his doubts. Why is that so? This is beyond his realm of understanding."
>
> After the World-Honored One had said these words, Brāhmin Jāṇussoṇi was delighted to hear the words of the Buddha and faithfully received this teaching and practice.
>
> ~From Fascicle 319 in the *Connected Discourses*

During the Buddha's lifetime, figures from other religions would call the Buddha by his name, Gautama. One day, a *brāhmin* who is known as Jāṇussoṇi approached the Buddha and asked: "What is the all?"

The Buddha replied, "The all refer to the twelve sense bases (the six sense organs and the corresponding six sense objects): the eyes to form, ears to sound, nose to scent, tongue to taste, body to touch, and the mind to mental objects. If a person was to say, 'This is not the all, I do not accept that the all are simply the twelve sense bases as spoken of by Śramaṇa Gautama. I feel that there are additional things beyond this...' then these are just empty words. If such a person was asked to further elaborate, they would find themselves unable to do so and they would just grow more and more confused. Why is that? It is because this would be beyond their capacity to experience."

From this we know that the Buddha's explanation of "the all" is the understanding of the mutual conditions arising from the six internal senses with the six external objects. Once the six sensory organs come into contact with the six external dusts, the arising feeling of pleasure or suffering is "all existence."

Thus have I heard:
One time the Buddha was residing at Anāthapiṇḍada's Park in Jeta's Grove near Śrāvastī.

At that time, Brāhmin Jāṇussoṇi went to visit the Buddha, after they greeted each other with a half bow, he sat to one side. He asked the Buddha: "Gautama! What is that which is called all existence?"

The Buddha asked the brāhmin, "Now I will ask you a question. Answer me as you will. Brāhmin, what do think: do the eyes exist?"

He replied, "Yes, they do, Śramaṇa Gautama!"

"Does form exist?"

"Yes, it does, Śramaṇa Gautama!"

"Brāhmin, when there is form, there is eye consciousness and visual contact. With visual contact, feeling arises due to the conditions, which can be suffering, pleasure, and neither suffering nor pleasure, right?"

"Yes, Śramaṇa Gautama!"

"The ears, nose, tongue, body, and mind are also the same as said. Going beyond such… it will not be within the realm of understanding."

After the World-Honored One had said these words, Brāhmin Jāṇussoṇi was delighted to hear the words of the Buddha and faithfully received this teaching and practice. He stood up and took his leave.

~From fascicle 320 in the *Connected Discourses*

Brāhmin Jāṇussoṇi asked the Buddha about all existence. The Buddha explained that the eye cognizes the visible objects, giving rise to eye consciousness; together that is called contact, followed by the arising of feelings – suffering, pleasure, and neither suffering nor pleasure. These are "all existence."

Animals depend on sensory nerves to perceive the external environment, giving rise to suffering and pleasure; this is all existence. In other words, the optical nerves (eye base), the auditory nerves (ear base), the olfactory nerves (nose base), the taste receptors (tongue base), the tactile nerves (body base), and cognitive perception (mind base). These sense bases cognize the corresponding sense objects – forms, sound, scent, taste, touch, and mental objects (feeling, mental formation, and memory), giving rise to six consciousnesses: eye consciousness, ear consciousness, nose consciousness, tongue consciousness, body consciousness, and mind consciousness. Subsequent mental states further develop into six contacts, six feelings, and six perceptions, which are the all existence.

After discussing the all existence, the Buddha mentioned the term "all *dharmas*." In fact, the two *suttas* are similar. In other words, when the Buddha spoke on "the all," "all existence," and "all *dharmas*," these terms referred to all worldly things, the 'twelve sense bases.' Aside from the 'twelve sense bases,' there is not much to learn or speak about and to practice or realize, the rest is metaphysics and from the Buddha's perspective, it is frivolous talk and not necessary to discuss or explain.

Thus have I heard:
One time the Buddha was residing at Anāthapiṇḍada's Park in Jeta's Grove near Śrāvastī.

At that time, Brāhmin Jāṇussoṇi went to visit the Buddha, after they greeted each other with a half bow, he sat to one side. He asked the Buddha: "Śramaṇa Gautama! What is that which is called all dharmas?"

The Buddha replied to the *brāhmin*, "With the eye, form, eye consciousness, and visual contact; visual contact gives rise to feelings due to the conditions: feelings of suffering, pleasure, and neither suffering nor pleasure. The ears, nose, tongue, body, mind, mental consciousness, and mental contact; gives rise to feelings due to the conditions: feelings of suffering, pleasure, and neither suffering nor pleasure. This is what is known as all dharmas. If someone is to say, 'These are not all dharmas, I do not accept the all dharmas taught by Śramaṇa Gautama but will accept other all dharmas.' While speaking as such and upon asking for elaboration, he has no understanding and only increases his doubt. Why is that so? It is not his realm of understanding."

After the World-Honored One had said these words, Brāhmin Jāṇussoṇi was delighted to hear the words of the Buddha and faithfully received this teaching and practice.

~From fascicle 321 in the *Connected Discourses*

In order to gain ease in body and mind, understand causes and conditions

Emotional management focuses on calming the mind and understanding that the reality of phenomena has no substance. The reason people experience suffering is because the mind is afflicted by greed, anger, and ignorance; it is frequently bombarded by temptations and distracted by the external environment, giving rise to worries. Our only way out is to learn how to observe worldly matters through the "eye of wisdom" and to understand the world and all phenomena arise and cease according to dependent origination and causes and conditions. By this understanding, we will be away from the entanglement of gains and losses, hence away from worries and attachments.

Once a king heard beautiful music from a lute that he had never heard before, giving rise to very strong craving in him. He asked his minister, "What is this sound? It is so wonderful to hear!"

The minister replied, "It is the sound of a lute."

The king ordered, "Go and get that sound for me here.'

The minister immediately brought the lute to the king, "Great king! This is the lute that made the beautiful sound."

The king said, "I'm not asking for this lute, but tell you to bring the sound of the lute that we just heard here."

The minister replied, "That sound was from someone playing the lute, furthermore, the sound of lute we just heard had already passed on, it is impossible to get!"

The king then said, "Tut! Why do we need such a fake and unreal thing! Lutes in the world are fake and unreal, making people crave and become attached to them. You now go destroy this lute and throw it away anywhere!"

If we correctly understand the reality of the world, the all, and all existence; knowing that the world is fragile, decaying, and empty, then we will not be concerned about gains and losses, making it easy to calm the mind.

Chapter Three
Observe the Phenomena of Arising and Ceasing of Body and Mind

Since birth, a person is subject to the intrusions and harassment of suffering due to aging, sickness, death, closeness to loathsome people, separation from loved ones, not getting what one wants, and the five aggregates. In order to completely resolve the life issue of endless transmigration, the Buddha decided to renounce the home life and progressed on the Way of practice, contemplating deeply the cause of human existence and transmigration, finally he realized the principle of dependent origination: "When this arises, that comes up. When this is present, that comes to be. When this is absent, that does not come to be. When this ceases, that is extinct." Ultimately, he was liberated from all suffering and worries, attaining the state of *nirvāṇa.*

"When this arises, that comes up" indicates that cause and condition already exist (this arises) and effect will come to exist (that comes up). "When this is present, that comes to be" means when cause and condition arise (this is present), effect will arise (that comes to be). The former focuses on when the "effect" arises in existence, and the latter emphasizes the moment the "effect" arises. In observing dependent origination, we will discover the world is impermanent. In studying the process of the Buddha attaining enlightenment, it is not difficult to discover that he departed from delusive thoughts and gained liberation and ease through observing how his body and mind arise and cease. In this chapter, I will explain how consciousness and emotional bondage develop. With understanding and realization, we will be able to improve self-control over our emotions and behaviors.

The mind will follow how six sense organs in contact with the six dusts to grasp and pursue

In Mahāyāna Buddhism, we often speak about the sense organs of the eyes, ears, nose, tongue, body, and mind. In the *Āgama Sutta,* these are known as the "six internal sense bases;"

the internal sense bases of the eyes, ears, nose, tongue, body, and mind. In modern terminology, these may be referred to the nerve systems of visual, auditory, smell, taste, tactile, and mental cognition.

> Thus have I heard:
> One time the Buddha was residing at Anāthapiṇḍada's Park in Jeta's Grove near Śrāvastī.
>
> At that time, the World-Honored One addressed the *bhikṣus*: "There are six internal sense bases. They consist of the internal sense bases of the eyes, ears, nose, tongue, body, and mind."
>
> After the Buddha had said these words, the *bhikṣus* were delighted to hear the words of the Buddha and faithfully received this teaching and practice.
>
> ~From Fascicle Number 323 from the *Connected Discourses.*

"The six internal sense bases" and "the six external sense fields" can be collectively referred to as "the twelve sense bases (*dvādaśâyatana*)." What are the "the six external sense bases?" Please read the following passage for an explanation.

> Thus have I heard:
> One time the Buddha was residing at Anāthapiṇḍada's Park in Jeta's Grove near Śrāvastī.
>
> At that time, the World-Honored One addressed the *bhikṣus*, "There are six external sense fields. Which six are they? Form, sound, smell, taste, touch, and mental objects. These are what are called the six external sense fields."
>
> After the Buddha had spoken the sutta, the *bhikṣus* were delighted to hear the words of the Buddha and faithfully received this teaching and practice!
>
> ~ From Fascicle Number 324 from the *Connected Discourses.*

The six external sense bases described in the *Āgama Sutta* are the bases of form, sound, smell, taste, touch, and mental objects. In Mahāyāna Buddhism these are usually referred to as the six dusts: the dusts of form, sound, scent, taste, touch, and mental objects. They are also known as "the six fields."

In short, the twelve sense fields describe cognitive abilities through the six sense bases of the eyes, ears, nose, tongue, body, and mind, toward the cognizable objects; the six dusts of form, sound, scent, taste, touch, and mental objects. In other words, these are "the all" as spoken by the Buddha.

Consciousness and its Development

Once the six sense organs are in contact with the six dusts giveing rise to the function of differentiation of the six consciousnesses, the three karmas of action, speech, and thought will be created unceasingly. Consciousness performs the functions of cognition and knowing. If you've seen a given person or a given object, it will leave a certain impression on your mind. This is the function by which the six types of consciousness rely on sensory nerve systems to leave behind visual, auditory, and gustatory sense impressions. With every encounter by the consciousness, an effect rises immediately and is able to influence our emotional state of mind. These sorts of phenomena are part of the seventh consciousness.

Every day we venture outward and this develops into actions and behaviors. These pursuits might be beneficial to our families and societies or they might be harmful to others. All of these are remembered and stored in our eighth consciousness. Therefore, the eighth consciousness is like our spiritual DNA and it determines our next rebirth.

The series of mental process can actually be divided into several stages. Below are related passages from suttas that I have selected to explain this process:

The six-consciousness body

The six sense bases (biological) cognize the six sense fields (physical) that generate the arising of the six consciousnesses (psychological). This is the meaning of "sense base and fields come together, consciousness arises." Six-consciousness body indicates the six kinds of consciousness (body means kinds.)

> Thus have I heard:
> One time the Buddha was residing at Anāthapiṇḍada's Park in Jeta's Grove near Śrāvastī.
>
> At that time, the World-Honored One addressed the *bhikṣus*: "There is the six-consciousness body. Which six? The eye consciousness of the body, the ear consciousness of the body, the nose consciousness of the body, the tongue consciousness of the body, the body consciousness of the body, and the mind consciousness of the body. These are called the six-consciousness body.'"
>
> After the Buddha had said these words, the *bhiksus* were delighted to hear the words of the Buddha and faithfully received this teaching and practice.
>
> ~ From Fascicle Number 325 from the *Connected Discourses.*

The six-contact body

When the three phenomena of internal sense bases, sense fields, and consciousness come together, contact arises. In this way, subsequent mental phenomenon can arise. For instance, the sense base of the eyes, the sense field of form, and eye-consciousness come together, therefore it is called "eye-contact." This same explanation applies to the other senses as well.

> Thus have I heard:
> One time the Buddha was residing at Anāthapiṇḍada's Park in Jeta's Grove near Śrāvastī.
>
> At that time, the Buddha addressed the *bhikṣus*, "There is the six-contact body. What is the six-contact body? They are the body of

visual contact, auditory contact, olfactory contact, gustatory contact, tactile contact, and cognitive contact. These are called the six-contact body."

After the Buddha had said these words, the *bhikṣus* were delighted to hear the words of the Buddha and faithfully received this teaching and practice.

~ From Fascicle Number 326 from the *Connected Discourses.*

In truth, Mahāyāna Buddhism rarely touches on the six-contact body. The main reason is, some may not cultivate the Dharma method of ceasing and contemplating meditation as taught by the Buddha. The feeling, perception, and volitional formations of the five aggregates and the six feelings, six perceptions, and six cravings from the Twelve Links of Dependent Origination are all triggered by the arising of contact. Four applications of mindfulness: contemplate that the body is impure, that feelings result in suffering, that thoughts are impermanent, and that all dharmas are due to the causes and conditions based on the dependent origination.

The six-feeling body

Next, consciousness develops into feelings.

Thus have I heard:
One time the Buddha was residing at Anāthapiṇḍada's Park in Jeta's Grove near Śrāvastī.

At that time, the Buddha addressed the *bhikṣus*, "There is the six-feeling body. Which six? They consist of feelings arising from visual, auditory, olfactory, gustatory, tactile, and mental contact. This is called the six-feeling body."

After the Buddha had said these words, the *bhikṣus* were delighted to hear the words of the Buddha and faithfully received this teaching and practice.

~ From Fascicle Number 327 from the *Connected Discourses.*

In the regions where Mahayana Buddhism was propagated, there is rare mention of how the six contacts give rise to the six corresponding feelings and how the connection between contact and feelings affect psychological changes and the development of emotional states, and not much spoken on the practice of "all feelings result in suffering." Nonetheless, this is how feelings; painful, pleasant, and neither painful nor pleasant unfold into emotions such as joy, anger, sorrow, pleasure, sadness, grief, affliction, anxiety, fear and longing.

The six-perception body

After the arising of six feelings the mind wants to understand, the mind wants to understand and analyze deeper; therefore, the integration and organizing functions of the cognitive process arise.

> Thus have I heard:
> One time the Buddha was residing at Anāthapiṇḍada's Park in Jeta's Grove near Śrāvastī.
>
> At that time, the World-Honored One addressed the *bhikṣus,* "There is the six-perception body. Which six? Perception from visual, auditory, olfactory, gustatory, tactile contact, and mental contact. This is called the six-perception body."
>
> After the Buddha had said these words, the *bhikṣus* were delighted to hear the words of the Buddha and faithfully received this teaching and practice.
>
> ~ From Fascicle Number 328 from the *Connected Discourses.*

The six perceptions come directly from contact. That is to say that perception analyzes, distinguishes, and cognizes the external sense fields, which trigger the arising of the psychological emotions such as joy, anger, sorrow, and pleasure. The distinction of right thought and incorrect deluded thought is such that right thoughts derive from right view and associate with wisdom; incorrect deluded thoughts derive from incorrect view and associate with ignorance. Ignorant and incorrect thought leads to the arising of craving (desirous thought), and thereby physical and verbal karma are created. The accumulation of these is called "becoming," the momentum which propels life and death and the cycle of rebirth.

The six-intention body

After this cognition takes place, it further initiates action. In this context, it refers to "mental actions," also called "craving."

> Thus have I heard:
> One time the Buddha was residing at Anāthapiṇḍada's Park in Jeta's Grove near Śrāvastī.
>
> At that time, the Buddha addressed the *bhikṣus*, "There is the six-intention body. Which six? They are intentions arising from visual, auditory, olfactory, gustatory, tactile, and mental contact. This is called the six-intention body."
>
> After the Buddha had said these words, the *bhiksus* were delighted to hear the words of the Buddha and faithfully received this teaching and practice.
>
> ~ From Fascicle Number 329 from the *Connected Discourses*.

The six-intention body is psychological actions arising from the six contacts of the sense organs. It has the same content as the aggregate of "mental formation" as in "feeling, perception, mental formation, and consciousness;" in the context of karma, it is "mental karma:" it is also the link of "craving" as in "craving, grasping, and becoming."

The six sense bases together with the six sense objects give rise to the six-consciousness body, six-contact body, six-feeling body, six-perception body, and six-intention body. These give rise to the emotional states of joy, anger, sorrow, and pleasure in our daily lives; the compound of these phenomena are referred to as humans. When the six sense bases come together with the six sense objects, we develop the perceptions with the notions of a person and sentient beings. Once we develop the notions of self and others, then subsequently onto the notions of sentient beings and longevity, worries come forth.

Nevertheless, we ought to understand that the twelve sense bases and the eighteen states (six sensory organs, six sense fields, and the six consciousnesses) are the "coming together of causes and conditions, arising from false perceptions." Therefore, when emotional turmoil comes and distress arises, we should learn the practice of "giving up." Let go of unwholesome habitual tendencies such as attachments, greed, and craving. By learning to accept the short end of the stick and letting go, we will benefit from the "supposed disadvantages that allow gaining the upper hand." If we can replace owning with sharing, then we will be the wealthiest person in the world.

With regards to all conditioned phenomena, we should understand clearly that all phenomena are impermanent and devoid of self-nature. Due to phenomena being devoid of self-nature, naturally they change in accordance with conditions. According to the *Diamond Sūtra*, "All conditioned phenomena are like dreams, illusions, bubbles, and shadows, like dew and lightning. One should contemplate them in this way." The *sūtra* also stated that the mind "should not be attached to form, sound, scent, taste, touch, or conditioned phenomena." If we clearly understand this principle, we will be free from all burdens and bindings, no longer be subject to the influence of external environments.

Understanding oneself from consciousness

If you truly wish to understand yourself, you can do so in depth through the understanding of consciousness. The mind is referred to sometimes as intention, sometimes as consciousness, or also as a conscious state of mind. The mind possesses the functions of cognition, differentiation, memorization, and decision-making.

The object that the consciousness is able to cognize and differentiate is "dharma dusts" which is, memory. When we are idle, the mind searches inward for memories of people, events, and things. The mind further analyzes, integrates, and forms concepts, then makes decisions. Through this process comes about verbal and physical behaviors; these then become mental karma, verbal karma, and physical karma.

People may ask, "Which consciousness is responsible for our day to day seeing, hearing, and cognizing?" In fact, everything in the world arises through dependent origination. When our optical nerves (eye sense organ) come into contact with an object through sight, the consciousness arises at almost the same time and a recording of the form is made. After a bird flies afar or a small animal skitters out of view and although you can no longer see the bird or animal, an impression of them remains in the consciousness. This is a memory and becomes a part of "dharma dust."

The functions of our consciousness are remarkably strong, and could be described as extraordinary powers. When the optical nerves (eyes sense organ) or auditory nerves (ear sense organ) come into contact with the respective dust of sight or dust sound, the separate consciousness simultaneously arises and immediately records the experience. At the same time, it searches for files stored in the memories (dharma dusts) for comparing and contrasting: "I saw some sort of bird flying by" or "I heard some sound." If there is no comparable sights or sounds in the memory database, it will simply inform us: "I have no idea what that was" or "what the sound was."

The remarkably strong capacity of the consciousness is most pronounced while encountering a quarrel or a fight, especially when people are hurling verbal abuse at one another. Before party A has even finished speaking, party B understands the gist of what will be said and is ready to immediately offer up a counter. This is because in our everyday lives, the consciousness relies on the contact between sense organs and sense objects for search of the memory database. The sense organs are optic nerves, auditory nerves, olfactory nerves, gustatory nerves, and tactile nerves and come into contact with the dust of form, dust of sound, dust of scent, dust of taste, and dust of touch; searching endlessly the database for memories and consciousness, the process able to differentiate and compare, give rise to emotional states such as joy, sadness, excitement, and melancholy, et cetera.

That which the consciousness finds agreeable is pursued with great desperation. On the other hand, that which the consciousness finds disagreeable will be avoided or destroyed by all means. Greed and anger naturally arise. With fear of gain and loss, people sometimes develop depression or bipolar disorder. In less severe cases, some encounter emotional states such as inhibition, worry, nervousness, or irritability, and others. If we do not apply the wisdom of the Dharma and diligently practice meditation, we will not be able to eradicate these psychological ailments. It can be said that the practice of meditation is the unsurpassed method for countering emotional instability.

In conclusion, what people have done and committed in their lives will enter into their memory and be brought along to their rebirth in another life. The endless attachments and concerns of such allow no peace of mind. Like an oil lamp, if oil or fuel is added continuously, the fire will keep burning unceasingly; it is only by removing oil or fuel that the fire will be extinguished. Similarly, with no attachments or worries and no tainting by cravings or desires, worries will then be possible to cease.

Chapter Four
The Place for Countering Worries: Gates of the Six Roots

Let me continue the explanation on the functions of consciousness. The "six roots" or sense bases of eyes, ears, nose, tongue, and body are the sensory nervous system, bringing about the corresponding visual consciousness, auditory consciousness, olfactory consciousness, gustatory consciousness, and tactile consciousness to help our mind understand the surrounding environment. Like seeds, when provided with soil and water, they are able to sprout and further continue to grow. Roots signify growth, so the sensory nervous system is called "root."

The six roots interact with form, sound, smell, taste, touch, and mental objects which are called the six states or six dusts. When our mind comes across the six dusts, it will give rise to six corresponding consciousness with joy, aversion, happiness, or anger. These serve to cover our true, pure wisdom like dust so we cannot see clearly.

Six Roots Contact with the Six Dusts and Give Rise to the Six Consciousness

Simply put, six roots are biological organs, six dusts are the physical world, and the six consciousnesses are psychological functions. If our visual nervous system (eyes) are not good, we will not be able to see what a flower is like. If we wish to know the fragrance of a flower or that of a fruit, we rely on our olfactory nervous system. If we wish to know what is sour, savory, or sweet, we rely on our gustatory nervous system. If we wish to know what is soft, hard, or hot, we rely on our tactile nervous system. Therefore, in order for the mind to learn, it takes the physical body to provide assistance. We cannot solely rely on the physical nor the mental because neither will make sense by itself.

Because they are helpful in the understanding of our mind,

these five sensory organs are called eye consciousness, ear consciousness, nose consciousness, tongue consciousness, and body consciousness. In addition, the function to think, cognize, differentiate, make decision, and remember is called the sixth consciousness.

On cognizing and differentiating (sixth consciousness), love will then develop, which is the function of the seventh consciousness. For things that we love or hate, emotions such as joy, anger, sorrow, happiness, anxiety, grief, or distress will arise. In other words, the seventh consciousness is filled with love; it is also very active, impulsive, and resilient. Affected by the differentiation from the six roots on encountering the six dusts, it consistently latches on to outside circumstances in the pursuit of external objects, similar to an ape or a wild horse. Consciousness is also equipped with the function of memory. Once the consciousness takes in external states, it contemplates endlessly; similar to viewing video or listening to audio recordings repeatedly, the impressions grow stronger; consequently, towards those which we find agreeable, then we incline to gain and possess.

Once there was a person who is not particularly wise but was quite determined in his studies, one time he heard someone say the word, preposterous and he thought to himself, preposterous is a rather good word. He then kept repeating this word to himself, hoping that he had memorized it. One day he needed to take a boat somewhere and just as he boarded the boat, it shook a little and he suddenly forgot the word. He thought he lost it and began pacing around the boat searching for it. The boatman yelled out to him, "Did you lose something?" The man called back, "I lost a word." The boatman replied, "You can even lose a word? That's utterly preposterous!" The man then piped up, "Hey! You found it and you didn't even tell me?"

For things we hold close to our hearts, should we miss it let alone losing it, we may very easily fall into deep anxiety. There was once a male student who over one vacation stayed with a classmate and brought along his homework. Once the vacation concluded and classes were set to start again, he had to return home. As he got aboard a bus to head home, he casually slipped his hand into his pocket and suddenly discovered that he had forgotten to take his keys. He immediately grabbed his mobile phone and called his classmate to say, "Hey! My key is in your home. Yeah... my key is in your home." In Chinese, this sentence sounds quite similar to "I want to die in your home." Overhearing the conversation, the bus driver felt alarmed and pulled over the bus to find out what was going on with the young student.

Maternal love is an example of impulses driven by love. For instance, in an unfortunate event such as a house fire. If her son is still trapped in the fire, the mother will risk her own life in the attempt to rush back to the burning building to bring him to safety. Although firefighters would hold her back, she will still exhaust herself in the struggle to do so.

Six-craving body

How is love depicted in the *Āgama Sutta?*

> Thus have I heard:
> One time the Buddha was residing at Anāthapiṇḍada's Park in Jeta's Grove near Śrāvastī.
>
> At that time, the World-Honored One addressed the *bhikṣus*, "There is the six-craving body. What is the six-craving body? Visual contact gives rise to craving; auditory, olfactory, gustatory, tactile, and mental contacts give rise to craving. This is called the six-craving body"
>
> After the Buddha had said these words, the *bhikṣus* were delighted to hear the words of the Buddha and faithfully received this teaching and practice.
>
> ~ From Fascicle Number 330 from the *Connected Discourses.*

According to teachings of the Buddha, contacts give rise to the six cravings. It belongs to the mental karma; in the Twelve Links of Dependent Origination, this is the link known as craving.

At this stage, the mind is entangled with the external sense fields, unable to let go, and hence not capable to resist the object. In this way, if we were to say that ignorance is the main cause for the cycle of rebirth, then craving is the momentum and a sustaining cycle of rebirth!

Six-clinging attachments

With a mind tainted by the six-craving, we tend to miss the good old days and at times, strongly attached to what is present. This will bring about physical or verbal behaviors. Consequently, this extends to "the six-clingings."

> Thus have I heard:
> One time the Buddha was residing at Anāthapiṇḍada's Park in Jeta's Grove near Śrāvastī.
>
> At that time, the World-Honored One addressed the *bhikṣus*, "There are six clingings. Which six? Clinging over sight, clinging over sound, clinging over smell, clinging over taste, clinging over touch, and clinging over thought. These are called the six clingings."
>
> After the Buddha had said these words, the *bhikṣus* were delighted to hear the words of the Buddha and faithfully received this teaching and practice.
>
> ~ From Fascicle Number 331 from the *Connected Discourses*.

Once the emotion drifts along with external sense fields, one thinks about them constantly and becomes preoccupied with everything in the past, including nostalgia, wealth, power, and everything one used to possess. It is especially true that if someone brings up your glory days, you will quickly become enraptured with those bygone days. Conversely, if you discuss sad tragedies from your past, you may well find yourself breaking into tears and lamenting immensely! These sorts of emotions are more common in the elderly. On the other hand, young people experiencing similar behaviors have a higher chance of developing depression.

Six-obscurations

It is not difficult to see when contact connects with ignorance, the arising six-feeling body, six-perception body, six-contemplation body, six-craving body, and six-clinging body will lead to conduct with outflows.

Thus have I heard:

One time the Buddha was residing at Anāthapiṇḍada's Park in Jeta's Grove near Śrāvastī.

At that time, the World-Honored One addressed the *bhikṣus,* "There are six obscurations. Which six? Outflow from form causes an obscured mind. Outflow from hearing, smelling, taste, touch, and mental objects give rise to obscured mind. These are called the six-obscurations."

After the Buddha had said these words, the *bhikṣus* were delighted to hear the words of the Buddha and faithfully received this teaching and practice.

~ From Fascicle Number 332 from the *Connected Discourses.*

Six-obscurations are the six kinds of obscure or covered circumstances. Due to the clinging resulting from our body and mind interacting with external states, which results in the rising ideology of a self, the origin of ignorance. When ignorance obscures our pure mind, then what is agreeable brings joy, while what is disagreeable brings sorrow. Furthermore, in the ceaseless pursuit of form, sound, scent, taste, touch, and metal objects, all the resulting conduct from the endless cravings and desires are all "outflows," phenomena with attachments and worries. Whether it be joy and excitement or pain and sorrow, day after day, we can only be carried away with the flow endlessly.

Six-joyful Conduct

When we encounter people, events, or things which we like, the six sense bases give rise to the conduct in forms of joyful, praising, and tainted conduct ('conduct' in this context means 'volitional actions').

> Thus have I heard:
> One time the Buddha was residing at Anāthapiṇḍada's Park in Jeta's Grove near Śrāvastī.
>
> At that time, the World-Honored One addressed the *bhikṣus*, "There is the six-joyful conduct. Which six? As such, *bhikṣus*! When the eyes see form of joy, will conduct according to the form. When the ears hear sound, nose smell, tongue taste, body touch, and mind mental objects of joy, one will conduct according the phenomena. *Bhikṣus*! This is called the six-joyful conduct."
>
> After the Buddha had said these words, the *bhikṣus* were delighted to hear the words of the Buddha and faithfully received this teaching and practice.
>
> ~ From Fascicle Number 336 from the *Connected Discourses*.

When the six external states are agreeable, we naturally feel delighted. Especially when our favorite people, events, or things suddenly appear, we might even find ourselves so elated that we cheer with delight or jump for joy. As the six sense bases pursue agreeable forms of the six sense objects, even simple lapses in attention can cause one to fall into over-indulgence. If unfortunately one becomes addicted to unwholesome habits, such as gambling, smoking, overeating, overdrinking, and soliciting prostitutes, it is quite difficult to give up these vices.

Six-sorrowful Conduct

The opposite of six-joyful conduct is the six-sorrowful conduct. These refer to all external states that are not agreeable with what we like.

> Thus have I heard:
> One time the Buddha was residing at Anāthapiṇḍada's Park in Jeta's Grove near Śrāvastī.

> At that time, the World-Honored One addressed the *bhikṣus*, "There is the six-sorrowful conduct. Which six? *Bhikṣus*! When the eyes see form of sorrow, will conduct according to the form. When the ears hear sound, nose smell, tongue taste, body touch, and mind mental objects of sorrow, one will conduct according to the phenomena. *Bhikṣus*! This is called the six-sorrowful conduct."
>
> After the Buddha had said these words, the *bhikṣus* were delighted to hear the words of the Buddha and faithfully received this teaching and practice.
>
> ~ From Fascicle Number 337 from the *Connected Discourses*.

When we see or hear people, events, things, or sounds for which they have an aversion, suffering or distress thus arises. The six-joyful conduct which cause joy occur when in contact with attractive external states. The six-sorrowful conduct occur when in contact with averse external states. A simple example would be when one wins a contest, it will be the six-joyful conducts; when we lose a contest, it will be the six-sorrowful conducts instead.

The Mind Should Not Change with the Environment

The mind should not turn with the environment is the key Dharma teaching of section four in the *Diamond Sutra*: "Moreover, Subhuti, within this phenomenal world, a bodhisattva should practice giving without abiding in anything. This means that he should not give abiding in form, nor should he give abiding in sound, smell, taste, touch, or dharmas." It is also the key practice within Humanistic Buddhism.

When our eyes see something wonderful or beautiful, giving rise to greed, then this is tainted attachment and such is called "abiding." Therefore, "without abiding in anything" means there is no tainted attachment to any phenomena. When we do not have greed or anger in facing the six sense objects, this is called "equanimity."

All suffering in the world arises from love. If we understand the physical body is the combination of causes and conditions, which is impermanent and not lasting forever and unchanging, then our mind can be at ease in following conditions and will not suffer. As long as the mind does not change with external states, then even though the body may suffer, the mind will not take it as suffering.

Six-equanimity Practice

Thus have I heard:
One time the Buddha was residing at Anāthapiṇḍada's Park in Jeta's Grove near Śrāvastī.

At that time, the World-Honored One addressed the *bhikṣus,* "There is the six-equanimity practice. Which six? *Bhikṣus!* When the eyes see forms and maintain equanimity for the form; when the ears hear sound, the nose smells scent, the tongue tastes a flavor, the body touches a texture, and the mind thinks a thought and maintain equanimity for the phenomena, such is called the six-equanimity practice of *bhikṣus.*"

After the Buddha had said these words, the *bhikṣus* were delighted to hear the words of the Buddha and faithfully received this teaching and practice.

~ From Fascicle Number 338 from the *Connected Discourses.*

Do not give rise to desire or greed when met with the six sense objects are attractive, enjoyable, memorable, and pleasing. In other words, a practitioner should be able to remain neutral to either the six-joyful or the six-sorrowful conducts. This is what is called "equanimity."

Six-continuous Practice

In order to protect the mind from regressing, it is important to maintain right mindfulness, right understanding, and right wisdom. Consequently, the Buddha explained as follows:

Thus have I heard:
One time the Buddha was residing at Anāthapiṇḍada's Park in Jeta's Grove near Śrāvastī.

At that time, the World-Honored One addressed the *bhikṣus,* "There is the six-continuous practice. Which six? When *bhikṣus* see forms with their eyes, there is neither suffering nor pleasure. The equanimous mind abides in right mindfulness and right wisdom; when the ears hear sound, the nose smell scent, the tongue tastes a flavor, the body touches a texture, and the mind thinks a thought, there is neither suffering nor pleasure, the equanimous mind abides in right mindfulness and right wisdom, such is called the six-continuous practice of *bhikṣus.*"

After the Buddha had said these words, the *bhikṣus* were delighted to hear the words of the Buddha and faithfully received this teaching and practice.

~ From Fascicle Number 339 from the *Connected Discourses.*

A *bhikṣu* must maintain right mindfulness and right wisdom in life at all times. Within the six sense objects, there should be no greed nor anger. Always maintaining a mind that is not abiding in anything. These practices are called the six-continuous practices of a *bhikṣu.*

If throughout all moments, a practitioner is able to maintain high awareness while walking, standing, sitting or lying down with the mind not changing with the external environment, it is the unsurpassed field of merits. If in addition, he practices the bodhisattva path without abiding in anything, it is even more remarkable. Therefore in the following *sutta* the Buddha praised his disciples in being able to accomplish the six-continuous practice, which is rare to achieve in the world and so is worthy of being attended to, respected, and offerings made to by everyone.

Thus have I heard:
One time the Buddha was residing at Anāthapiṇḍada's Park in Jeta's Grove near Śrāvastī.

At that time the World-Honored One addressed the *bhikṣus*: "There are six continuous practices. Which six? When a *bhikṣu's* eyes see a form, there is neither suffering nor pleasure. The renouncing mind abides in right mindfulness and right wisdom. When the ears hear a sound, the nose smells a scent, the tongue tastes a flavor, the body touches a texture, or the mind thinks a thought, there is neither suffering nor pleasure. The renouncing mind abides in right mindfulness and right wisdom. If a *bhikṣu* accomplishes the six-continuous practices, then he has done something rarely achieved in this world. He is worthy of being attended to, respected, and offerings made to; the unsurpassed field of merit in the world."

After the Buddha had said these words, the *bhikṣus* were delighted to hear the words of the Buddha and faithfully received this teaching and practice.

~ From Fascicle Number 341 from the *Connected Discourses.*

Unsurpassed Field of Merit in the World

The Buddha further took Śāriputra as an example for he always maintained right mindfulness and right wisdom; further, he was able to practice the six equanimity and the six-continuous practices. This achievement was truly remarkable and was therefore called the highest field of merits in the world worthy of offering by future generations.

Thus have I heard:
One time the Buddha was residing at Anāthapiṇḍada's Park in Jeta's Grove near Śrāvastī.

At that time, the World-Honored One addressed the *bhikṣus*, "There are six-continuous practices. Which six? When a *bhikṣu's* eyes see a form, there is neither suffering nor pleasure. The renouncing mind should abide in right mindfulness and right wisdom. When the ears hear a sound, the nose smells a scent, the tongue tastes a flavor, the body touches a texture, or the mind thinks a thought, there is neither suffering nor pleasure. The renouncing mind abides in right mindfulness and right wisdom. When *bhikṣus* achieve the six-continuous practices, you should know it is accomplished by Śāriputra and other advanced *bhikṣus*. When Bhikṣu Śāriputra's eyes see a form, there is neither suffering nor pleasure; his renouncing mind abides in right mindfulness and right wisdom. When his ears hear a sound, his nose smells a scent, his tongue tastes a flavor, his body touches a texture, and his mind thinks a thought, there is neither suffering nor pleasure. His renouncing mind abides in right mindfulness and right wisdom. Due to Bhikṣu Śāriputra accomplishing the six continuous practices, it is something rarely achieved in this world. He is worthy of being attended to, respected, and made offerings to; the unsurpassed field of merit in the world."

After the Buddha had said these words, the *bhikṣus* were delighted to hear the words of the Buddha and faithfully received this teaching and practice.

~ From Fascicle Number 342 from the *Connected Discourses*.

The above *sutta* was not the only *sutta* which Buddha praised Śāriputra. From fascicle number 236 from the *Connected Discourses*, it can be seen as well.

Thus have I heard:
One time the Buddha was residing at Anāthapiṇḍada's Park in Jeta's Grove near Śrāvastī.

At that time, the Honorable Śāriputra donned his robes in the morning and carried his alms bowl, entering Śrāvastī to beg for food. When he was done collecting alms, he returned to the monastery and put away his robes and bowl. When he finished washing his feet, he carried his meditation mat and entered a nearby forest for a daytime meditation. Then Śāriputra exited his meditation and went to visit the World-Honored One. He prostrated before the Buddha's feet and sat to one side.

At that time, the Buddha spoke to Śāriputra, "From where have you come?"

Śāriputra replied, "World-Honored One, I have come from

sitting in daytime meditation."

The Buddha asked further, "What meditative abode do you abide?

Sariputra answered, "World-Honored One, today I practice in the forest, abiding in *Sunyata Samādhi.*"

The Buddha said to Sariputra, "Excellent! Excellent! Sariputra, you now abide in *maha-purisa-vihara*. If *bhikṣus* wish to enter *maha-purisa-vihara,* they should learn as such.

When entering the city to collect alms, and when exiting the city after collecting alms, you should contemplate as such: 'Now my eyes see forms, are there the arising of desire, passion, or attachment?

Sariputra, when *bhikṣus* contemplate in this manner, if the eye consciousness is tainted with attachment of desire, these *bhikṣus* should eradicate the negative and unwholesome by striving for skillful means in order to be mindful of their practice. It is like a man whose head-dress caught fire, in order to extinguish the fire, he should expediently apply all skills and means to put out the fire. *Bhikṣus* should be as such, they should expediently apply all diligence, skills, and means in being mindful of their practice.

When *bhikṣus* observe on the road, entering the village to beg for alms, or while exiting the village, their eye consciousness has no tainted attachment of desire for forms within, these *bhikṣus* apply these roots of joy and wholesomeness with diligence day and night to be mindful of their practice, it is called the pure alms begging of *bhikṣus* while walking, standing, sitting, or lying down. Therefore, this *sutta* is called *Pure Alms Begging Sutta*."

After the Buddha had said these words, the *bhikṣus* were delighted to hear the words of the Buddha and faithfully received this teaching and practice.

~ From Fascicle Number 236 from the *Connected Discourses.*

The key points of this *sutta* passage is that one morning after Śāriputra finished his meditation, he went to where the Buddha resided and asked for further instruction. The Buddha asked him where he had come from. Śāriputra answered that he had come from the forest after finishing his meditation. The Buddha further asked him which state of meditative concentration he had entered, and Śāriputra replied, "In the forest I entered into *Sunyata Samādhi*."

On hearing this, the Buddha praised Sariputra's practice of *Sunyata Samādhi* as the top level of meditation method *(maha-purisa-vihara)* and emphasized that for people wishing to enter into such meditative concentration, they should at all times observe their own thoughts arising. It is as if the clothes we wear caught fire, the most efficient way is to put out the fire quickly.

Sunyata Samādhi is the meditation method of cultivating "contemplate the five aggregates of form, feeling, perception, volition, and consciousness are impermanent." It is one of the three kinds of *samādhi* (*Sunyata Samādhi, Anamitta Samādhi,* and *Ākiṃcanyāyatana Samādhi*); also one of the major meditation methods in the *Agamas.*

Simply put, *Sunyata Samādhi* is empty of the five aggregates, *Anamitta Samādhi* is empty of the six dusts, and *Ākiṃcanyāyatana Samādhi* is empty of the three poisons of greed, anger, and ignorance. In fascicle 342 of the *Connected Discourses,* the Buddha praised Sariputra for accomplishing the six-continuous practice to be the unsurpassed field of merits in the world; in fascicle 236, the Buddha further praised Sariputra for abiding in *maha-purisa-vihara* in meditation, it is certain that Sariputra had eradicated greed, anger, and ignorance for all states of the six sense objects and realized *Ākiṃcanyāyatana Samādhi.*

Moreover, in section ten of the *Diamond Sūtra* it reads: "For this reason, Subhūti, all bodhisattvas should give rise to purity of mind in this way: They should not give rise to a mind that abides in form, they should not give rise to a mind that abides in sound, smell, taste, touch, or *dharmas.* They should give rise to a mind that does not abide in anything." This excerpt is actually an extension of the teaching that Buddha gave to the noble Śāriputra on 'states of meditative concentration and seated meditation.' That is why the Buddha said that this teaching is to be known as the *'Purification of Alms Food Sūtta.'*

Ākiṃcanyāyatana Samadhi: Non-arising of Greed, Anger, and Ignorance – Three Poison Defilements

Ākiṃcanyāyatana Samādhi refers to the complete cessation of pleasure, displeasure, annoyance, greed, anger, or ignorance when the mind encounters the states of the six sense objects. From Sunyata Samādhi, the five aggregates are empty; and from Anamitta Samādhi, all in the world are empty. All in the world are fragile and decaying, arising and ceasing rapidly and are devoid of real substance. Therefore, on encountering such states that are illusory and unreal, which will extinguish in the end, what is there to be greedy for? What is there to be angry over? As such, we can progress by not having greed, anger, or ignorance for these states. Since "all phenomena arise through dependent origination and are of an empty nature," one knows that all phenomena are empty, false, and not real; all phenomena arise and cease rapidly; all phenomena are fragile and decaying, eventually fall into cessation. Only through this wisdom is one able to arrive upon a state free from greed and anger.

Chinese Buddhism has always taught that practitioners to "practice morality, meditative concentration, and wisdom to extinguish greed, anger, and ignorance." In other words, we cultivate by steps the morality, meditative concentration, and wisdom in order to extinguish greed, anger, and ignorance. In actuality, greed and anger arise due to ignorance. Therefore, we should first rid ourselves of ignorance and then proceed from there! Once ignorance has been extinguished, greed will be extinguished; once greed has been extinguished, anger will naturally be extinguished as well. After all, without greed, it is not possible for anger to take root. The meditative concentration of having cutoff greed, anger, and ignorance is precisely "Meditative Concentration Focused on the Nothingness."

Chapter Five
The Stages of Practicing Meditation: Nine Stages of Mental Focus

Our thoughts are usually scattered and distracted because the eyes, ears, nose, tongue, body, and mind connect with the self-delusion, self-view, self-love, and self-arrogance within the seventh consciousness. As the six sense bases keep pursuing from the outside, the mind will become agitated, always craving for and having greed for what is seen, smelled, heard, and tasted from the external surrounding.

Once the mind comes into contact with the external environment, it will immediately give rise to the feelings of either agreeable or adverse. When the feeling is agreeable, then the thought of "can you give me some more" will instantly arise. If what we want is not given to us, anger and hate will take place.

In our daily life, when the six sense bases are influenced by the seventh consciousness in craving for what is outside is a very natural phenomenon. When the daily craving becomes a habit, the mind within will give rise to delusional thoughts at every turn. In order to subdue such delusional thoughts, the most basic and thorough method is to engage in "self-empty contemplation" for breaking the seventh consciousness through "contemplate the five aggregates are empty."

Nonetheless, when the principle of wisdom of emptiness is not yet accomplished, we first have to apply effort at the mundane phenomena state. That is to use various methods to master or control our eyes, ears, nose, tongue, body, and mind so as to "see no evil, hear no evil, speak no evil, and act no evil." As such, through the practice of upholding precepts and reciting the Buddha's name to help us see less, hear less, speak less, and act less, then naturally, our worries will also lessen.

The Process of Focusing the Mind and Subduing Worries

A reminder here: when we practice we must concurrently uphold precept, practice concentration, and contemplate wisdom; while the three complement one another, upholding precepts comes first. Because by not transgressing others, our mind will not have regret, shame, guilt, vexation, or annoyance, making it easier to enter into concentration. This is why in cultivating concentration, we must first uphold precepts. Therefore, when we are mindful in our practice of meditative concentration, our mind will not become agitated, impulsive and our conduct will naturally be in accordance with the Dharma and conforms with the precepts.

With concentration we can restrain the worries within the mind and our conduct will be pure. When the strength of concentration is within our speech and conduct, our mind will be very clear on every thought arising, knowing whether it is wholesome or unwholesome, pure or tainted, and further guard against worries. In this chapter I will explain the "nine stages of mental focus" so that we will not be confused in our cultivation of meditative concentration and be clear of the progress in our practice.

1. *Internal Focus*

The stages of practicing meditative concentration follow a set sequence; we first should decide on a state or object of focus so be able to concentrate. When the six sense bases come across the six sense objects, they are seeking externally; it is called "the mind is released" as the mind is completely let go outwardly. So delusional thoughts always arise and the mind is unable to settle. When we begin to practice, we must "gather the mind and guard the intention" to abide on a state or object of focus. As such, the mind directs inwards and no longer engages in the six sense bases seeking six sense objects externally. This is called "internal focus," the first stage of practice.

2. *Continuous Focus*

Naturally, one cannot become fully accustomed to inner abiding overnight. It is like moving to a new city and living in a new house. It is not possible to be immediately accustomed to your new surroundings, and that is why when training in meditative concentration, deluded thoughts are unavoidable. Dealing with this involves a response to the arising of a deluded thought by immediately recalling that you are cultivating meditative concentration, and then, bring your concentration back to the task at hand. Anything that drifts outward from your mind, bring it back and refocus your concentration.

This is like ox herding. If your ox starts eating someone else's grains, you have to give it a tug on its bridle and bring it back where you want it. If you do not keep paying attention to it, your ox will go back to someone else's field and start eating their crops until you take notice and bring it back once more. At this time in the cultivation of meditative concentration, this action of having one's focus stray and then bring it back to its proper object is "continuous focus."

3. *Calm Focus*

As you examine your state of focus, for instance breath-counting, have you ever found yourself 'counting' something else as deluded thoughts carry your attention elsewhere? Once you observe that this has happened, you can bring your attention back slowly. When training oxen or horses, they can only be tamed slowly and only then becoming relatively obedient. They can even learn to identify which crops belong to which farmers and demonstrate their obedience by eating the crops on their master's land. However, sometimes, just like humans, greed easily arises in their minds and they might start eating crops that they like even if those crops are on a neighboring farmer's land. It is truly hard to decline the allure and therefore they sometimes eat crops that belong to others. When this happens they should be brought back home. After a while, they will get better and progress at adapting to this.

After some time, you will know all your neighbors, be familiar with your environment, and have attained a certain degree off peace of mind. This is called "tranquil abiding." Even though it is still unavoidable that thoughts may still wander outward, but it is very easy to be aware of it, knowing that we need to come back within, we will not stray too far from the state or object of focus.

4. *Close Focus*

For instance, if you see something or someone you like, an emotional impulse will arise in that moment, however, since you have cultivated meditative concentration, your concentration arises and then you quickly realize that you should not act impulsively. With regards to protecting your state of focus, you are able to cause right mindfulness to arise, and when you do so, you are able to abide quite closely to your state of focus. This level cannot be described as being free from the arising of deluded thoughts, but it is close to such a state. That is why this level is called "close focus." The levels of internal focus, continuous focus, calm focus, and close focus are skills that one should diligently train in day by day and night by night.

Cultivating meditative concentration requires diligence. This is like how, in order to hatch baby chicks, a mother hen must sit on her eggs, not allow them to grow cold, and keep their temperature warm for the proper amount of time. Diligence is precisely this meticulous. In one's daily life one must take care of right mindfulness wherever and whenever it is needed. We practice this skill in meditation halls so that in our daily lives after we leave our meditation halls, when we meet with external states, we can immediately return to our state of focus. This kind of skill is "close abiding," and through it, we are able to overcome worries.

5. *Compliance*

Within "close focus," we will feel more focused in dealing with matters and we will be able to concentrate more easily. When reading Buddhist sutras, we will also feel more invested, focused and feel that our understanding and realization has increased. We will like to continue practicing concentration even more, and gradually grow less enchanted with the five desires and six sense objects offered by the external surroundings. This is not to say that once situations emerge, emotional impulses do not arise. It is rather that we appreciate the wondrous merits of meditative concentration, we feel it is better to let go of the five desires and six sense objects. As such, our mind will calm down and the gates of our senses are closely guarded. On reaching this stage, our six sense bases are under our control and well disciplined, meaning we are able to tame our body and mind to comply with the state or object of focus. It is called "compliance," the stage of our learning the Dharma and cultivating the Way where worries can quickly be subdued.

From this stage onwards, we will be able to achieve what Early Buddhism has taught regarding the "four right efforts" as follows:

1. Increase wholesomeness that has already been produced: the wholesome thoughts that have arisen in the mind or wholesome deeds that have committed, sustain their growth and strengthen their effect.
2. Generate wholesomeness that has not yet been generated: we should give rise to the resolve to do so if wholesome thoughts are not yet risen.
3. Eliminate unwholesomeness that has already been produced: unwholesome deeds already committed must be ceased immediately, not allowing to continue growing or expanding.
4. Not to produce unwholesomeness that has not been produced: unwholesome deeds that have not arisen should not be allowed to develop. Once an unwholesome thought arises, it should not be allowed to proliferate but eradicated immediately.

It is at this stage the four right efforts can be truly applied and effectively eradicate our worries and habitual tendencies.

6. *Quiescence*

The compliance in the previous stage refers to the mind being able to subdue the seductive power of the external environment and to comply with the state or object of focus. The sixth stage is quiescence of the mind; it is the beginning of concentration and the ability completely hold on to the state or object of focus. So on the arising of irrelevant thoughts and delusions, we will be able to differentiate them clearly and eradicate them cleanly. Therefore, this stage is where we specifically differentiate whether the arising thoughts within our minds are good or bad, pure or tainted, wholesome or deviant.

We need to take note that the "*nirvāṇa* quiescence" of the Three Dharma Seals is the description of the state of *nirvāṇa* which sages realize on entering into meditative concentration and eradicating all defilements. Here, the quiescence indicates not yet entering into meditative concentration, when past seeds within the Eighth Consciousness begin to sprout, we are able to detect them right away. So we are to increase the wholesomeness that has already been produced, not to produce the unwholesomeness that has not been produced, and to eliminate the unwholesomeness that has already been produced.

7. *Supreme Quiescence*

When thoughts arise at the sixth stage of quiescence, the mind is still in an ambiguous state, still differentiating whether they are tainted or agreeable and still debating if we should accept them or not? We are unable to eradicate these delusional thoughts right here and now with wisdom. However, on reaching the seventh stage of supreme quiescence, awareness is even higher. Once a thought arises, we can cease it immediately, subduing delusional thoughts and not allowing them to continue breeding. When cultivation has reached this stage, the mind is almost entirely trained on the state or object of focus.

At this time, we will have clear knowledge of our thoughts as they arise; whether they are wholesome or unwholesome, tainted or pure, and right or deviant. We will know if thoughts should be subdued or ceased. Equipped with the strength of concentration and further fortified with the strength of awareness, so we are able to subdue them immediately. This is "supreme quiescence." It could be said that upon reaching the sixth level, quiescence, and the seventh level, supreme quiescence, our meditative concentration is such that we rarely ever do or say something wrong in daily life. In this stage we abide in right understanding; when thoughts arise, we can differentiate them very clearly.

8. *One-pointed Focus*

If we are able to continue holding our mind to the state or object of focus, then we will be able to enter into the eighth stage of one-pointed focus. This point refers to "focal point," meaning the mind is completely focused on one point, the state or object of focus.

9. *Equilibrium*

Most people that do not practice meditation will experience rising and ceasing within their minds. When met with matters they like they will keep thinking about them, their thoughts rising endlessly. When tired, they become fuzzy and have no wisdom, getting drowsy and just wanting to doze off. So the inner mind is "not in equilibrium."

On reaching the ninth stage when practicing meditation, we should be able to maintain a state of quiescence and equality. There is not the slightest rising, agitation, or confusion; there is not the slightest drowsiness or ambiguity, it is a state of equality, and being able to sustain as such, it is called equilibrium.

On reaching the eighth stage of one-pointed focus and the ninth stage of equilibrium, physically there is the feeling of relaxing ease like floating on air which is very soothing and comfortable. With this experience, it can be said we have reached non-regression in the practice of meditation. However, this is only non-regression for practicing meditation and not non-regression in the gate of wisdom.

We choose our own state or object of focus in our practice, and after reaching the state of equilibrium if we experience relaxing ease then we are nearing the states of "close to concentration" or "not yet to concentration," the preparatory stage for basic concentration. When continuing to apply effort, we can enter basic concentration, meaning the four kinds of concentration of first *dhyāna*, second *dhyāna*, third *dhyāna*, and fourth *dhyāna* within the Realm of Form and Realm of Formlessness.

The above are the steps of cultivating meditation and we all should know how to apply them. As such, we are able to understand our progress and further prevent arrogance within ourselves. For some people, especially for those practicing Chan, they become wildly arrogant on achieving some concentration, almost becoming obsessed. Therefore, in practicing meditation, the nine stages of mental focus must be clearly understood. We should observe ourselves well from now on and self-examine from time to time to check what stage we have progressed into.

Sutric Teachings have Clear Structure of Stages in Learning Buddhism

Some people lacking a deep understanding of Sutric teachings often go to learn Tantric teachings with a curious mind, thinking that Tantric teachings are very well-structured in stages. In reality, Sutric teachings are truly well-structured. For instance, on the understanding of principles, starting from knowing how suffering accumulates to the state of happiness when suffering dissipates, and then further explains the causes and reality of suffering. In the cultivation of meditation, there are the "close to concentration" and "not yet to concentration" stages. There are also the basic concentration stages of first *dhyāna*, second *dhyāna*, third *dhyāna*, and fourth *dhyāna*. More so are the levels of nine stages of mental focus, which describe how to focus the mind and how to subdue worries, all the way to how to eradicate habitual tendencies. All of which are clearly explained and described.

On realizations, it starts from the "four foundational practices" to the first attainment, second attainment, third attainment, and fourth attainment. For the Bodhisattva Path, first off it needs to be the Ten Levels of Faith for cultivating merits. On completion of the cultivation, next is the non-regression Bodhisattva Path for abiding in the Ten Levels of Abiding, all the way to the Ten Levels of Grounds: first level is perfection of Giving Paramita, second level is perfection of Precepts Paramita etc., all of which are very structured in various stages.

Chapter Six
Practice Self-Reconciliation

A practitioner of Buddhism should not mistake the Dharma for common knowledge and should truly actualize the teachings. So "letting go" is not being apathetic for that which has been let go, we should instead diligently apply ourselves towards making positive changes wherever we are able.

There are many things in life that people have difficulty letting go. When pet owners have a dog die, they cry very sadly in their grief. Some people file lawsuits over an odd plot of land; or on hearing a single criticism of themselves, they embed the hate in their hearts and never let it go. Buddhism teaches that there is not a self and that all are unreal and illusory. However, sentient beings think there is a self which is eternal, unchanging, and capable of being one's own master. No wonder they are often worried about gains and losses, always troubled and in suffering. In truth though, our physical bodies undergo changes every day. For example, as we age, we become more susceptible to health problems such as high blood pressure and diabetes; our emotional states are often at the mercy of how inflation rates fluctuate. This is impermanence, there is nothing in the world that stays unchanging forever; all phenomena are changing endlessly.

If we are able to understand the true forms of phenomena within the world, knowing that originally there is no self nor objects of self. As such, we will no longer give rise to attachments and be at ease here and now. In dealing with people and matters, we will not be fighting with others as if it is a life or death struggle. We just follow conditions; what is there is there, what is not there is not there, accepting things as they are is true freedom. When the mind is free, we will be able to let go.

All phenomena arise from causes and conditions and cease due to causes and conditions; all phenomena come into existence from causes and conditions. The world is impermanent and not real, so we need to let go of all matters. Unable to let go, we alone suffer; able to let go, we can live in happiness.

Correct Understanding of the Law of Causality

Thus have I heard:
One time the Buddha was residing at Anāthapiṇḍada's Park in Jeta's Grove near Śrāvastī.

At that time, the World-Honored One addressed the *bhikṣus*: "There are five appropriated aggregates. Which are taken as the five? They consist of the appropriated aggregate of form, and the appropriated aggregates of feeling, perception, mental formations, and consciousness. Excellent! *Bhikṣus* who do not take pleasure in form, give praise to form, cling to form, or become attached to form. Excellent! *Bhikṣus*! They do not delight in form, feeling, perception, mental formations, and consciousness. They do not give praise to consciousness, do not cling to consciousness or become attached to consciousness. Why is that so? If *bhikṣus* do not delight in form, do not give praise to form, do not cling to form, due to their not delighting in form, their minds will be liberated. The same is true of feeling, perception, mental formation, and consciousness; do not delight in consciousness, do not give praise to consciousness, do not cling to consciousness, do not become attached to consciousness, due to their not delighting in consciousness, the mind attains liberation. For *bhikṣus* not delighting in form, the mind is liberated. The same is true for feeling, perception, mental formation, and consciousness. The mind attains liberation, neither ceasing nor arising, abiding in equanimity, right mindfulness, and right wisdom.

Bhikṣus who understand and view as such have viewed their previous lifetime, forever eliminated without remainder; view through their previous lifetime and forever eliminated without remainder, they view their future lifetime, also eliminated without remainder; having viewed their future lifetime and eliminated without remainder, they have viewed their past and future lifetimes, eliminated without remainder, they have no attachments. Those with no attachments do not cling to anything in any world and also have no desire. Those without desires self-realize *nirvāṇa*: I have completed my final birth and established my pure practice; all there that is to be done is now done. I know I will no longer be subject to rebirth."

After the Buddha had said these words, the *bhikṣus* were delighted to hear the words of the Buddha and faithfully received this teaching and practice.

~From Fascicle Number 60 in the *Connected Discourses.*

This *sutta* explains that practitioners should "understand the five aggregates and not be attached to the five aggregates," then their mind is liberated. I will now explain the terms, "having seen through their past lifetime, having seen through their future lifetime, having seen through their past and future lifetimes." The time periods here correspond to "past, present, and future," and "view" means the ability to "see through." In the *Treatise on the Stages of Yogâcāra Practice* in part 785 of section 30, 87th scroll of the *Taishō Tripiṭaka*, it further explains: "There are three parts in forming *satkāyadṛṣṭi*, also known as, the view of the body and view of the self, wrong views of having substantial existence: Fundamental view of all: 1) Due to all in the past lifetime, 2) Due to all in the future lifetime, 3) Due to all in the past and future lifetimes.

Due to all in the past lifetime is giving rise to attachment of the self. Wherein one contemplates as such, "Did I exist in a previous life? Did I not exist in a previous life? Who was I in my previous lives? How was it that I came to exist in those lives?"

Due to all in the future lifetime is giving rise to attachment of the self. Wherein one contemplates as such, "Will I exist in a future life? Will I not exist in future life? Who will I be? How is it that I will become as such?"

Due to all in the past and future lifetimes is giving rise to attachment of the self. Wherein one contemplates, "Who was I in past lives? Who was me in past lives? Where did I now, come from? At the end of this lifetime, after I die, where will I go?"

Additionally, in fascicle number 296 in the *Connected Discourses* it reads:

"Noble disciples who have often heard the Dharma have attained right view and wholesome understanding regarding the

> principle of causality and phenomena arisen through dependent origination. They perceive phenomena well and do not seek for knowing past lifetime by asking, "Did I exist in past lives? Did I not? What kind of existence did I belong to? How were my past lives?" They do not seek for knowing future lifetimes: "Will I exist in future lifetimes? Or will I not? What kind of existence? How will my future lifetimes be?" They do not waver within: "What are these around me? Why did they exist previously? Who were they in previous lifetimes? Where do these sentient beings come from? What form will they take after death?" If *śramaṇas* or *brāhmins* give rise to attachment due to worldly views such as the view of permanent self, view of sentient beings, view of longevity, or view of auspicious and inauspicious omens. Then, such views should be eradicated on awareness of them. Sever such views at their roots as though chopping down the head of a *tāla* tree, then in future lifetimes, they will become a non-arising phenomenon. This is how noble disciples who have often heard the Dharma attain from the principle of causality and phenomena arisen through dependent origination: right understanding, right view, right awakening, right cultivation, and right reception."

In this *sutta*, the Buddha reminds his disciples that they should have a correct understanding of the law of causality and dependent origination. They definitely should not reflect on whether or not they existed in a past life and do not look for what type of sentient being they will be reborn as in their next life. In their minds, they should not wonder about why they exist in this life, or where they will go after they die. If *śramaṇas* or *brāhmins* become bound by these deluded mundane views, then they are bound to the false notions of view of the self, view of sentient beings, view of longevity, and view of taboo and auspicious actions, which are subjected to the perspectives of culture and mores.

The most significant difference between the cultivation of the Dharma practiced by monastics and the Dharma teachings practiced by the laity is that monastics strive to eradicate all of their desires and greed. The deepest held forms of desire and greed are centered on each individual's body and mind. If the notion of body and mind cannot be given up within our thinking, we will always, to a greater or lesser degree, express ourselves verbally in a manner tainted by greed and desire. We may use flattery, pandering, clever language, or ingratiating behaviors.

If we are truly able to cultivate, not through restraint but through practice of the practitioner, to the stage of non-grasping, non-attachment, non-abiding, and then we will have no grasping for anything in the world. Having no grasping, we will have no desires. Those without desires (individuals whose minds clearly understand the power of being without desire) can self-realize enlightenment and *nirvāṇa.* With no regard or seeking for the past or future, we are very free and at ease, our body and mind are liberated! What is stated in the *Diamond Sūtra*: "The mind of the past cannot be obtained, the mind of the present cannot be obtained, and the mind of the future cannot be obtained" should be related to the two *suttas* above.

During the Buddha's lifetime, instructions to disciples in their cultivation were either simultaneously cultivating morality, meditative concentration, and wisdom or the dual cultivation of meditative concentration and wisdom. In fascicle number 60 in the *Connected Discourses* contains the emphasis on non-abiding and turning away from notions are the key teachings of the *Diamond Sūtra.*

"Nothing to Grasp" is a Converging Point between the Śrāvaka Path and the Bodhisattva Path

Practitioners who correctly observe that the five aggregates have no self and no objects of the self, are able to not grasp on to anything within the world, and have no attachments.

> Thus have I heard:
> One time the Buddha was residing at Anāthapiṇḍada's Park in Jeta's Grove near Śrāvastī.
>
> At that time the World-Honored One addressed the *bhikṣus:* "Form is impermanent, impermanence is suffering, suffering is not self. As for no-self, none of it is self, not different from self, nor

> mutually existing. By knowing as such, it is called right contemplation. Feeling, perception, mental formations, and consciousness are also as such. Noble disciples who have often heard the Dharma observe the five aggregates have no-self and not objects of self. Contemplating as such, there is nothing to grasp in the world, and hence there are no attachments, and since there are no attachments, there is self-realization of *nirvāṇa*: I have completed my final birth and established my pure practice; all there that is to be done is now done. I know I will no longer be subject to rebirth."
>
> After the Buddha had said these words, the *bhikṣus* were delighted to hear the words of the Buddha and faithfully received this teaching and practice.
>
> ~From Fascicle Number 84 in the *Connected Discourses*

The *sutta* opens with observation of impermanence and then concludes with suffering, emptiness, and non-self.

"Throughout the world, there is nothing to grasp; with nothing to grasp there are no attachments, and since there are no attachments, there is self-realization and *nirvāṇa*"; this means that on observing the five consciousnesses are impermanent and the five aggregates, have no self and not objects of the self, we are able to have no grasping or attachments, progressing to the state of *nirvāṇa.* It should be noted here that this level of *arhatship* is equivalent to that of a bodhisattva on the eighth ground, "the ground of unperturbedness." In other words, having no grasping or attachments is the key leading to *arhats* or bodhisattvas.

The most significant difference is that due to the great power of the bodhisattva's compassionate vows, they do not enter into the state of cessation in *nirvāṇa.* It is the state of meditative concentration wherein the effects of all appearances and feeling have been extinguished. At that point, the mind enters into a perfect state of tranquil oneness. If bodhisattvas enter into this state, they will not be able to deliver sentient beings in *saṃsāra.* Furthermore, when bodhisattvas reach the eighth ground, even the Buddha will come to advise them "Do not become *śrāvakas* or *pratyekabuddhas!* You cannot enter into *nirvāṇa!*"

The Sūtra of Great Wisdom states: "When bodhisattvas cultivate to reach the stage of having no attachments, they can increase their practice of giving, morality, patience, and the other six perfections of diligence, meditative concentration, and wisdom, as well as the myriad practices which exist within those perfections. If bodhisattvas are not otherwise fulfilling compassionate vows and have reached the stage of having no attachments, then they enter *nirvāṇa*, the same state as *arhats*."

Because there is Nothing to Grasp, Nirvāṇa Can be Attained

Thus have I heard:
One time the Buddha was residing at Anāthapiṇḍada's Park in Jeta's Grove near Śrāvastī.

At that time, the World-Honored One addressed the *bhikṣus*, "*Bhikṣus*! What is it which is not viewed as the self, separate from the self, or mutually existing with the self?"

The *bhikṣus* answered the Buddha, "World-Honored One, you are the Dharma root, the Dharma eye, and the Dharma refuge; our only wish is to be taught! On hearing your teaching, all *bhikṣus* will sincerely practice as you have instructed."

The Buddha told the bhikṣus, "Listen carefully! Contemplate well! I will speak on this for you. In form, there is no self, not separate from self, and not mutually existing with self, is it not? It is the same for feeling, perception, mental formations, and consciousness. Bhikṣus, is form permanent or impermanent?"

The *bhikṣus* replied to the Buddha, "Impermanent, World-Honored One!"

"*Bhikṣus*! If form is impermanent, is it suffering or not?"

The *bhikṣus* replied to Buddha, "It is suffering, World-Honored One!"

"*Bhikṣus*! If it is impermanent, suffering, and subject to change, should noble disciples who have often heard the Dharma perceive within a self, no-self, or mutually existing in the self or not ?"

The *Bhikṣus* replied to Buddha: "No, World-Honored One!"

> "Feeling, perception, mental formations, and consciousness are also as such. Because of this, *bhikṣus*, all form which exists whether in the past, present, or future, whether internal or external, whether coarse or fine, whether attractive or ugly, whether far or near, all of these are not a self, separate from self, or mutually existing with self. *Bhikṣus*! Noble disciples who have often heard the Dharma observe the five aggregates, that they have no self and no objects of self. For those having observed as such, they have nothing to grasp in all the world; with nothing to grasp there is no attachment, and with no attachment there is self-realization of *nirvāṇa*: I have completed my final birth and established my pure practice; all there that is to be done is now done. I know I will no longer be subject to rebirth."
>
> After the Buddha had said these words, the *bhikṣus* were delighted to hear the words of the Buddha and faithfully received this teaching and practice.
>
> ~From Fascicle Number 85 in the *Connected Discourses*

Whether it is the three time periods of past, present, and future, whether internal or external, fine or coarse, attractive or ugly, near or far, the five aggregates still have no self and no objects of self. There is no self in the five aggregates and the five aggregates are not within a self... Observing as such, we have right view and see the Dharma. Therefore, the mind attains peace and ease in all the world!

With Nothing to Grasp, Able to Enter the Bodhisattva Path

Since bodhisattvas are without attachment, they are able to enhance themselves by practicing all wholesome practices. Bodhisattvas denounce the five desires of form, sound, smell, taste, and touch, eliminating greed, anger, and ignorance, and know that all phenomena are nominal names to become free from attachment. These stages of cultivation are similar to the practice of the *śrāvaka* path: no grasping to anything in the world and no attachments. These paths need to follow the Middle Way of dependent origination as stated in the Noble Eightfold Path in order to realize enlightenment.

When *arhats* achieve *nirvāṇa* all defilements are eradicated. For the bodhisattva path, it is the beginning to be motivated by their own original aspiration, or rely on the empowerments of all buddhas in protection and instructions, commencing to extensively practice the bodhisattva path. This is why I have referred to this as the converging point of the *śrāvaka* path and the bodhisattva path.

The Middle Way of Dependent Origination is a Unique Characteristic of Buddhism

The Middle Way of dependent origination explains that everything in the world could not have arisen without causes and conditions. All matters and objects rely on a multitude of causes and conditions in order to be as they are. On the other hand, once the causes and conditions that make up a phenomenon disperse or no longer adhere to one another, that phenomenon will change or even cease to be. Consequently, arising and changes are both due to causes and conditions. There is not a "real self-existence" in the world. In Buddhist sutras, it is often said that all phenomena have no intrinsic self, 'no self-nature' is neither a state of existence or nonexistence; there is no actual state of increasing or decreasing. This is emptiness, the philosophy of the Middle Way.

The Five Aggregates Have No Self-Mastery (1)

Thus have I heard:
One time the Buddha was residing at Anāthapiṇḍada's Park in Jeta's Grove near Śrāvastī.

At that time, the World-Honored One addressed the *bhikṣus*: "There is no self within form. If there was a self within form, then it would not be subject to sickness or the arising of suffering. Likewise, if that self wishes to make form act this way or that way, it could do so. Since form has no self, so there is sickness and suffering in form, and form cannot order itself to act this way or that way. Feeling, perception, mental formations, or consciousness are the same. *Bhikṣus*! What do you think? Is form permanent or impermanent?"

The *bhikṣus* replied to the Buddha, "Impermanent, World-Honored One!"

"*Bhikṣus*! If form is impermanent, is it suffering?"

The *bhikṣus* replied to Buddha, "Yes, it is suffering, World-Honored One!"

"Given that form is impermanent, suffering, and is a phenomenon subject to change, should noble disciples who have often heard the Dharma perceive within form a self, separate from self, or mutually existing with self?"

The *bhikṣus* replied to Buddha: "No, World-Honored One!"

"Feeling, perception, mental formations, and consciousness are also like this. Because of this, *bhikṣus*, all form which exists whether in the past, present, or future, whether internal or external, whether coarse or fine, whether attractive or ugly, whether far or near, all of these are not a self, separate from self, or mutually existing with self. Observation as such reveals that feeling, perception, mental formations, and consciousness are also the same.

"*Bhikṣus*! With regard to the five aggregates, noble disciples who have often heard the Dharma understand that they are not self, not objects of self, and observe as such. Having observed as such, there is nothing to grasp in all the world, and hence there are no attachments; and since there are no attachments, there is self-realization and *nirvāṇa*: I have completed my final birth and established my pure practice; all there that is to be done is now done. I know I will no longer be subject to rebirth."

After the Buddha had said these words, the *bhikṣus* were delighted to hear the words of the Buddha and faithfully received this teaching and practice.

~From Fascicle Number 33 in the *Connected Discourses*.

This *sutta* explains how form is unable to have self-mastery and therefore there is no self. Feeling, perception, mental formations, and consciousness are likewise unable to have self-mastery and there is no self. Those who understand and view as such do not grasp or attach themselves to anything, realizing *nirvāṇa*.

The Buddha emphasized that "the five aggregates have no self" because the five aggregates depend on causes and conditions for their continual existence and do not have self-mastery. Therefore, there is no way for us to wish we will not get sick and then be freed from sickness, to hope to be without suffering and then be freed from suffering, or to wish to have our way in what we do. We need to understand that the five aggregates have no self and are not objects of self so as to be free from attachments.

The Five Aggregates Have No Self-Mastery (2)

The *sutta* below also explains how form has no self-mastery and therefore has no self. Feeling, perception, mental formations, and consciousness also have no self-mastery and have no self. Right view requires understanding of no self and so no grasping to anything, without attachments is the attainment of *nirvāṇa*.

> Thus have I heard:
> One time the Buddha was residing at the Deer Park of Ṛṣipatana near Vārāṇasī.
>
> At that time, the World-Honored One spoke to a group of five *bhikṣus*: "Form has no self, if form has a self, then it would not be subject to sickness or the arising of suffering. Likewise, if that self wishes to make form act this way or that way, it could do so. Due to form having no self, so there is sickness and suffering, and form cannot order itself to act this way or that way. Feeling, perception, mental formations, or consciousness are also the same. *Bhikṣus*! What do you think? Is form permanent or impermanent?"
>
> The *bhikṣus* replied to the Buddha, "Impermanent, World-Honored One!"
>
> "*Bhikṣus*! If form is impermanent, is it suffering?"
>
> The *bhikṣus* replied to Buddha, "Yes, it is suffering, World-Honored One!"
>
> "*Bhikṣus*! Given that form is impermanent, suffering, and a

phenomenon subject to change, should noble disciples who have often heard the Dharma perceive within form a self, separate from self, or mutually existing with self?"

The *bhikṣus* replied to Buddha: "No, World-Honored One!"

"Feeling, perception, mental formations, and consciousness are also like this. *Bhikṣus*, all form which exists whether in the past, present, or future, whether internal or external, whether coarse or fine, whether attractive or ugly, whether far or near, all of these have no self and are not objects of self. Actual observation reveals that feeling, perception, mental formations, and consciousness are also as such.

Bhikṣus! With regard to the five aggregates, noble disciples who have often heard the Dharma understand that they have no self, not objects of self, and contemplate as such. There is nothing to grasp in all the world, and therefore no attachments; since there are no attachments, there is self-realization and *nirvāṇa*: I have completed my final birth and established my pure practice; all there that is to be done is now done. I know I will no longer be subject to rebirth."

When the Buddha finished speaking this discourse, the group of five *bhikṣus* no longer gave rise to any outflows, attaining liberation in their minds.

After the Buddha had said these words, the *bhikṣus* were delighted to hear the words of the Buddha and faithfully received this teaching and practice.

~From Fascicle Number 34 in the *Connected Discourses*.

The Buddha Taught No Self to Three Bhikṣus

Thus have I heard:
One time the Buddha was residing in Veṇuvana-vihāra on Mount Jeta.

At that time, there were three excellent practitioners who had only recently renounced. They were known as the Honorable Aniruddha, Honorable Nandiya, and Honorable Kimphilla. Thereupon, the World-Honored One knew what they were thinking and began instructing them, "*Bhikṣus*, this mind, this intention, this consciousness; you should contemplate as such. Not to contemplate to eradicate this desire, this form, the body is testimony of realization. *Bhikṣus*, could there be a form which is permanent, unchanging, and abiding?"

The *bhikṣus* replied to the Buddha, "No, World-Honored One."

The Buddha spoke again to the *bhikṣus*, "Excellent! Excellent! Form is impermanent, a phenomenon which is subject to change, it is to be weary of, to depart from desire, to be extinguished, and to cease. Form has always been as such, all of which are impermanent, suffering, and a phenomenon subject to change. If you know as such, form is the condition by which all harmful defilements, vexations, and worries arise; it is also the condition by which they are eradicated. On eradication, there are no attachments; with no attachments, there is abidance in peace and happiness; on abiding in peace and happiness, one attains *nirvāṇa*. Feeling, perception, mental formations, and consciousness are also as such."

When the Buddha spoke this discourse, the three excellent practitioners no longer gave rise to any outflows and their minds attained liberation.

After the Buddha had said these words, the *bhikṣus* were delighted to hear the words of the Buddha and faithfully received this teaching and practice.

~From Fascicle Number 35 in the *Connected Discourses*.

The non-self as spoken in Buddhism is teaching us to be just and unselfish in dealing with people and situations. In our cultivation, non-self is contemplating the five aggregates are empty. To observe this from within a quiet state, it is the tranquility of *nirvāṇa*. "Self" means it is eternal, unchanging, singular, and characterized by self-mastery, being in complete control of itself, independent with a real nature. For instance, when the "I" eats, dresses itself, and goes about its other daily tasks should be spoken of as a "nominal self."

The Buddha's teaching on non-self aims to eliminate the ignorance of sentient beings. Ignorance is wrong thinking, it is inverse. Because ordinary beings believe there is the existence of a self, they give rise to incorrect thinking.

Take the Right Dharma as Refuge

The world is impermanent and money cannot buy true and lasting friendship, power, affection, or happiness. This insight can also be proven through the truth of the Three Dharma Seals: All conditioned phenomena are impermanent, all phenomena are without an independent self, and *nirvāṇa* is perfect tranquility. When we understand the truth of impermanence, we can achieve ease of body and mind because we are able to let go of the self. The mind is free from worries, attaining premier happiness, the tranquility of *nirvāṇa.*

In understanding this principle, we can also understand the empty nature of all phenomena, and to have further appreciation of the principle of "should give rise to a mind that does not abide in anything," liberating the body and mind to be free from obstructions. We will not lose our grounding in success and not lose our spirit in failure. We will be able to get back on our feet and strive forward on the path of happiness and fulfillment in life.

A fulfilled life is not a matter of cultivating as an *arhat* for gaining self-realization, but is instead a matter of benefiting sentient beings by cultivating the six perfections and the myriad practices of the bodhisattva path. In brief, life is a matter of self-reliance, helping others, believing deeply in cause and effect, and building a right view of life. In the following *sutta*, the Buddha tells us "Abide in own self-nature, abide in own refuge, abide in Dharma nature, abide in Dharma."

The meaning of the above is to rely on ourselves, be our own refuge, rely on the right Dharma, and take refuge in the right Dharma. Do not rely on others, and do not take refuge in others. In other words, "rely on yourself, rely on the Dharma, and rely on nothing else."

The main point of the following *sutta* is that the five aggregates are impermanent, suffering, and phenomena subject to change.

Thus have I heard:
One time the Buddha was residing near Ajitavatī River in Āmravana Park in Madhurā.

At that time, the World-Honored One addressed the *bhikṣus*, "Abide in yourselves, abide in own refuge; abide in Dharma, abide in refuge of the Dharma; not on another, not rely on another. *Bhikṣus*, observe correctly as such: abide in yourselves, abide in own refuge, abide in Dharma, abide in refuge of the Dharma; not on another, not rely on another. What is the cause giving rise to worries, sorrow, affliction, and suffering? Why are there these four? What is the cause, what are the tethers? Why is it that worries sorrow, affliction, and suffering arise before we see them? Why is it that after they have arisen, they only expand and increase?"

The *bhikṣus* beseeched the Buddha: "World-Honored One, you are the Dharma root, the Dharma eye, and the Dharma refuge. We wish you teach us! Hearing your teachings, we will sincerely practice as you have instructed."

The Buddha told the *bhikṣus*, "Listen carefully! Contemplate well! I now speak for you. *Bhikṣus*, with form, be bound by form. Worries sorrow, affliction, and suffering arise before we see them. After they have arisen, they only expand and increase. Feeling, perceptions, mental formations, and consciousness are also as such. *Bhikṣus*, is there form which is permanent, unchanging, and always exist?"

The *bhikṣus* replied, "No, World-Honored One."

The Buddha spoke further to the *bhikṣus*: "Excellent! Excellent! *Bhikṣus*! Form is impermanent. If good men know that form is impermanent, suffering, and a phenomenon subject to change; it is to be weary of, to depart from desire, to be extinguished, and to cease. Since the beginning, all forms have been impermanent, suffering, and phenomena subject to change. Form is the condition by which all harmful defilements, vexations, and worries arise; it is also the condition by which they are eradicated. Upon eradication, there are no attachments; with no attachments, there is abidance in peace and happiness; on abiding in peace and happiness, one attains *nirvāṇa*.

Feeling, perception, mental formations, and consciousness are also as such."

When the Buddha spoke this discourse, sixteen *bhikṣus* ceased all outflows and their minds attained liberation.

After the Buddha had said these words, the *bhikṣus* were delighted to hear the words of the Buddha and faithfully received this teaching and practice.

~From Fascicle Number 36 in the *Connected Discourses.*

Marvelous Methods for Emotional Relief: Practices of Letting Go and Joy

The six *suttas* above explain practitioners should have no grasping, no attachment to the five aggregates, whether in form or in mind. As such we can attain peace, ease, and liberation. Most importantly, bodhisattvas also cultivate in the same way at this point, and are not different from that of *arhats.*

This is the same as in the second half of the sixth section of the *Diamond Sūtra*: "And why is this? If a sentient being clings to a notion with his mind, then he will cling to self, others, sentient beings, and longevity. If he clings to the notion of phenomena, then he will cling to self, others, sentient beings, and longevity. And why is this? If he clings to the notion of non-phenomena, he will cling to self, others, sentient beings, and longevity. Thus, he must not cling to phenomena or non-phenomena. This is why I have often said to you, *bhikṣus,* that even my teachings should be understood to be like a raft. If even the Dharma must be let go of, what about what is not the Dharma?"

To state this simply, we should have no attachments to anything and this includes the conditioned phenomena of the five aggregates, which should be let go; and the unconditioned phenomenon that is *nirvāṇa.* Then we can peacefully and happily abide in the state of *nirvāṇa*, our emotions will be stable and we are able to live a life of great ease.

I often teach in my talks that everyone must learn well the

practice of letting go. Let go of our attachments, let go of our greed, and let go of our unwholesome habitual tendencies. Learn to let go and to accept losses, then we will understand the happiness that we are looking for. After completed learning the practice of letting go, we need to cultivate the practice of joy. Just set aside fifteen minutes each day in the morning and evening to practice lifting up the corners of your mouth, just enough to continually maintain a gentle smile.

The practice of joy enables us to reduce stress and clear junk from the mind. This will not only smoothen out our circulation, it will also improve general health, and there will be less need to worry about high blood pressure, heart disease, and other such ailments. Should insomnia strike, try the practice of joy and we will be able to fall asleep in no time.

Chapter Seven
Give Me Courage Without Fear

The essence of life is suffering and therefore, many worries, fears, and anxieties exist in the human subconscious. Consequently, the pursuit of happiness has become the momentum that drives life. However, the majority of matters and events in people's life are not in accord with their wishes, and suffering results from failure to gain what is liked. Even if they are able to gain what is liked, but concern over losing it results in fear. Often times, people come into contact with those they dislike, and hate ensues. Transmigration in samsara is like floating on a massive ocean, and this is called "the limitless ocean of suffering."

In the *Agamas*, the Buddha teaches us about liberating the body and mind through the five aggregates of form, feeling, perception, mental formations, and consciousness, the six sense organs and the six sense objects; and the six elements of earth, water, fire, wind, space, and consciousness; also known as the six great elements.

The five aggregates focus on the psychology; the sensory and nervous systems of the six sense bases are focused more on physiology, while the six sense fields are focused mainly on physicality. If we are able to understand through analyzing the five aggregates that have no self and are empty of a self; the six sense bases such as the eyes have no self and "internally empty;" the six sense fields have no self and "externally empty;" and the six elements have no self and "all empty," then we can depart from inverse dreams and delusional thinking to have no fear!

For most people, it is inevitable that we will encounter challenging situations and individuals whom we are not fond of. Consequently giving rise to fear, attachments, worries, distress, and other such negative emotional states. If this stress is not properly dealt with, it will almost certainly lead to chronic illnesses.

A devotee discovered that after his new house was completed, his little dog became sick. After an examination by a veterinarian, it was discovered that the dog had diabetes. It turned out that when his owner's home was being remodeled, workers who were all strangers to the dog had been coming and going all the time, resulting in a considerable amount of stress for the dog.

The major contributor to the perpetuation of life is the errors in thinking and behaviors. Due to the misperception that phenomena in the world have a real existence, as long as love and sentiments expand endlessly, strong attraction, aversion, and tainted attachments will arise. The life-philosophy of Buddhism is to understand ourselves from the mind, knowing clearly the source of stress, improve our outlook, rectify our behaviors, and perfect our character. Furthermore, we come to understand the true form of worldly phenomena so that even when facing death, it will not be so fearful.

Remember: The view, "there is no I to love, and no objects of the self" must be our perspective of life, we can then be able to let go of the tainted attachments and worries of love. After all, the body is empty and nothing truly exists, what is there worth getting angry over? Moreover, it is crucial that we understand causes, conditions, and effects, practice the three acts of goodness, and accumulate merits and virtues. Being able to understand these principles, we will be able to enjoy happiness in future rebirths in heaven.

Honorable Upasena: Ease in Life and Death

Death has always been feared most by humankind and also a topic of discussion that we are afraid to face. What is the Buddhist perspective on death?

> Thus have I heard:
> One time the Buddha was residing in Elder Karaṇḍa's Garden in Rājagṛha.
>
> At that time, a *bhikṣu*, named Upasena who lived in a cemetery underneath Snakehead Cliff. There, the Honorable Upasena was

inside sitting alone in meditation.

At that time, a poisonous snake more than a foot long had fallen from within the rocky cliff onto Upasena's body. Upasena called out to Śāriputra and other *bhikṣus*, "A poisonous snake fell on me, my body is poisoned. Quickly come to lift my body away from here, not allowing it to spoil and decompose in here like a pile of bran and chaff."

Thereupon, the Honorable Śāriputra, who was residing under a tree nearby, heard Upasena's words and quickly went to his whereabouts. He asked Upasena, "I now observe your appearance and the sense organs do not seem out of the ordinary. Yet you said, 'I am poisoned. Quickly come to lift my body away from here, not allowing it to spoil and decompose in here like a pile of bran and chaff.' What is the matter?"

Upasena replied to Śāriputra, "If someone was to say, 'My eyes are self, objects of a self; ears, nose, tongue, body, and mind are self, objects of a self; sight, sound, smell, taste, touch, and dharmas are self, objects of the self; earth realm is self, object of the self; the elements of water, fire, wind, space, and consciousness are self, objects of the self; aggregate of form is self, object of the self; feeling, perception, mental formations, and consciousness are self, objects of self.' The person's color and sense organs should be changing. I am not that way. Eyes are non-self, not objects of self… to the extent that the aggregate of consciousness is not self, not objects of self. That is why my color and sense organs have not changed."

Śāriputra replied, "As such, Upasena! If after a long period of dark ignorance you abandon the attachments to the notion of self, objects of self, and self-arrogance, sever them at the roots as though chopping down a tāla tree, they will not arise again in future lives. Why would the color and sensory organs change?" Thereupon, Śāriputra immediately turned to carry the body of Upasena outside where the poison in Upasena caused his body to spoil and decompose like a pile of bran and chaff. There, Śāriputra recited a *gāthā:*

"Long cultivate all pure practices, practicing well the Noble Eightfold Path;

Happy to give up life, like discarding a poisoned alms bowl.

Long cultivate all pure practices, practicing well the Noble Eightfold Path;

Happy to give up life, like a person cured of serious illness.

Long cultivate all pure practices, practicing well the Noble Eightfold Path;

Like exiting a burning building, no sorrow or regrets on death.

Long cultivate all pure practices, practicing well the Noble Eightfold Path;

Observe the world with wisdom, it is a heap of filthy trees and grasses,

Not seeking any further rebirths, any remainder will not be continued."

There, the Honorable Śāriputra paid homage to Upasena's remains and went to visit the Buddha. He prostrated before the Buddha's feet and retreated to one side, he spoke to the Buddha, "World-Honored One! The Honorable Upasena had a small venomous snake, the size of a small bamboo piece that is used to remove rheum from the eyes, drop upon him. His body decayed straightaway like a pile of bran or chaff."

~From Fascicle Number 252 in the *Connected Discourses.*

One day, while Bhikṣu Upasena was practicing meditation in a cave at Snake Grotto, he was inadvertently bitten by a snake. He then asked the Honorable Śāriputra for help. Seeing that Upasena to be well-composed and his expressions had no panic or fear, at first Śāriputra did not believe that Upasena had been bitten by a snake and was on the verge of dying. Śāriputra asked, "How is it that there is venom in your body, Honorable, and yet your complexion has not changed?" Upasena answered, "If I believed that any of the six sense bases, six sense objects, or five aggregates, were a self or were objects of self, I would be seized with panic. However, I deeply know that these are neither a self nor are they objects of self, and therefore, my body and mind are at ease as such."

It is clear that Upasena had already realized that the eyes and other organs of the six sense organs, that sight and the other fields of the six sense fields, that the six elements of water, fire, wind, space, and consciousness, that form and the other aggregates of the five aggregates... that all these phenomena are non-self and nor objects of the self, so his complexion and other faculties remained unchanged, remaining well-composed and at ease. This is something that we should all learn from.

Right Observation of the Five Aggregates as Non-self

Because Upasena had 'achieved the realization that the body and mind is non-self and not object of self,' even when facing death, his complexion remained unchanged. In other words, because he did not attach to the five aggregates, the mind will have no fear. The *Connected Discourses* contain the following *sutta* with an explanation of how not to engage in clinging or attachment:

> Thus have I heard:
> One time the Buddha was residing at Anāthapiṇḍada's Park in Jeta's Grove near Śrāvastī.
>
> At that time, the World-Honored One addressed the *bhikṣus*: "Because of clinging, attachment arises. If one does not cling, there will be no attachment. Listen carefully! Contemplate well! I will now speak for you."
>
> The *bhikṣus* replied to the Buddha, "Please do so. We are ready to receive your teachings!"
>
> The Buddha spoke to the *bhikṣus*, "Why is it that clinging give rise to attachment? Foolish beings who have not heard the Dharma see form as self, being separate from self, or mutually existing with self. They see form as self and object of self and they cling to it. Clinging to it, if that form changes, their minds also turn and change. On changing, the mind gives rise to clinging and attachment. These changes gather in the mind and the mind abides in them. As the mind abides in the gathering of changes, fear, obstructions, and vexation arise; consequently, there is clinging and attachment. Foolish beings who have not heard the Dharma regard feeling, perception, mental formations, and consciousness as a self, separate from a self, or mutually existing with a self. They view consciousness as a self, and

object of self and cling to it. Clinging to it, if it changes, their minds also turn and change. On changing, the mind gives rise to clinging and attachment. These changes gather in the mind and the mind abides in them. As the mind abides in this gathering of changes, fear, obstructions, and vexation arise; consequently, there is clinging and attachment. This is called 'clinging and attachment.'

"What is not clinging and not becoming attached? With regard to form, noble disciples who have often heard the Dharma do not perceive it as a self, separate from self, or mutually existing with self. They do not see form as self or object of self to which they can cling. Not clinging to it, if that form changes, their minds do not turn and change. Not changing, the mind does not give rise to clinging and attachment. Since changes do not gather in the mind, the mind does not abide in them. When the mind does not abide in this gathering of changes, fear, obstructions, and vexation do not arise; consequently there is no clinging and no attachment. With regard to feeling, perception, mental formations, and consciousness, these are not perceived as a self, separate from self, or mutually existing with self. They are not perceived as self, objects of self to cling to. If consciousness changes, their minds do not turn and change. Not changing, the mind does not give rise to clinging or attachment. Since changes do not gather in the mind, the mind does not abide in them. When the mind does not abide in this gathering of changes, fear, obstructions, and vexation do not arise; consequently, there is no clinging and no attachment and is called 'no clinging and no attachment.' Such is called attachment and no attachment"

After the Buddha had said these words, the *bhikṣus* were delighted to hear the words of the Buddha and faithfully received this teaching and practice.

~From Fascicle Number 43 in the *Connected Discourses.*

In the *sutta*, it is written, ".... If form changes, the mind does not turn and change. Not turning and changing, the mind does not give rise to clinging or attachment. Since the changes do not gather in the mind, the mind does not abide in them. When the mind does not abide in the gathering of changes, fear, obstructions, and vexation do not arise." This means no matter how form or the external states change, the mind will not turn and change. Once the mind is no longer tethered or bound, it no longer gives rise to attachments from thinking "This is mine" or "I possess this." Emotions such as fear, obstructions, and vexation will no longer arise.

If clinging and attachment grows stronger in the body and mind (five aggregates), in facing sudden changes such as a physical examination revealing a tumor, then we will undoubtedly experience an onslaught of different feelings and even great fear! Only with clear recognition that 'the five aggregates are not real, are non-self, and do not belong to a self,' are we able to attain newfound strength and wisdom for the mind to calm down.

Method 1:

Observe as such; Arising, Cessation, Desire, Danger, and Liberation

The following *sutta* also guides us in how not to cling and be attached, using a different verb to describe "being attached."

> Thus have I heard:
> One time the Buddha was residing at Anāthapiṇḍada's Park in Jeta's Grove near Śrāvastī.
>
> At that time, the World-Honored One addressed the *bhikṣus*: "There will be attachment on arising, without arising, there will be no attachment. Listen carefully! Contemplate well! I will now speak for you.
>
> Why is there attachment on arising? Foolish beings who have not heard the Dharma do not understand the reality of the arising of form, cessation of form, desire of form, danger inherent in form, and liberation from form. Since they do not understand this reality, they delight in form, praise it, cling to it, and become attached to it. They see form as self, objects of self and cling to it. Clinging to it, if that form changes to be different, their minds turn in changing to be different. When their minds turn in changing to be different, the changes gather in the mind and the mind abides in them. As the mind abides in the gathering of changes, fear, obstructions, and vexation

arise. Feeling, perception, mental formations, and consciousness are also this way. This is called 'arising of attachment.'

Why is it that with no arising there is no attachment? Noble disciples who have often heard the Dharma understand the reality of the arising of form, cessation of form, desire of form, danger inherent in form, and liberation from form. Because they understand as such, they do not delight in form, praise it, cling to it, and become attached to it. Because they do not become attached to it, if that form changes to be different, their minds do not turn and change. Because their minds do not turn and change to be different, their minds have no attachments. These changes do not gather in the mind and the mind does not abide in them. As the mind does not abide in the gathering of changes, fear, obstructions, and vexation do not arise. Feeling, perception, mental formations, and consciousness are also this way. This is called 'no arising, no attachment.'

After the Buddha had said these words, the *bhikṣus* were delighted to hear the words of the Buddha and faithfully received this teaching and practice.

~From Fascicle Number 44 in the *Connected Discourses.*

This fascicle is basically the same as the preceding fascicle, number 43. They differ in the focus on understanding the reality of the arising of form, cessation of form, desire for form, danger inherent in form, and liberation from form. These words appear frequently in the *Connected Discourses.* Their meaning is as follows:

Arising of form: How does it arise?
Cessation of form: How does it disintegrate, extinguish, and cease?
Desire for form: What is attractive about it?
Danger inherent in form: What danger is hidden within it?
Liberation from form: How to gain liberation from it?

The Buddha taught us the methodology on how not to be bound by any external states. We must contemplate these five points above carefully. After we have gained an understanding, then when we encounter changes in our body and mind or when the external environment is not in accordance with our wishes, we are still able to live life happily.

Method 2:

Not be Tainted as the Six Sense Organs Encounter the Six Sense Objects, and the Six Consciousnesses will Not Arise

There was an old man in the last moments of his life, but he just could not close his eyes to leave. His son asked if he had any regrets. The old man said that two years ago he was eating with someone and there was a piece of pork he wanted that was taken by his dining companion. It was a shame because at the time, he had a piece of pork in his mouth and a piece in his chopsticks, and so he could not get the other piece... Think about it, he was unable to let go of a piece of pork for two, three years. How could he be happy?

"Virtuous sages have no attachments or obstructions on their minds, ordinary beings are obstructed everywhere they go." Ordinary beings and virtuous sages have different views. When faced with changes of the six sense objects, ordinary beings give rise to despair and suffering. In dealing with death and separation, they wail and cry and fall into deep pain and sorrow. Virtuous sages or buddhas and bodhisattvas understand well that all phenomena is subject to change and are impermanent, so when the six sense objects undergo changes, they maintain their freedom and ease.

Life is like a suitcase. When it is time to pick it up, we should pick it up; and when it is time to put it down, we should also be able to put it down. In other words, the mind should not be overly tainted with attachments. Seeing something good, do not give rise to greed or craving; seeing something bad, do not be troubled and worried. As such, we will not overly exhaust ourselves, and instead enjoy true happiness.

Next, we will take another look at a fascicle from the *Connected Discourses* that will teach us how to not be tainted by attachments and the disadvantages of tainted attachments.

Thus have I heard:
One time the Buddha was residing at Anāthapiṇḍada's Park in Jeta's Grove near Śrāvastī.

At that time, the World-Honored One addressed the *bhikṣus:* "All *devas* and worldly people are tainted by form and abide in craving and delight. If form is impermanent, subject to change and cessation, it will give rise to great suffering to all *devas* and humans. They crave and delight in sound, smell, taste, touch, and mental objects, abiding in them. These phenomena are impermanent, subject to change and cessation, all *devas* and humans abide in great suffering.

"The Tathāgata understands the reality of form, arising of form, cessation of form, desire of form, danger inherent in form, and liberation from form. Understanding this reality, he is no longer tainted by form and do not crave or delight in form nor abiding in it. Such form is changing, impermanent, and will cease, giving rise to delight and abiding. With sound, smell, taste, touch, mental objects, and their arising, cessation, desire, inherent danger, and liberation the Tathāgata likewise understands their reality. Understanding their reality, the Tathāgata is no longer tainted or delighted by nor abide in them. Such form is changing, impermanent, and will cease, giving rise to delight and abiding. Why is that so? The conditions of eye and form give rise to visual consciousness; the three factors combine in contact, contact is the condition for feeling which can be suffering, pleasure, or neither suffering nor pleasure. Understanding as such that the arising of these three feelings, their cessation, desire, inherent danger, and liberation will give rise to obstructions due to the conditions of such form, when obstructions cease, it is called unsurpassed tranquil *nirvāṇa.* Eyes, ears, nose, tongue, body, and mind give rise to conditions for consciousness. When these three factors combine in contact, giving rise to the conditions for feeling: one feels suffering, pleasure, or neither suffering nor pleasure. The Tathāgata understands the reality of feeling, the arising of feeling, cessation of feeling, desire for feeling, danger inherent in feeling, and liberation from feeling. Understanding that the reality will give rise to obstructions due to the conditions of such phenomena, when obstructions cease, it is called unsurpassed tranquil *nirvāṇa.*

Thereupon, The World-Honored One recited the *gāthā:*

"The six sense fields of form, sound, smell, taste, touch, and mental objects,

Give rise to pleasure and delight, tainted by craving and attachment.

Devas and humans take only this as their happiness,

When these phenomena change and cease, giving rise to great suffering for them.

Only wise sages view their cessation as happiness,

What are worldly happiness, all are bitterness on observation.

What wise sages see as suffering, the world mistake it for happiness,

What the world takes as suffering, wise sages take as happiness.

This deep and difficult to understand Dharma,

The deluded and ignorant beings in the world,

Submerged within murky darkness, blind and cannot see anything.

It is only the wise sages, who can open up the deluded to great illumination.

Such profound teachings, who but the sages can understand?

Those no longer subject to rebirths, can understand deeply the truth."

After the Buddha had said these words, the *bhikṣus* were delighted to hear the words of the Buddha and faithfully received this teaching and practice.

~From Fascicle Number 308 in the *Connected Discourses.*

This *sutta* mainly explains how *devas* and humans (ordinary beings) become tainted by form, sound, smell, taste, touch, and mental objects. They are tainted and become attached, guarding them and unwilling to give up. When sudden changes occur, their minds are thrown into disarray. However, Buddha and bodhisattvas know that all phenomena are impermanent and subject to change, so they are not tainted by becoming attached. Only by losing all external shackles, they can achieve purification of mind and liberation. This is the difference between tathāgatas and ordinary beings.

We regard all people, matters, and objects as being real and our "mind abides on something." For example, if a given object is ours and if we know others have a great desire to possess it, then we will become preoccupied with it at every turn and not wanting others to see. This is called having your mind "abide in" this object, frequently recollecting and being concerned with it.

Before ordinary beings attain enlightenment, in dealing with all matters, especially when we interact with people, things, and situations we find pleasing, our minds will often move towards such. This is known as the "mind abides in something." It never hurts to learn from the teaching of "not abiding in anything" from the *Diamond Sūtra*. With regards to people, matters, and objects, the mind should not give rise to tainted attachments. We should observe whether any given phenomenon has a real existence, including our cultivation and upholding precepts. We should not misunderstand this cultivation as having an unchanging innate nature!

The following *sutta* explains how the six sense bases interact with the six sense objects that are deemed pleasurable, acceptable, agreeable, and desirable. If the mind gives rise to tainted attachments, then suffering also arises; if there is no tainted attachments, then suffering ceases.

> Thus have I heard:
> One time the Buddha was residing on the shore of Lake Gaggarā near Campā.
>
> At that time, the Honorable Migajala came to visit the Buddha. He prostrated before the Buddha's feet and then sat to one side. He spoke to the Buddha, "Excellent! World-Honored One! Please speak the Dharma to me. After hearing it, I will go alone to a place of quietude. I will contemplate with diligence and not abide in slackness… till when I know, I will no longer be subject to rebirth."
>
> The Buddha replied to Migajala, "Excellent! Excellent! Migajala! Being able to ask the Tathāgata the meaning of suchness. Listen carefully! Contemplate well! I will now speak for you."

The Buddha told Migajala, "If the eyes see forms which are attractive, enjoyable, pleasing, or desirable, they develop desire towards them. Having seen such, praise them, become attached to them, and regard them as agreeable; having praised them and become attached, there is an accumulation of happiness. Due to the accumulation of happiness, there is an accumulation of suffering. Ears, nose, tongue, body, and mind are also this way. Migajala, if *bhikṣus* see forms with their eyes which are attractive, enjoyable, pleasing, or desirable, they do not develop desire towards them. Having seen such forms, they do not praise them, become attached to them, or regard them as agreeable. Since they did not praise them or become attached to them, there is no accumulation of happiness. Due to no accumulation of happiness, then there is cessation of suffering. The phenomena of ears, nose, tongue, body, and mind are also this way."

At that time, Migajala, who had heard the Buddha's teaching, felt blissful joy and acceptance. He paid his respects and took his leave.

Thereupon, Migajala, having heard the Buddha speak Dharma and teaching, went alone to a place of quietude, contemplated with diligence and did not abide in slackness... till attaining *arhatship*, for his mind to be liberated.

~From Fascicle Number 310 in the *Connected Discourses.*

The Honorable Migajala asked the Buddha to instruct him an easy method for him to practice and even achieve *arhatship.* The Buddha began explaining that when the eyes see something which is pleasing, attractive, and agreeable, the defilement of greed for form increases. If *bhikṣus* do not delight in such things, do not welcome them, and do not become attached to or clinging to them, then there will not be any sorrow, distress, suffering, or worries. The other sense bases of ears, nose, tongue, body, and mind are also this same way. After the Honorable Migajala finished listening, he set off to diligently contemplate these principles. Indeed, before long he achieved liberation and became an *arhat.*

Method 3:

Let Go of the Craving and Attachment for the Body and Mind

Aside from letting go of external states, one must also let go of the nominal self of the body and mind, the self which is controlled by greed, anger, and ignorance. How can it be let go? The following two *suttas* contain some interesting analogies:

> Thus have I heard:
> One time the Buddha was residing at Anāthapiṇḍada's Park in Jeta's Grove near Śrāvastī.
>
> At that time, the World-Honored One addressed the bhikṣus: "Whatever you do not have, relinquish it entirely. After relinquishing that phenomena, you will have lasting peace and happiness. Bhikṣus! What do you think? If someone took all of the trees, branches, leaves, and grass here in Jeta's Grove and left, would any of you think or say 'Everything he took was mine. How could he just take those things and leave?'"
>
> The bhikṣus answered, "No, World-Honored One."
>
> What is the reason for this? These things are non-self and are not objects a self. You bhikṣus are also this way. Whatever you do not have, relinquish it entirely. After relinquishing that phenomenon, you will have lasting peace and happiness. What are the things which do not belong to you? They are the eyes, the eyes do not belong to you. Relinquish them entirely. After relinquishing them, you will have lasting peace and happiness. The ears, nose, tongue, body, and mind are also this way. Bhikṣus! Are the eyes permanent or impermanent?"
>
> They replied, "Impermanent."
>
> The World Honored-One again asked, "If impermanent, is it suffering?"
>
> They answered, "Yes, it is suffering, World-Honored One!"
>
> "Given that form is impermanent, which is suffering, and subject to change, should noble disciples who have often heard the Dharma perceive within form a self, separate from self, or mutually existing with self?
>
> "They answered: "No, World-Honored One!"
>
> "Ears, nose, tongues, body, and consciousness are also like this. Noble disciples who have often heard the Dharma contemplate

the bases of the six sense organs as non-self and not objects of a self. Observing as such, there is nothing to which one clings in all the world, and there is no attachment, when there is no attachments, there is self-realization of nirvāṇa: I have completed my final birth and established my pure practice; all there that is to be done is now done. I know I will no longer be subject to rebirth."

After the Buddha had said these words, the *bhiksus* were delighted to hear the words of the Buddha and faithfully received this teaching and practice.

~From Fascicle Number 274 in the *Connected Discourses.*

Thus have I heard:
One time the Buddha was residing at Anāthapiṇḍada's Park in Jeta's Grove near Śrāvastī.

At that time the World-Honored One addressed the *bhikṣus*: "Phenomena which is not yours should be discarded in their entirety. After discarding them, you will have lasting peace and happiness! *Bhikṣus*! What kind of phenomena are not yours and should therefore be swiftly discarded? In this way, form, feeling, perception, mental formations, and consciousness are not phenomena which are yours. You should discard them in their entirety. Having discarded these phenomena, you will have lasting peace and happiness. For instance, if someone came into Jeta's Grove to chop down trees or cut off branches, and then leave carrying them away, you would not find yourselves distraught. What is the reason for this? It is because those trees and branches are not yours and they are not objects of yours.

"As such, *bhikṣus*! Phenomena which is not yours should be discarded in their entirety. After discarding them, peace and happiness are finally gained! What kind of phenomena are not yours? Form is not yours; it should be discarded in its entirety. After discarding it, lasting peace and happiness are finally gained. Feeling, perception, mental formations, and consciousness are also this way. They are not yours and should be discarded in their entirety. After discarding them, peace and happiness are finally gained. *Bhikṣus,* is form permanent or impermanent?"

The *bhikṣus* replied to the Buddha, "It is impermanent, World-Honored One."

"*Bhikṣus,* regarding that which is impermanent, is it suffering?"

They answered, "It is suffering, World-Honored One."

The Buddha spoke to the *bhikṣus,* "Given that form is impermanent, is suffering, and subject to change, should noble disciples who have often heard the Dharma perceive within form a self, separate from self, or mutually existing with self?

"They replied: "No, World-Honored One!"

"And what of feeling, perception, mental formations, and consciousness? Are they permanent or impermanent?"

They replied, "Impermanent, World-Honored One!"

"If they are impermanent, are they suffering?"

They replied, "Yes, they are suffering, World-Honored One!"

The Buddha spoke to the *bhikṣus,* "Given that they are impermanent and suffering and subject to change, should noble disciples who have often heard the Dharma perceive within them a self, separate from self, or mutually existing with self?"

They replied, "No, World-Honored One."

"*Bhikṣus!* Therefore, all forms whether in the past, present, or future, whether internal or external, whether coarse or fine, whether attractive or ugly, whether far or near, all of these have no self, separate from self, or mutually existing with self. Feeling, perception, mental formations, and consciousness are also as such, whether in the past, present, or future, whether they are internal or external, whether they are coarse or fine, whether they are attractive or ugly, whether they are far or near; all of these have no self, separate from self, or mutually existing with self.

Noble disciples who have often heard the Dharma observe the five aggregates and as have no self and not objects of self. Having observed as such, there is nothing to cling to and no attachments in all the world; having nothing to cling to and no attachments, there is self-realization of *nirvāṇa*: I have completed my final birth and established my pure practice; all there that is to be done is now done. I know I will no longer be subject to rebirth."

After the Buddha had said these words, the *bhiksus* were delighted to hear the words of the Buddha and faithfully received this teaching and practice.

~From Fascicle Number 269 in the *Connected Discourses.*

The whole entity of our body and mind are eyes, ears, nose, tongue, body, and mind. The former five parts are form, whereas the last part refers to feeling, perceptions, mental formations, and consciousness.

How to contemplate the six internal sense bases as empty? We can rely on the perspective of impermanence in observing the six sense bases of the eyes, ears, nose, tongue, body, and mind. For instance, in a forest where someone is chopping down trees, we will not be unhappy about it because we know that "those trees are not mine, and they do not belong to me." Through observing impermanence, practitioners can understand the five aggregates are empty and proceed to have no attachments and cling to nothing, understanding how to let go to gain lasting peace and happiness.

Relinquish Heavy Burdens and be Reborn No More

In explaining the arising and eradication of worries and suffering, the Buddha repeatedly employed different analogies. The following *sutta* uses heavy burdens as a metaphor for the five aggregates.

> Thus have I heard:
> One time the Buddha was residing at Anāthapiṇḍada's Park in Jeta's Grove near Śrāvastī.
>
> At that time, the World-Honored One addressed the *bhikṣus*: "I will now speak to you about heavy burdens, taking up of burdens, letting go of burdens, and the carrier of burdens. Listen carefully! Contemplate well! I will now speak to you. What are burdens? They are known as the five defilements of aggregates. Which five? The defilements of aggregates to form, feeling, perception, mental formations, and consciousness.
>
> What is taking up of heavy burdens? When there is craving, greed, and joy and delight in them.
>
> What is letting go of burdens? It is when there is craving, greed, and joy and the delight in them, and are eradicated without remainder; on cessation, suffering ends, separated from desire, and cessation complete.

Who are carriers of burdens? Human beings being called a given name, being born, being in a clan, eating a given food, feeling suffering and joy, having a long life, and abiding a long time. However, lifespan has a limit, and this is called a 'heavy burden, taking up a burden, letting go of a burden, and the carrier of burden.'

Thereupon, the World-Honored One recited a *gāthā:*

"On letting go of the heavy burden, take it up again no more,

The heavy load is great suffering, unloading it is great joy;

One should eradicate all desire, then ending all mental formations,

Awaken to the conditioned states, not transmigrating again into becoming."

After the Buddha had said these words, the *bhiksus* were delighted to hear the words of the Buddha and faithfully received this teaching and practice.

~From Fascicle Number 73 in the *Connected Discourses.*

The Buddha instructed us, "The heavy burden we have let go of should not be taken up again because hoisting up heavy burdens is painful. Only by discarding heavy burdens are we able to attain great happiness. We should eliminate all greed and desire in order to end all mental formations for future becoming. Understanding the principle of the origination of suffering, we will no longer be subject to birth and death in the future."

It is worth noting, such is the name and such is being: "the notion of human being." Such is the clan, such is food taken, and such is the feelings of suffering and joy: "the notion of sentient beings." Such is longevity, such is abiding a long time, and such is longevity span: "the notion of longevity." In other words, on letting go of this heavy burden and the four notions, it is known as bodhisattva!

Chapter Eight
Six Perspectives for Resolving Worries

In our daily lives, what will give rise to deluded thoughts most easily? Perhaps you have heard about the famous carving known as "The Three Wise Monkeys" at Nikkō Tōshō-gū Shrine in Japan. One monkey is plugging its ears, one blocking its eyes, and the remaining monkey is covering its mouth. The allusion here is that we should not be careless in speaking, listening, or looking, because our eyes, ears, and mouths are the easiest means in giving rise to deluded thoughts!

So while in the course of delivering sentient beings, bodhisattvas are unable "not to see, not to listen" in the here and now of the six sense organs coming in contact with the six sense fields; the mind is very clear about "see no evil, hear no evil, speak no evil, and do no evil." This is what Confucianism called "decorum" and Buddhism, "precepts;" cultivation is to manage our six sense organs well.

Therefore, sutras tell us to: "tightly guard the gates of sense organs." The meaning of which is to carefully look after our eyes, ears, nose, tongue, body, and mind, not allowing them to come into contact with environments of strong temptations. Moreover, we need to appreciate moderation in food and drink, knowing the limit of our intake and not giving rise to greed or anger; be diligent in practicing sleeping yoga, contemplating bright light when asleep; and abide in right understanding, maintaining high awareness at all times and in all places. As such, we will be able to have the strength for ceasing delusional thoughts.

> Thus have I heard:
> One time the Buddha was staying in the Ox-Taming Village of the Kurus.
>
> Thereupon, the World-Honored One addressed the *bhikṣus*: "I will now speak the Dharma for you. The content will be excellent throughout; from beginning, middle, and end. Wholesome meaning, wholesome essence; pure and fulfilled, the pure practices of which

are untarnished and true. Listen carefully! Contemplate well! This is called the 'teaching on causes, conditions, and bondage.'

Why do you think it is called 'the teaching on causes, conditions, and bondage?' Eyes have causes, conditions, and bondage. What are the causes, conditions, and bondage of the eyes? They are the eye-based karmic causes, karmic conditions, and karmic bondage. Karma has causes, conditions, and bondage. What are the conditions, causes, and bondage of karma? They are the causes, conditions, and bondage of karmic craving. Craving has its causes, conditions, and bondage. What are the causes, conditions, and bondage of craving? They are the causes, conditions, and bondage of craving due to ignorance. Ignorance has its causes, conditions, and bondage. What are the causes, conditions, and bondage of ignorance? They are the causes, conditions, and bondage of ignorance due to incorrect thought. Incorrect thought has its causes, conditions, and bondage. What are the causes, conditions, and bondage of incorrect thought? They are the eyes and form which produce incorrect thought due to delusion and ignorance.

Due to the conditions of eyes and form, giving rise to incorrect thought within delusion. Those who are deluded are afflicted with ignorance. Through delusion they pursue desires and this is called craving. What is generated through craving is called karma. As such, *bhikṣus!* Incorrect thought is the cause for clinging to craving. Ignorance is the cause for craving, and craving is the cause for karma. Eyes are the cause for karma. Ears, nose, tongue, body, and mind are also spoken of as such. These are called the teaching on causes, conditions, and bondage."

After the Buddha had said these words, the *bhikṣus* were delighted to hear the words of the Buddha and faithfully received this teaching and practice.

~From Fascicle Number 334 in the *Connected Discourses*.

The Buddha said to the *bhikṣus*, "So, what is the '*Causes, Conditions, and Bondage Sutta*?' It is eyes which have causes, conditions, and bondage. What are the causes, conditions, and bondage of the eyes? They are physical and verbal karma which are the causes, conditions, and bondage of the eyes; and physical and verbal karma also have causes, conditions, and bondage.

What are the causes, conditions, and bondage of karma? They are craving. Craving is the causes, conditions, and bondage for karma. Craving has its own causes, conditions, and bondage. What are the causes, conditions, and bondage of craving? They are ignorance. Ignorance is the causes, conditions, and bondage of craving. Ignorance has its own causes, conditions, and bondage. What are the causes, conditions, and bondage of ignorance? They are incorrect thought. Incorrect thought is the causes, conditions, and bondage of ignorance. Incorrect thought has its own causes, conditions, and bondage. What are the causes, conditions, and bondage of incorrect thought? They are the eyes seeing form giving rise to incorrect thinking, resulting in ignorance.

Due to eyes seeing form and giving rise to incorrect thinking, ignorance arises; ignorance is delusion. From delusion to the pursuit of greedy desires, it is called "craving." The actions resulting from craving are known as "karma." *Bhikṣus!* Incorrect thinking is the cause that gives rise to ignorance, ignorance is the cause for craving; craving is the cause that gives rise to karma, and karma is the cause that gives rise to eyes; ears, nose, tongue, body, and mind are also as such.

In short, all ignorance and worries are results of the interaction between the six sense organs and six sense objects, giving rise to delusional thinking. Consequently, in cultivation we must tightly guard our sense organs and should not latch onto outside conditions casually. Then we can reduce our worries; as it is said, "One less matter is better than having one more matter."

Perspective 1: Practice the Four Bases of Mindfulness

Thus have I heard:
One time the Buddha was residing at the Deer Park of Ṛṣipatana near Vārāṇasī.

At that time, the World-Honored One addressed the *bhikṣus*: "The world speaks of beauties. Can beauties attract a gathering of many spectators?"

The *bhikṣus* replied to the Buddha, "Indeed, World-Honored One."

The Buddha asked the *bhikṣus*, "If there were those considered by the worldly as beautiful, and they were further able to perform various songs, dances, and music; could an even larger gathering of spectators be attracted?"

The *bhikṣus* replied to the Buddha, "Indeed, World-Honored One!"

The Buddha told the *bhikṣus*, "If such beauties in the world were to perform songs, dance, and music with a large group of people gathering at one place to watch; and if there was a man who was neither foolish nor ignorant, who enjoys happiness and avoids suffering, and who fears death in the effort to survive; should someone say, 'You here! You are to carry a bowl filled to the brim with oil on your head, and walk past singing and dancing beauties with the gathering of people. A sword-wielding killer will follow behind you, and if you spill even a drop of oil, the killer will kill you right away!' *Bhikṣus!* Would the man carrying the oil bowl not be mindful of the oil bowl and the killer, but watch the performing beauties and the audience?

The *bhikṣus* replied to the Buddha, "No, World-Honored One! Why is that so? World-Honored One! Seeing a sword-wielding killer behind him, he would keep thinking, 'If I spill even one drop of oil, the sword-wielding killer behind me will cut off my head.' The only matter on his mind would be the oil bowl, walking steadily by the beauties and the gathering of people, dare not looking here and there."

"It is indeed, *bhikṣus!* If *śramaṇas* and *brāhmins* were upstanding and self-disciplined, focus their minds, pay no heed to sensory objects, concentrate well on all practices of the mind, and abide their bodies on mindfulness, they are my disciples and are following my teachings. Why should *bhikṣus* be upstanding and self-disciplined, focus their minds, pay no heed to sensory objects, concentrate on all practices of the mind, and abide their bodies on mindfulness? It is indeed, *bhikṣus!* Abide in contemplation and apply efforts for skillful means, with right wisdom and right mindfulness, overcome worldly greed and craving. The same is true of contemplating the body, feelings, the mind, and phenomena; abide in contemplation. These are known as *bhikṣu* who are upstanding, self-disciplined, focus their minds, pay no heed to sensory objects, concentrate well on all practices of the mind, and abide on the four applications of mindfulness. Thereupon, the World-Honored One recited a *gāthā*:

"Concentrate in right mindfulness, safeguarding a bowl of oil,
The mind follows in protection, while not yet reaching the destination,
Very difficult to overcome, being wondrous and subtle.
Teachings spoken by all buddhas, the words teach like sharp swords,
Should focus the mind, concentrating in diligent protection.
It is not ordinary people, not matters of slackness;
If able to gain entry, do not be slack with the teachings."

After the Buddha had said these words, the *bhikṣus* were delighted to hear the words of the Buddha and faithfully received this teaching and practice.

~From Fascicle Number 623 in the *Connected Discourses*.

A man balancing a bowl of oil on his head who feared being killed if so much as a single drop was spilled. Even though he had to walk by a crowd and beautiful women, he would not dare to look this way and that way. Through this analogy, the Buddha is telling us that in cultivation we should focus all of our thoughts for our minds to abide in contemplation of the body, contemplation of feelings, contemplation of the mind, and contemplation of Dharma.

The four applications of mindfulness also known as the four abodes of mindfulness are means of focusing the mind and thoughts on "contemplating the body is impure, contemplating feelings result in suffering, contemplating the mind as impermanent, and contemplating phenomena are non-self." This is to prevent deluded thoughts from arising and to eliminate defilements.

Perspective 2:
Maintaining Right Mindfulness

Thus have I heard:
One time the Buddha was residing at Anāthapiṇḍada's Park in Jeta's Grove near Śrāvastī.

At that time, Māluṅkyaputra came to visit the Buddha. He prostrated before the Buddha's feet and then sat to one side. He spoke to the Buddha, "Excellent! World-Honored One! Please speak the Dharma to me. After hearing the Dharma, I will go alone to a place of quietude. I will focus my thoughts diligently, not slacking in abidance… till I will no longer be subject to rebirth."

At that time, the World-Honored One told Māluṅkyaputra, "All those who are young and intelligent with sharp faculties cultivate my Dharma and Vinaya, although they have not renounced for long, they do not slack in cultivating my Dharma and Vinaya. Now you are advanced in age and mature in your faculties, you wish to hear me speaking briefly on the teachings and instructions!"

Māluṅkyaputra replied to the Buddha, "World-Honored One, although I am advanced in age and mature in my faculties, I still wish to hear the World-Honored One speak briefly on the teachings and instructions. My only wish is the World-Honored One speak briefly on the teachings and instructions. After hearing the Dharma, I will go alone to a place of quietude. I will focus my thoughts diligently, not slacking in abidance… till I will no longer be subject to rebirth." He beseeched the Buddha twice and then a third time.

The Buddha told Māluṅkyaputra, "You stop now!" After repeating three times, he did not speak.

Thereupon, the Buddha spoke to Māluṅkyaputra, "Now I will ask you a question, answer me as you will."

The Buddha asked Māluṅkyaputra, "If the eyes have yet to see form which you wish to see, would you give rise to desire, craving, longing, and tainted attachment for that form?"

He answered, "No, World-Honored One! Ears and sound, nose and scent, tongue and taste, body and touch, and mind and mental objects are also spoken of in this way."

The Buddha told Māluṅkyaputra, "Excellent! Excellent! Māluṅkyaputra! You take seeing as just seeing, hearing just as hearing, sensation just as sensation, and consciousness just as consciousness." The Buddha then recited a *gāthā*: "You are not by this, and that is not this; neither is it in between, it is the boundary of suffering."

Māluṅkyaputra spoke to the Buddha: "I have understood, World-Honored One! I have understood, Immaculately Departed One!"

The Buddha told Māluṅkyaputra, "How would you explain in further detail with my brief teaching of the Dharma?

Thereupon, Māluṅkyaputra recited a *gāthā* to the Buddha:

"If the eyes see form, losing right mindfulness;

Then from the form seen, notions of craving, clinging, and longing develop.

Those with notions of craving and delight, their minds are often bound;

From the various craving, immeasurable forms arise.

Greed, desire, and anger harm awareness, allowing the mind to digress;

Nourishes myriad forms of suffering, forever separated from *nirvāṇa*.

Seeing forms and not clinging to their notions, the mind follows right mindfulness,

Not tainting the mind with craving, not giving rise to attachments;

Not arising to any form of craving, immeasurable forms arise;

Greed, desire, and anger harm awareness, unable to harm the mind;

Less nurturing of suffering, gradually gaining proximity to *nirvāṇa*,

Cultivating what the Honored One has spoken, depart from craving to enter *nirvāṇa*.

If the ears hear all sounds, the mind loses right mindfulness,

Clinging to notions of sound, grasping firmly and not relinquishing;

The nose and scents, the tongue and tastes, the body and touch, the mind and dharmas;

Losing right mindfulness, the same for clinging to their notions.

Such a mind gives rise to craving, abiding firmly in attachments,

Giving rise to various craving, immeasurable phenomena accumulate;

Greed, desire, and anger harm awareness, allowing the mind to digress;

Nourishes myriad forms of suffering, forever separated from *nirvāṇa*.

Not tainted by phenomena, abide in right wisdom and right mindfulness,

Such a mind is not defiled, no longer delighted and attached;

Not arising to any form of craving, immeasurable Dharma arise;

Greed, desire, and anger harm awareness, do not allow the mind to digress;

All suffering diminishes, gradually gaining proximity to *nirvāṇa*,

Crave ceases attaining *nirvāṇa*, as taught by the World-Honored One."

"This is called the Dharma the World-Honored One has spoken briefly explained in detail."

The Buddha told Māluṅkyaputra, "You truly explained in detail the Dharma I spoke briefly. Why is that so? Just as what you said in the *gāthā:* "If the eyes see form, losing right mindfulness; then from the form seen, notions of craving, clinging, and longing develop… as explained in detail earlier."

At that time, Māluṅkyaputra, who had heard the Buddha's teaching, felt joy and acceptance, paid his respects, and took his leave.

Thereupon, the Honorable Māluṅkyaputra, having explained in detail the Dharma the Buddha had briefly spoken, went alone to a place of quietude and focused his thoughts diligently, not slacking in abidance…till attaining *arhatship* and liberation of the mind.

~From Fascicle Number 312 in the *Connected Discourses.*

The elderly householder, Māluṅkyaputra went to the Buddha one day to beseech him for teachings. The majority of the Buddha's disciples were young, yet intelligent, sharp in their faculties, and diligent in their studies. The Buddha had no intention to teach the old, dim Māluṅkyaputra (he had already expressed his dissatisfaction with the Buddha's avoidance in an earlier debate; for more details, read the *Arrow Analogy Sutta*, fascicle number 221 in the Middle Length Discourses).

Even after being beseeched three times, the Buddha did not agree to speak the Dharma to him, but he did ask him the following question: "If the sense base of your eyes has not yet seen something beautiful, would you have already given rise to desire, craving, longing, and defiled attachment for that form?" Māluṅkyaputra replied, "No, World-Honored One! Even the ears and sounds, nose and scents, tongue and tastes, body and touch, and mind and mental objects are also this way."

The Buddha praised him by saying, "You have truly answered well! Māluṅkyaputra! It is to take seeing to just be seeing, hearing to just be hearing, sensation to just be sensation, and thinking to just be thinking." This means that when the six sense bases come into contact with the six sense objects, we should maintain right mindfulness and observe them as such, and worries will not arise. In other words, all seeing, hearing, feeling and cognition require the coming together of the six sense bases with the six sense objects in order to give rise to awareness, differentiation, and the arising of longing, desire, and tainted attachments. If we maintain right mindfulness, we can prevent the arising of desire and gain closer proximity to *nirvāṇa!*

Ordinary beings give rise to joy, aversion, and suffering due to their self-consciousness. For instance, when it is clear that they are doing a good deed but were misunderstood and criticized by others, displeasure arises in their minds. How to subdue our minds? We should know that when the mind "departs from all notions" and has no attachments and no tainted desire for external states, then we are able to attain true ease and happiness!

Perspective 3: Uphold the Middle Way Attitude of Not Suffering and Not Joy

In cultivation, only upholding the middle path can be regarded as proper practice. Cultivation is not endlessly reciting sutra all day and night, however, one should not regard sutra as unapproachable just because of its immense vastness. It is like the saying, "opening a book reaps benefits." Just being willing and receptive will be helpful.

Thus have I heard:
One time the Buddha was residing in Elder Karaṇḍa's Garden in Rājagṛha.

At that time, the Honorable Śroṇakoṭīviṃśa was living at Vulture Peak where he often diligently cultivated the factors of enlightenment.

One time, the Honorable Śroṇakoṭīviṃśa was alone in quiet meditative contemplation and thought to himself, "I am one of the Buddha's disciples who is diligent in cultivating themselves as a *śrāvaka*. But now, I have yet to cease all outflows. I was born into a high caste, and my family has an excess of wealth and treasures. I would rather return to a life of the five desires, and could extensively practice charity and accumulate merits."

Thereupon, the World-Honored One knew what Śroṇakoṭīviṃśa had thought, and told a *bhikṣu*, "You go to Śroṇakoṭīviṃśa and tell him: 'the World-Honored One has summoned you!'"

That *bhikṣu* heard the Buddha's order and went to visit Śroṇakoṭīviṃśa, saying, "The World-Honored One has summoned you!"

Śroṇakoṭīviṃśa heard this order from his great master and immediately went to visit the World-Honored One. He prostrated before the Buddha's feet, and sat to one side.

Thereupon, the World-Honored One spoke to Śroṇakoṭīviṃśa, "When you were recently alone in a quiet meditative contemplation, you thought, 'I am one of the Buddha's disciples who exerts themselves as *śrāvaka*. But I have yet to cease all outflows. I was born into a high caste, and my family has an excess of wealth and riches. I would rather return to a life of the five desires, and could extensively practice charity and accumulate merits,' right?"

At that time, Śroṇakoṭīviṃśa thought, "The World-Honored One has read my mind." Startled and fearful, his hair stood on end. He replied to the Buddha, "That is really so, World-Honored One!"

The Buddha told Śroṇakoṭīviṃśa, "Now I will ask you a question, answer me as you will. Śroṇakoṭīviṃśa, when you still lived in the secular world, you were skilled at playing the *vīṇā*, right?"

He answered, "Yes, World-Honored One!"

The Buddha asked again, "What do you think? When you played the *vīṇā* and your strings were too tight, were you still able to play wondrous, subtle-sounding notes?"

He answered, "No, World-Honored One."

The Buddha asked again, "What about this? When you played the *vīṇā* and your strings were too loose, were you able to play wondrous, subtle-sounding notes?"

He answered, "No, World-Honored One!"

The Buddha asked again, "How to tune the strings well? Not loose, not tight, and will wondrous, subtle-sounding notes be played?

He answered, "It is so, World-Honored One!"

The Buddha told Śroṇakoṭīviṃśa, "Being too hurried in applying efforts, vexations and anxieties will increase; being too slack in applying efforts, people fall into indolence. Therefore, you should apply equanimity to your cultivation and focus. Do not be hurried, do not be slack, and do not cling to notions."

At that time, the Honorable Śroṇakoṭīviṃśa was delighted to hear the words of the Buddha and faithfully received this teaching and practice. He paid his respects and took his leave.

Thereupon, the Honorable Śroṇakoṭīviṃśa often contemplated the *vīṇā* metaphor as spoken by the World-Honored One. Alone in quiet meditative concentration in accordance with the above, till he ceased all outflows, liberating the mind and attaining *arhatship.*

Thereupon, the Honorable Śroṇakoṭīviṃśa attained *arhatship,* having inner joy of liberation. He thought to himself, "I should go visit the World-Honored One."

Thereupon, the Honorable Śroṇakoṭīviṃśa went to visit the Buddha. He prostrated before the Buddha's feet and then sat to one side. He spoke to the Buddha, "World-Honored One, by the Dharma of the World-Honored One, I have attained *arhatship,* ceasing all outflows, done all there is to be done, letting go of the heavy burden, accomplished my goal, severed all bonds of existence, achieved liberation of the mind with right wisdom, and was liberated from six bondages. Which six? The liberation of abandoning desire, the liberation of abandoning anger, the liberation of being detached, the liberation of eliminating craving, the liberation from all clinging, and the liberation from delusional thinking."

"World-Honored One! If only relying on a little faith and to speak of "liberation of abandoning desire," this is not a reliance. Only the extinguishing of greed, anger, and ignorance can be called true liberation of abandoning desire. Moreover, if a person relies on a little upholding of precepts and claims 'I have achieved the liberation of abandoning anger,' this is not a reliance. Only the extinguishing of greed, anger, and ignorance can be called true liberation. Moreover, if a person cultivates the detachment from personal gains and speaks of the 'liberation of detachment,' it is also not a reliance. Only the extinguishing of greed, anger, and ignorance can be called true 'liberation of detachment.'

The extinguishing of greed, anger, and ignorance is also called separation from craving, also called separation from clinging, and also called liberation of separation from delusional thinking. As such, World-Honored One! If *bhikṣus* who have yet to become *arhats* and have not yet ceased all outflows, it is due to them having yet to liberate themselves from these six places.

Moreover, *bhikṣus* still at the learning stage and have yet to attain supreme bliss of *nirvāṇa*, they should abide their mind in practice; eventually, they will succeed in the study of precepts and accomplish the faculties of learning. Afterwards, they will cease all outflows; without outflows, they gain the liberation of the mind… till they realize they are no longer subject to rebirth. They should have nothing more to learn with regards to precepts and faculties. It is like an infant who is young and ignorant, only able to lie on his back until he masters all the faculties of childhood. Thereafter, he will gradually grow to master all faculties, then he will further master the faculties of adulthood. Those in the learning stage are similar, they have yet to attain advanced ease and happiness, till there is nothing more to study with regard to precepts and faculties.

Even if eyes are often engaging eye consciousness with form, it cannot obstruct the mind from attaining liberation or the liberation of wisdom. It is due to strong abidance of the mind, the internal cultivation of immeasurable wholesomeness for liberation, and observation of arising, ceasing, and the impermanence within. Even if ears consciousness engage with sound, nose consciousness engage with scent, tongue consciousness engage with taste, body consciousness with touch, and mind consciousness with mental objects, they cannot obstruct the mind from attaining liberation or the liberation of wisdom. It is due to strong abidance of the mind, the internal cultivation of immeasurable wholesomeness for liberation, and observation of arising and ceasing. Similar to the great rock mountain close to the village which has no breaks, no erosion, no cracks, completely thick and dense. Even if winds from the four directions were to blow, the winds cannot move nor penetrate the mountain. Those without further learning are also as such. If they always engage eye consciousness with form… to the mind engaging in consciousness with dharmas, these cannot obstruct the mind from attaining liberation or the liberation of wisdom. It is due to strong abidance of the mind, the internal cultivation of immeasurable wholesomeness for liberation, and observation of arising and ceasing. At that time, Śroṇakoṭīviṃśa recited a *gāthā*:

"Liberation of abandoning desire, likewise the liberation of abandoning anger;

Liberation of being detached, craving eradicated forever without remainder.

Liberation of the mind from all clinging, with no delusional thoughts;

Understanding the sense bases, thus liberation of the mind.

Those with minds liberated, *bhikṣus* who have ceased their minds;

All there is to do is done, they do not do no more.

Like a great rock mountain, winds from four directions cannot move,

Form, sound, scent, taste, touch, and good or bad dharmas,
Which the six sense bases often encounter, unable to move their minds,
Their minds are strong in abidance, truthfully observing phenomena arise and cease."

When the Honorable Śroṇakoṭīviṃśa spoke this teaching, his great master was pleased. On hearing what Śroṇakoṭīviṃśa had spoken, the many practitioners of pure practice felt great joy. At that time, the Honorable Śroṇakoṭīviṃśa heard the Buddha's teaching, felt great joy, paid his respects, and took his leave.

Thereupon, the World-Honored One knew that Śroṇakoṭīviṃśa had just recently departed, told the *bhikṣus*, "Those who excel at liberation of the mind should remember teachings which are spoken. Just as Śroṇakoṭīviṃśa remembered the teachings with wisdom. He did not use the teachings to elevate himself or to disparage others, and just explain the right meaning of the teachings. Unlike arrogant practitioners who are slow in progress, unable to understand the meaning of the teachings, but praise themselves over others, doing themselves harm."

~From Fascicle Number 254 in the *Connected Discourses*.

The Buddha had the ability to read the minds of others, and he realized that Śroṇakoṭīviṃśa was digressing from the Way and preparing to leave for mundane life. Therefore, the Buddha employed skillful means to guide Śroṇakoṭīviṃśa through the teachings. Knowing that before Śroṇakoṭīviṃśa renounced home life, he was gifted at playing the *vīṇā*. So the Buddha used the analogy of tuning the strings of a lute to admonish him; that cultivation should neither be too hurried nor too slack and he should make appropriate adjustments. After Śroṇakoṭīviṃśa heard the instructions, he eventually gained the fruit of *arhatship*. He later returned to visit the Buddha to report that he had realized the state of *arhatship*. The Buddha offered him verification, high praise, and encouragement!

Perspective 4: Realize Dependent Origination from the Body and Mind

Thus have I heard:
One time the Buddha was residing in Ghoṣilārāma Garden in Kauśāmbī.

At that time the World-Honored One addressed the *bhikṣus*: "Having hands, you know how to pick up and set down objects. Having feet, you know how to walk to and fro. Having joints, you know how to flex and stretch. Having stomachs, you know hunger and thirst. As such, *bhikṣus!* Having eyes, feelings arise through eye contact. There are feelings of suffering, pleasure, or neither suffering nor pleasure. Ears, nose, tongues, body, and consciousness are also like this.

Bhikṣus! If you have no hands, you would not know how to pick up or set down objects. If you have no feet, you would not know how to walk to and fro. If you have no joints, you would not how to flex and stretch. If you have no stomachs, you would not know hunger or thirst. As such, *bhikṣus!* If you have no eyes, then no feelings arise through eye contact. There would not be feelings of suffering, pleasure, or neither suffering nor pleasure. Ears, nose, tongues, body, and consciousness are also like this.

After the Buddha had said these words, the *bhiksus* were delighted to hear the words of the Buddha and faithfully received this teaching and practice.

~From Fascicle Number 1,166 in the *Connected Discourses.*

The Buddha told the *bhikṣus*, "Having hands, you are able to grasp and let go of things. Having feet, you are able to walk about. Having joints, you are able to flex and stretch. Having stomachs, you are able to feel hungry and thirsty. *Bhikṣus*, having a pair of normal eyes, you can look upon all phenomena, giving rise to feelings of happiness or aversion and such emotional states. Ears, nose, tongue, body, and mind are also this way."

This *sutta* explains how the six sense bases give rise to feelings due to causes and conditions. Therefore, "cultivation of the six sense bases" is the most fundamental in our practice, so that we will not be enslaved by external states.

Perspective 5: Be Like a Turtle Guarding Its Head, Tail, and Four Limbs

The following *sutta* is quite interesting. The Buddha uses a turtle as an analogy for retracting the six sense organs so that Māra cannot seize advantage to gain entry.

> Thus have I heard:
> One time the Buddha was residing in Ghoṣilārāma Garden in Kauśāmbī.
>
> At that time the World-Honored One addressed the *bhikṣus*: "In the past, there was a river with plants; there were turtles residing within. One time, a hungry *śṛgāla* was out looking for food. On seeing the turtle, the *śṛgāla* swiftly moved in to seize it. The turtle saw it coming and immediately retracted its six protruding parts. The *śṛgāla* waited by the side, looking for the head and limbs to reach out so as to eat it. After a long wait, the turtle's head did not come out, nor its limbs. The *śṛgāla* became tired and hungry, leaving in anger.
>
> "*Bhikṣus!* Today you all are as such. Knowing that *Māra-pāpīyān* is always waiting, hoping your eyes will become attached to form, ears to sound, nose to scent, tongue to taste, body to touch, and mind to dharmas; that you will give rise to tainted attachment to the six sense fields. Therefore, *bhikṣus!* From today on, you should firmly uphold precepts of the eyes and abide within. Upon firmly upholding precepts of the eyes and abiding within, evil *Māra-pāpīyān* will not be able to have the opportunity, and whether the eyes reach out or follow conditions, there are no attachments. Ears, nose, tongue, body, and mind are also as such. So if the six sense bases are to reach out or follow conditions, there is no opportunity for Mara due to no attachments. Similar to the turtle, the *śṛgāla* had no opportunity.

Thereupon, the World -Honored One recited a *gāthā:*

"Turtle fears the *śṛgāla,* hiding its six parts within the shell,
Bhikṣus excel at focusing the mind, safely hide all feelings and thoughts,
No reliance and no fear, covering their minds and refrain from speech."

After the Buddha had said these words, the *bhiksus* were delighted to hear the words of the Buddha and faithfully received this teaching and practice.

~From Fascicle Number 1,167 in the *Connected Discourses.*

There was once a *śṛgāla,* a fox-like animal that is smaller, and it saw a turtle near the waterside and was about to snatch it for a hearty meal. However, the turtle quickly retracted its head and four limbs into its shell. The *śṛgāla* could not do anything except linger by its side and wait, hoping for the turtle to stick out its head and legs to eat it. Unfortunately for the *śṛgāla,* however, he waited a long time without any success and eventually left disappointed.

The Buddha used the head, tail, and four legs of a turtle as an analogy for the six sense organs, not allowing them to be in pursuit of sounds and forms to avoid the intrusions of *Māra-pāpīyān; Māra,* actually refers to greed and desires within the mind.

Perspective 6: Guard the Field of Seedlings; Do Not Allow Fenced Oxen to Enter

The Buddha used the analogy of "guard the field of seedlings, do not allow fenced oxen to enter" to admonish his disciples to guard the field of the mind, do not allow form and the rest of the six sense fields to invade the body and mind. We should know that all phenomena are impermanent and conditioned, and all are not real. All Dharma friends, we should observe as such in our daily lives!

Thus have I heard:
One time the Buddha was residing in Ghoṣilārāma Garden in Kauśāmbī.

At that time the World-Honored One addressed the *bhikṣus*: "If *bhikṣus* and *bhikṣuṇīs*, with their eye consciousness and form through causes and conditions give rise to desire, greed, affection, longing, or points of attachment, and they excel in protecting their minds; why is that so? These are all paths of fear with obstacles and difficulties; these are followed by deviant people, and not by good people. Therefore, one should protect oneself from them. Ears, nose, tongue, body, and mind are also this way. For example, a farmer who owns a field of good seedlings, but the person guarding the field is lazy and slack, so that oxen that were fenced off came to feed on the seedlings; foolish beings are also the same with the six points of contact and the internal sense bases… till slacking to be as such.

If the field of good seedlings with the person guarding the field is not slack, the fenced off oxen would not be able to feed on it; even though they may enter the field, they would be chased away. For their minds, intentions, or consciousness, noble disciples who have often heard the Dharma should protect well their virtues from the five sensual desires, eradicating them from the mind. Similar to the field of good seedlings, the person protecting the field should not be slack. Should the fenced off oxen enter, his left hand should grab the oxen by their snouts and his right hand holding the whipping stick to beat them all over to drive them out of the field. *Bhikṣus!* What do you think? After these oxen meet with pain from the village to home and from home to the village, do you think they will ever try eating the seedlings in the field again?"

They answered, "No, World-Honored One!"

"Why is that so? Because the oxen remember when they entered the field and were met with the suffering from lashings of a stick. As such, *bhikṣus!* For their minds, intentions, or consciousness, noble disciples who have often heard the Dharma are weary and fearful of the six contacts with sense fields. Their minds abide and concentrate on single-mindedness.

"*Bhikṣus!* In the past there was a king who had heard the unsurpassed pleasing sound of a lute. He gave rise to extreme delight for it, indulging himself and became tainted with attachment. He asked his ministers, 'What is that sound? It is absolutely delightful!' The minister answered, 'That is the sound of a lute.' He ordered the minister, 'Bring that sound here to me.' The minister obeyed the command and immediately brought the lute to the king, saying 'Great king! This is the lute which produced the pleasing sound.' The king replied to the minister, 'I have no need for a lute. Bring me the delightful sound I just heard.' The minister answered, 'Lutes like this have many component parts such as a neck, fretboard, decorative fixtures, strings, and a resonator. When someone is playing it, these causes and conditions produce the sound. Without these component parts, that sound does not come into being. The sound you heard has already gone away some time ago. It has faded and completely ceased; it cannot be brought here.'

Thereupon, the great king spoke: 'Tsk! What use do I have for such an artificial thing? The music instruments of this world are artificial, leading people to indulge in them and become tainted with attachments. You take it away, smash it into pieces, and scatter them in the ten directions.' The minister obeyed this command and broke the lute into a hundred pieces, scattering them about in all directions. As such, *bhikṣus!* Form, feeling, perceptions, thoughts, desires, these phenomena are impermanent, conditioned, and arise in the mind through causes and conditions. So when saying, 'this is me' and 'this belongs to me.' It was another time, but are spoken no more. *Bhikṣus!* You should have equanimity and right wisdom in observing as such."

After the Buddha had said these words, the *bhiksus* were delighted to hear the words of the Buddha and faithfully received this teaching and practice.

~From Fascicle Number 1,169 in the *Connected Discourses.*

The Buddha said that the result of slacking toward the six sense bases is like the person guarding the field who is irresponsible, allowing oxen locked inside the fence to run out and feed on seedlings in the field. Only by diligently guarding the oxen, driving them away from the field paths so that the seedlings will not be ruined. Moreover, due to the oxen fear being whipped, they will not dare come to trample the field of seedlings again.

Chapter Nine
Cultivate Cessation and Contemplation to Calm the Mind

The principle of liberation in Buddhism is inseparable from cessation and contemplation. Cessation in Sanskrit is "*śamatha*" which refers to ceasing of all deluded thoughts and focus the mind to a state of concentration. Contemplation in Sanskrit is "*vipaśyanā*" which means developing right wisdom to observe all phenomena correctly for eradicating all worries.

In cultivation, Buddhism often teaches applying ceasing and contemplating in place of "meditation and wisdom." Hence, there are what is called the "dual practice of cessation and contemplation" and the "equal upholding of meditation and wisdom." Taking it a step further, from beginning to practice meditation till entering into concentration is the cultivation of ceasing and concentration. From observing dependent origination relying on concentration is the cultivation of wisdom and contemplation. By integrating both practices, the mind should always sustain the thinking of impermanence and non-self, then in practicing concentration the mind will be easily calmed and settled. Use wisdom to help cultivate concentration and use concentration to develop *nirvāṇa* and cessation, which is the wisdom of an empty and tranquil nature that is without outflow. By integrating and supporting one another as such, is called the "equal practice of concentration and wisdom."

True realization of the Way needs cultivation of meditation and wisdom, attaining super-natural powers and leading to the wisdom of no outflows. Given all this, how should we practice in order to succeed? Please refer to the *sutta* that follows.

Observe Form, Feeling, Perceptions, Mental Formations, and Consciousness as Impermanent

Thus have I heard:
One time the Buddha was residing in Chicken Grove in the Kingdom of Pāṭaliputra.

At that time, the Honorable Ānanda went to visit the Honorable Mahā-cunda. After they both bowed to one another with joined palms, they sat to one side. Thereupon, the Honorable Ānanda asked the Honorable Cunda, "There are some questions I wish to ask. Do you have time to answer them?"

The Honorable Cunda replied, "Ask as you will. I will answer them in accordance with my knowledge."

Thereupon, the Honorable Ānanda asked the Honorable Cunda, "In accordance with what was realized and observed by the World-Honored One, Tathāgata, Arhat, and the Perfectly Enlightened One, who said that form is made up of the four great elements, and further described and explained for better understanding that these four great elemental forms are non-self. The Tathāgata, Arhat, and the Perfectly Enlightened One also said that consciousness is also non-self?"

Honorable Cunda spoke to the Honorable Ānanda, "Kind Venerable, you have heard the most of the teachings. I came a far distance to visit you and ask you about this Dharma. I only ask that today, Honorable One! You explain the meaning of the teachings to me."

The Honorable Ānanda replied to Cunda, "Now I will ask you a question, Honorable One. Reply as you wish. Honorable Cunda! There are eyes, form, and eye consciousness, right?"

He answered, "Yes, there are."

The Honorable Ānanda asked, "Conditioned by the eyes and form, eye consciousness arises, right?"

He answered, "It is as such."

The Honorable Ānanda asked further, "Conditioned by the eyes and form, eye consciousness arises. Are these causes and conditions permanent or impermanent?"

He answered, "Impermanent."

The Honorable Ānanda asked, "If these causes and conditions give rise to eye consciousness and that these causes and conditions are impermanent and subject to change, will this consciousness abide?"

He answered, "No, Honorable Ānanda!"

The Honorable Ānanda asked, "What do you think? If it is known that these phenomena arise and cease, should noble disciples who have often heard the Dharma perceive within a self, separate from self, or mutually existing with the self?

He answered, "No, Honorable Ānanda!"

"Ears, nose, tongue, body, and mind, what do you think of these phenomena? Is there a mind, phenomena, and consciousness?"

He answered, "Yes, Honorable Ānanda!"

Again asked, "Conditioned by the mind and phenomena, consciousness arises, right?"

He answered, "It is as such, Honorable Ānanda!"

He asked further, "Given that being conditioned by the mind and phenomena, consciousness arises, are these causes and conditions permanent or impermanent?"

He answered, "Impermanent, Honorable Ānanda!"

He further asked, "If causes and conditions give rise to consciousness, and that these causes and conditions are impermanent and subject to change, will this consciousness abide?"

He answered, "No, Honorable Ānanda!"

"What do you think? If it is known that these phenomena arise and cease, should noble disciples who have often heard the Dharma perceive within these phenomena a self, separate from self, or mutually existing with self?

He answered, "No, Honorable Ānanda!"

The Honorable Ānanda spoke to the Honorable Cunda, "Therefore, Honorable One! In accordance with what was realized and observed by the World-Honored One, Tathāgata, Arhat, and the Perfectly Enlightened One, who said that consciousness is also impermanent. It is similar to a man carrying an axe into to the mountains, and upon seeing a banana tree, he thought it is fit for use as timber. He chopped it from the roots, cut off its leaves, hacked away the branches, and stripped the bark, looking for a solid core; but even when completely stripped down, there is nothing solid. As such, noble disciples who have often heard the Dharma should correctly observe eye consciousness and the consciousnesses of ears, nose, tongue, body, and mind. On correct observation, they see that there is nothing to cling to; since there is nothing to cling to, there is nothing to become attached to; with nothing to become attached to, there is self-realization and *nirvāṇa*: I have completed my final birth and established my pure practice; all there that is to be done is now done. I know I will no longer be subject to rebirth."

When these two excellent individuals spoke this teaching, both felt blissful joy and then returned to their own places.

~ From Fascicle Number 248 in the *Connected Discourses*

Bhikṣu Cunda was Śāriputra's younger brother. He is also known as "Mahācunda." Śāriputra had three brothers who became *bhikṣus* in renunciation under the Buddha; the other two brothers were Upasena and Revata.

One time, Cunda went to request instruction from Ānanda, the one foremost in hearing the Dharma by asking, "The Buddha has previously taught that the physical bodies of sentient beings are comprised of the four great elements; earth, water, fire, and wind. He has taught that 'form is non-self,' so is 'consciousness' also 'non-self'?"

Ānanda answered with a question by asking Cunda, "Are there eyes, form, and eye-consciousness?" Cunda answered, "Yes, there are." Ānanda asked further, "It is because of eyes and form that eye-consciousness arises, is that correct?" Cunda answered, "Yes!" Ānanda asked further, "So if eye-consciousness arises due to the causes and conditions of having the sense bases of the eyes and the sense field of form; is this state of causes and conditions permanent or impermanent?" Cunda answered, "It is impermanent." Ānanda asked further, "When that state of causes and conditions changes, is eye-consciousness able to maintain itself and not change?" Cunda answered, "No, it cannot!"

Ānanda continued, "Since eye-consciousness arises and ceases following causes and conditions, can noble disciples who have often heard the Dharma still see a self, separate from self, or mutually existing with self within this phenomenon?" Cunda answered, "No, they cannot!"

Ānanda continued by explaining that the other five consciousnesses are in the same situation. In the end, he offered an analogy: "There was a person carrying an axe who went into the mountains to chop lumber and saw a banana tree. He thought it would make for good lumber. He then chopped it down and peeled away the outside layers, looking for solid wood. It never occurred to him that on peeling away the entire banana tree, that there was no timber to be found." Ānanda concluded by saying, "Noble disciples who have often heard the Dharma should observe the six consciousnesses as such and understand that there is nothing to cling or be attached to."

I have heard others say, "My heart never ever changes." This is a deluded and inverted thought! It is because consciousness arises from sense bases interacting with sense fields; this is impermanent. It is impossible to remain unchanging forever, so there is not an always-abiding 'self.'

In this *sutta*, we see the disciples of the Buddha discussing the Dharma together. This is emblematic of the constant turning of the Dharma wheel. So the teachings of the Buddha really make it easy for people to become enlightened!

Pay Attention to the Arising and Cessation of the Thought

Before Sakyamuni Buddha attained enlightenment, he was alone in a quiet place in deep contemplation, "Why do people have different forms of suffering such as aging, sickness, death, worries, sorrow, and fear?" Only afterwards did he discover that because there is "birth," there is "suffering," and realized the Way to become Buddha.

"Becoming" refers to memories. The Buddha understood that sentient beings, in order to fulfill what they need in living, their pursuit of desires such as money, wealth, and fame gives rise to "becoming." All the positive and negative states that people come in contact will accumulate to form memories and the energized embodiment of memories collected never perishes with the death of the body. Instead, it will lead into rebirth for the next life.

In order to have a better next life, the only wondrous method is to create a perfect embodiment of memories. At the same time, we should all practice what Venerable Master Hsing Yun advocates, the Three Acts of Goodness: the body should do good deeds, the mouth should say good words, and the mind should think good thoughts. As such, we will be able to transform the DNA of our spirit and to become the engineer of our own life. So how did the Buddha think about the question regarding living and dying in life?

Thus have I heard:
One time the Buddha was residing at Anāthapiṇḍada's Park in Jeta's Grove near Śrāvastī.

At that time, the World-Honored one addressed the *bhikṣus:* "I recall that once during my existence prior to attaining right enlightenment, I was alone in a quiet place in deep meditative contemplation. I thought, 'It is difficult to enter the world; there are birth, aging, sickness, death, transmigration, and rebirth. However, sentient beings do not truly understand birth, aging, sickness, and death or what they depend on.

I contemplated: 'What phenomenon causes becoming? What phenomenon causes the existence of becoming? With right thought, giving rise to unimpeded understanding: when becoming exists, there is becoming; when condition exists, there is becoming.

I contemplated again: 'What phenomenon causes becoming? What phenomenon causes the existence of becoming? With right thought, giving rise to unimpeded understanding: when there is clinging, there is becoming; when there is clinging as condition, becoming exists.

Again I contemplated: 'What is the condition of clinging and the phenomenon for clinging to exist? What is the conditioning phenomena for clinging to exist?

With right thought, giving rise to unimpeded understanding:

clinging to a phenomenon giving rise to attachment, longing, binding, and the increase of craving; with craving, there is clinging; clinging is the condition for becoming, becoming the condition for birth; birth is the condition for aging, sickness, death, anxiety, sorrow, affliction, and suffering. Such is a massive culmination of suffering.

Bhikṣus! What do you think? If there are the conditions of oil and a wick, a lamp can keep burning bright. If more oil and wicks are added more times, could the lamp continue to burn bright for long?"

"It will indeed, World-Honored One!"

"As such *bhikṣus!* When clinging to form and giving rise to attachment, longing, binding, and affection, it will increase craving. With craving, there is clinging; clinging is the condition for becoming, becoming the condition for birth; birth is the condition for aging, sickness, death, anxiety, sorrow, affliction, and suffering. Such is the massive culmination of suffering.

I contemplated again: 'What is the phenomenon that is absent so that there is no aging, sickness, and death? What phenomenon is to cease so aging, sickness, and death also cease? With right thought, giving rise to unimpeded understanding: with no birth, there is no aging, sickness, and death; with cessation of birth, aging, sickness, and death also cease.

I contemplated again, 'What is the phenomenon that is absent, so that there is no birth? What phenomenon is to ceases so birth also ceases? With right thought, giving rise to unimpeded understanding: with no becoming, there is no birth; when becoming ceases, birth also ceases.'

Again I contemplated, 'What is the phenomenon that is absent, so that there is no becoming? What phenomenon is to cease so becoming also ceases? With right thought, giving rise to unimpeded understanding: with no clinging, there is no becoming; when clinging ceases, becoming also ceases.

I contemplated again: 'What is the phenomena that is absent, so that there is no clinging? What phenomenon is to cease so clinging also ceases? With right thought, giving rise to unimpeded understanding: the phenomenon clinging is impermanent, arising and ceasing, abandoning desire cessation completes, and to be given up; the mind has no longing and not bound by attachments;

craving will cease. With craving ceased, clinging ceases; with clinging ceased, becoming ceases; with becoming ceased, birth ceases. With cessation of birth, aging, sickness, death, anxiety, sorrow, affliction, and suffering cease. Such is the cessation of the massive culmination of suffering.

Bhikṣus, what do you think? Like the oil and wick which keep a lamp burning, if oil is not added and the wick not replaced, will the lit lamp cease to burn and exhaust itself to be extinguished in the future?

The *bhikṣus* replied to the Buddha, "Yes, as such, World-Honored One!"

"It is so, *bhikṣus!* Observe the phenomena as impermanent, arising and ceasing, abandoning desire cessation completes, and to be given up; the mind has no longing and not bound by attachments; craving will cease. With craving ceased, clinging ceases…till the cessation of the massive culmination of suffering."

After the Buddha had said these words, the *bhiksus* were delighted to hear the words of the Buddha and faithfully received this teaching and practice.

~ From Fascicle Number 285 in the *Connected Discourses*

From the moment of birth, a person begins to come across all kinds of suffering, including birth, aging, sickness, death, and separation from loved ones etc. To thoroughly resolve the source of suffering, the Buddha renounced the home life to focus on cultivation until he realized the truth of the principle of dependent origination: "When this arises, that comes up; when this is present, that comes to be; when this is absent, that does not come to be; when this ceases, that is extinct." He had thoroughly realized how the suffering of human existence comes about (the gate of transmigration), and how to eradicate suffering and afflictions to realization of the truth (the gate of cessation).

This *sutta* explains: the Buddha began from the Noble Truth of Suffering (birth, aging, sickness, and death) to the Noble Truth of the Cause of Suffering (craving, clinging, and becoming). He discovered that craving is the causal momentum of transmigration of birth and death. Then from the gate of cessation, the method for liberation from birth and death, he realized that when the Noble Truth of the Cause of Suffering (craving, clinging, and becoming) ceases, then the Noble Truth of Suffering (birth, aging, sickness, and death) will cease. He taught and guided his disciples with the above principle.

In this *sutta,* there are: "attachment in clinging, longing, and binding in affection for form increase the conditions for craving, clinging arises" and "with attachment in clinging, longing, binding in affection for dharmas increase craving and desire."

Here, "form" and "dharmas" should mean the six sense fields of form, sound, scent, taste, touch, and dharmas (mental objects). When our mind turns and changes with external states, endless tainted attachments, longing, craving, and desire will quietly grow and develop. Therefore, we must always observe the mind.

Thoroughly Observe the Essence of All Phenomena as Non-self

The "non-self" spoken of in Buddhism means we must deal with people and matters with a just and selfless mind. In cultivation, non-self is contemplating that the five aggregates are all empty. Viewed from the state of quietude and tranquility, it is quiescent *nirvāṇa.* The original meaning of "self" is always abiding, fixed, and unchanging; it is singular, free, and in control, existing by itself with a substantial nature. The "self" spoken of which eats, puts on clothes, and does the day-to-day matters in daily living is actually the "nominal self," the body and mind born relying on causes and conditions.

The following *sutta* explains how one goes from the nominal self to recognition of non-self. I believe it is a prelude that later developed into the content of the *Diamond Sūtra* wherein Subhūti beseeches the Buddha to answer two major questions: "What should they abide in?" and "How should they subdue the mind?"

Thus have I heard:
One time the Buddha was residing at Anāthapiṇḍada's Park in Jeta's

Grove near Śrāvastī.

At that time, a *bhikṣu* was alone in quiet contemplation: "What is self? What is the self for? What phenomenon is the self? Where does the self abide?" When he came out of his meditative state, he went to visit the Buddha. He prostrated before the Buddha's feet, sat to one side, and spoke to the Buddha, "World-Honored One! When I was alone in quiet contemplation, I contemplated as such: 'What is the self? What is the self for? What phenomenon is the self? Where does the self abide?'

The Buddha told the *bhikṣu,* "I will now speak the dual phenomena to you. Listen carefully! Contemplate well! Which two? The eyes and form are dual, the ears and sound, the nose and scent, the tongue and taste, the body and touch, and the mind and dharmas are all dual, and is called dual phenomenon. *Bhikṣu!* If someone said, 'Śramaṇa Gautama speaks of dual phenomena. These are not dual. I now abandon this notion and further establish another dual phenomena.' He spoke as such, whereupon someone asking further he could not answer, only adding to their doubt because it is beyond his state of understanding. Why is that so? The conditions of eyes and form give rise to eye consciousness.

"Bhikṣu! Eyes are of a fleshly form, they are internal, are causes and conditions, are solid, are feelings, and is called inner earth element of the eye fleshly form. *Bhikṣu!* Eyes are of a fleshly form, they are internal, are causes and conditions, are liquid, are feelings, and is called the inner water element of the eye fleshly form. *Bhikṣu!* Eyes are of a fleshly form, they are internal, are causes and conditions, are bright and warm, are feelings, and is called inner fire element of the eye fleshly form. *Bhikṣu,* eyes are of a fleshly form, they are internal, are causes and conditions, are light and moving, are feelings, and is called inner wind element of the eye fleshly form.

Bhikṣu! Just as two hands clapping together to make sound, similarly, the conditions of eyes and form give rise to eye consciousness. When these three factors combine with contact, contact will give rise to feeling, perceptions, and thoughts; these phenomena are non-self and impermanent. The impermanent self is not constant, a self that is unstable and subject to change. Why is that so? *Bhikṣu!* They are the phenomena of birth, aging, sickness, death, cessation, and becoming born.

Bhikṣu! All conditioned phenomena are like an illusion, like a flickering flame, and all can decay completely in an instant; there is neither really coming nor going. Therefore, *bhikṣu!* In the emptiness of conditioned phenomena, you should understand, be joyful, and contemplate. Empty all conditioned phenomena of their permanence, constant, abidance, and not subject to change; empty non-self and objects of self. Similar to a man with clear vision carrying a bright lamp into an empty room and can observe the empty room clearly.

As such, *bhikṣu!* Contemplate joy with regards to all empty phenomena and the empty mind; in empty phenomena are permanence, constant, abiding, not subject to change, are empty of self and objects of self. As such, eyes, ears, nose, tongue, body and mind are causes and conditions giving rise to consciousness; contact will give rise to feeling, perceptions, and thoughts; these phenomena are non-self and impermanent. All these phenomena are non-self and impermanent…till to be empty of self and objects of self. *Bhikṣu!* What do you think? Are eyes permanent or impermanent?"

He answered, "Impermanent, World-Honored One!"

The Buddha continued, "If it is impermanent, is it suffering?"

"Yes, it is suffering, World-Honored One!"

The Buddha again asked, "If it is impermanent, suffering, and subject to change, should noble disciples who have often heard the Dharma perceive within form a self, separate from self, or mutually existing with self?"

He answered, "No, World-Honored One!"

"Ears, nose, tongue, body, and mind are also this way. As such, noble disciples who have often heard the Dharma give rise to aversion for eyes. With aversion, they do not have delight; when they do not have delight, they are liberated. Upon liberation, they know and perceive: I have completed my final birth and established my pure practice; all there that is to be done is now done. I know I will no longer be subject to rebirth. Ears, nose, tongue, body, and mind are the same way."

Thereupon, the *bhikṣu* who had heard the World-Honored One's discourse on the sound of clapping, went alone to a place of quietude, focused his thoughts, not abiding in slackness; till he knew he no longer be subject to rebirth and attained *arhatship*.

~ From Fascicle Number 273 in the *Connected Discourses*.

Master Yìn Shùn had a very good and accurate interpretation of this sutra: Fascicle number 273 of the *Connected Discourses* contains questions like the following: *"What is the self? What is the self for? What phenomenon is the self? Where does the self abide?"*

1. **What is the self?**

The first question is about the intrinsic self. In other words, what did the self rely on to become self? The Honorable Śākyamuni answered, "Eyes and form, ears and sound, nose and scent, tongue and taste, body and touch, and the mind and mental objects are all dual... it is like two hands clapping together to make a sound. As such, the conditions of eyes and form give rise to eye consciousness. When these three factors combine with contact, contact gives rise to feeling, perception, and thought." This divides the twelve fields into two categories, the inner sense bases and external sense fields.

It is from the contact between inner and external phenomena that consciousness arises. In the sutta, the analogy is on two hands, the sense bases, clapping to become sound, the consciousness. The two coming together give rise to consciousness, and the three combine to become contact. Through the relationship between sense organs, sense fields, and consciousness, there is contact. According to the original meaning of the Agamas, the connection between consciousness and sense organs is contact. It is similar to the nominal term of contact as used by the Sautrāntika School.

In this way, the "six feelings," "six perceptions," and "six intentions" all arise following one another. This is the 'self,' built upon where the inner and external combine and is called 'self.' The teachings of the six inner sense bases are different from the principle of the five aggregates. It begins with the intrinsic nature of sentient beings, a combination of the six bases. Dependent origination's existence is not singular on its own. With human existence, there is inevitably existence of the world; so the six sense states will exist with material objects of the six sense bases.

With the intrinsic body of life, when there is contact of the self's external states and internal sense bases, there will be mental activities of the consciousness. Consequently, the "six points of contact," "six feelings," "six perceptions," and "six intentions" all arise. What is called the 'self' is as such.

2. What is the self for?

The second question asks about a person's actions, functions, and undertakings. The Honorable Śākyamuni offered an explanatory answer: "All these phenomena are non-self and impermanent; the self is impermanent, not constant and unstable, subject to change. Why is that so? Bhikṣu! This is the principle of birth, aging, sickness, death, ceasing, and becoming born." The combination of what is internal and external is nominally a 'self' within the continuous flow of changes, there are no permanence or joy as considered by other religions. The function of this 'self' is being reborn, aging, falling ill, and dying.

3. What phenomenon is the self?

Regarding the third question, "what phenomenon is the self?" the Buddha answered, "Bhikṣu! All conditioned phenomena are like an illusion, like a flickering flame, and all can decay completely in an instant; there is neither really coming nor going." Within the twelve sense fields, the six sense bases are especially emphasized and are called "all conditioned phenomena" which are made up of the eyes and other sense organs. Their nature is like an illusion, a mirage, deteriorating in an instant. It is the principle of causes and conditions, coming together in giving rise to phenomena. Therefore, their existence does not come from anywhere.

When those conditions scatter these phenomena cease to exist, therefore, in cessation there is nowhere to go. Although phenomena exist, they are not truly existent. The six sense bases are illusory conditioned phenomena. They are empty and have arisen due to dependent origination, without a self-nature. What is called the 'self' is just a combination of activities from the six sense organs giving rise to consciousness, feelings, perceptions, and intentions on interacting with the conditioned sense fields. This is the 'self' which exists within conventional truth; just this and nothing more.

4. **Where does the self abide?**

This illusory and nominal self is in accordance with the principle of non-self, empty and tranquil. In the answer to the fourth question, "Where does the self abide?" this concept is explained clearly and correctly.

"As such, bhikṣu! Contemplate joy with regards to all empty phenomena and the empty mind; in empty phenomena are permanence, constant, abiding, not subject to change, are empty of self and objects of self." This is to say that the self has no place for abiding; if the self had a place for abiding (a foothold somewhere), then that abode would have to be truly existing, permanent, and unchanging. However, all phenomena is a combination of causes and conditions, not real and not constant. Consequently, the pursuit for a truly existing self is unattainable. The self is just a nominally designated self, a combination and function of the six sense organs, but a truly existing inherent body is unattainable. The Dharma teachings of the internal sense bases emphasize the establishing of the 'self,' which has no truly existing entity of self, only the arising and cessation of the nominally designated conditioned phenomena. Birth is a birth of empty phenomena, and cessation is a cessation of empty phenomena. The meaning of this is more obvious than that of the Dharma teachings of the five aggregates.

(Abstracted from Master Yìn Shùn's *A Study of the Origins of the Emptiness of Nature,* beginning from page 44)

Contemplate the Law of Dependent Origination

Prior to attaining Buddhahood, the Buddha was originally a prince. Due to seeing people experiencing much pain and suffering and that this could not be thoroughly resolved by power, wealth, medicine, or general learning and knowledge. Consequently, he gave rise to limitless great compassion and loving-kindness, giving up the nobility and honor of the throne for renunciation and cultivation of the Way.

Before the World-Honored One awakened to the truth about the universe, within meditative concentration, he used contemplation to understand the process of life and death. He discovered the law of Dependent Origination: "When this arises, that comes up; when this is present, that comes to be; when this is absent, that does not come to be; when this ceases, that is extinct." This law is universally valid for myriad phenomena, the dependent origination principle has always been as such, is commonly as such, and is inevitably as such. The Buddha was awakened to the Noble Truth of Suffering which is a fact of life which must be experienced.

Why are there immeasurable forms of suffering? They all exist due to the Noble Truth of the Cause of Suffering: craving, clinging, and becoming. Craving, clinging, and becoming originate from incorrect thought: the belief that our body and mind is permanent, mistaking the impermanent for permanent; pleasurable, mistaking pain for pleasure; a self, mistaking the non-self for a self; and pure, mistaking what is defiled for what is pure. These are called the "four kinds of inversion."

The main inversion is mistaking that our body and mind have a "true self" which is permanently abiding and unchanging, truly existing, able to be in control, and can be its own master, called "self-delusion." A strongly tainted attachment to our body and mind and all which is related to our body and mind is called "self-love." The above life perspectives are known as "self-view." In Buddhism, self-delusion, self-view, and self-love are collectively called "ignorance."

With the element of ignorance, various behaviors are conducted which though bring various forms of pleasure, in the end it is still suffering. Because of the interaction of cognition and behaviors, there will be a memory body for rebirth into another life. Hence, transmigration between birth and death develops, and the endless ocean of suffering truly knows no bounds!

Although the main cause of transmigration between life and death is ignorance, the Buddha discovered that the momentum propelling transmigration is "craving" and "clinging." He became enlightened to the method for liberating from transmigration: "When this is absent, that does not come to be; when this ceases, that is extinct." When ignorance ceases, mental formations cease; when mental formations cease, consciousness ceases. Further on till birth, aging, death, afflictions, sorrow, worries, suffering, and the massive culmination of suffering cease. In the end, there is attaining of liberation from life and death.

In learning Buddhism, we need to understand dependent origination and the empty nature of the universe through Dependent Origination, the Three Dharma Seals, the Four Noble Truths, the Noble Eightfold Path, and the Twelve Links of Dependent Origination. Because all phenomena are just the coming together of causes and conditions.

The following *sutta* describes how the Buddha upheld these practices and realized the unexcelled, perfect enlightenment.

> Thus have I heard:
> One time the Buddha was residing at Anāthapiṇḍada's Park in Jeta's Grove near Śrāvastī.
>
> At that time, the World-Honored One addressed the *bhikṣus:* "I recall that once during my existence prior to attaining right enlightenment, I was alone in a quiet place in deep meditative contemplation. I thought to myself, 'What is the phenomena which causes aging and death? What phenomenon conditions aging and death? With right thought, giving rise to unimpeded understanding: with birth, there is aging; with birth as the condition, there is aging. It is as such for clinging, craving, feeling, contact, the six sense

organs, and name and form. What is the phenomena which causes name and form? What phenomenon conditions name and form? With right thought, giving rise to unimpeded understanding: with consciousness, there is name and form; with consciousness as the condition, there is name and form. When I was thinking as such, I found that the limits of consciousness could not be traced back further than this point, known as consciousness conditions name and form. Name and form then conditions the six sense bases, and the six sense organs conditions contact; contact then conditions feeling, and feeling conditions craving. Craving conditions clinging, and clinging then conditions becoming; becoming then conditions birth, and birth conditions aging, sickness, death, anxiety, sorrow, affliction, and suffering. As such, as such, a massive culmination of suffering.

I then thought to myself, 'What is the phenomena which if absent, would cause aging and death to be absent? What phenomenon if ceases would bring aging and death into cessation? With right thought, giving rise to unimpeded understanding: If birth was absent then aging and death would be absent; if birth ceases, then aging and death cease. As such, birth, becoming, clinging, craving, feeling, contact, the six sense organs, name and form, and consciousness can all be explained in this way.

I then further thought to myself, 'What is the phenomena which if absent would cause mental formations to be absent? What phenomenon if ceases would bring mental formations into cessation?" With right thought, giving rise to unimpeded understanding: If ignorance was absent then mental formations would be absent. If ignorance ceases, then mental formations cease. If mental formations cease, then consciousness ceases. If consciousness ceases, then name and form cease. If name and form cease, then the six sense organs cease. If the six sense organs cease, then contact ceases. If contact ceases, then feeling ceases. If feeling ceases, then craving ceases. If craving ceases, then clinging ceases. If clinging ceases, then becoming ceases. If becoming ceases, then birth ceases. If birth ceases, then aging, sickness, anxiety, sorrow, affliction, and suffering cease. As such, as such, a massive culmination of suffering ceases.

I then thought to myself, 'I have attained the Way of the

ancients, the path of the ancients, and the track of the ancients. The ancients had gone along this path, now I follow. It is like a person wandering through the wilderness, seeking a path in the wild. Suddenly, he came across an old path which had been traveled by ancients. He followed the path, advancing gradually when he saw an ancient city, a royal palace, gardens, ponds, and serene groves and trees. He thereby thinks to himself, 'Now I should go and tell the king about this.' He immediately went to tell the king, 'Great king, you should know that when I was traveling in the wilderness looking for a path, I suddenly discovered an old path which had been traveled by ancients. I immediately followed along and saw an ancient city, a royal palace, gardens, ponds, and serene groves and trees. Great king, you could go there to live.' After that, the king went to live there where all were plentiful, joyful, peaceful, and tranquil, and the king's subjects flourished.

Now I am as such. I have attained the Way of the ancients, the path of the ancients, and the track of the ancients. The ancients had gone along this path, now I follow. It is this Eightfold Noble Path: right view, right intention, right speech, right action, right livelihood, right skillful means, right mindfulness, and right meditative concentration. I learn from that path aging and death, the cause of aging and death, the cessation of aging and death, and the path that leads to the cessation of aging and death. I have seen birth, becoming, clinging, craving, feeling, contact, the six sense organs, name and form, consciousness, mental formations and their causes, cessation, and the path to their cessation. Through this Dharma, I have gained knowledge and awakening and have attained supreme enlightenment by myself. I have taught and explained this Dharma for *bhikṣus*, *bhikṣuṇīs*, *upāsakas*, *upāsikās*, the *śramaṇas* of other religions, *brāhmins*, householders, and renunciants. The four groups of practitioners hear the Dharma, turn to the right way, have joyous faith, know the wholesome Dharma, advance in pure practices, and gain a multitude of great benefits.

After the Buddha had said these words, the *bhiksus* were delighted to hear the words of the Buddha and faithfully received this teaching and practice.

~ From Fascicle Number 287 in the *Connected Discourses*.

The Buddha sometimes spoke of reverse contemplation of dependent origination or sequential contemplation of dependent arising; he sometimes taught right contemplation of the Four Noble Truths for attaining realization of the supreme bodhi. The contents of Dependent Origination and the Four Noble Truths are similar; it is just the way of interpretation that is different. What is key in Dependent Origination and the principle of causes and conditions is the explanation of the transmigration of birth and death and the reversal or cessation of birth and death. The gate of transmigration is the Noble Truth of Suffering and the Noble Truth of the Cause of Suffering. The gate of cessation is the Noble Truth of the Path Leading to the Cessation of Suffering. Being able to contemplate Dependent Origination: "When this arises, that comes up; when this is present, that comes to be; when this is absent, that does not come to be; when this ceases, that is extinct;" this is *prajñā*-wisdom, which is right view and right thought.

When the followers of the Buddha learn the Dharma, it is likely that many of them approached Dependent Origination and the Four Noble Truths separately. In actuality, when the Buddha contemplated the Noble Truth of Suffering, he traced back the cause of suffering which are craving, clinging, and becoming (the Noble Truth of the Cause of Suffering). He further reasoned that these were caused by wrong thought (ignorance) which propels desire (craving) and the mental formations of the three types of karma: physical, verbal, and mental. With mental formations, there is consciousness; with consciousness, there is name and form. This continues to birth, aging, and death; it is an inevitable principle.

Everything in the universe is like this. "When this arises, that comes up; when this is present, that comes to be." Realizing this principle is to understand Dependent Origination: 'in order to get a given effect or result, there must have been given causes and conditions.' It is: ignorance is the condition for mental formation, which is the condition for consciousness, which is the condition for name and form... until birth, the condition for aging, death, sorrow, worries, affliction, suffering, and a massive culmination of suffering. Moreover, if certain causes and conditions do not come to be, then the certain effect will not come to be. Consequently, the gate of cessation is: ignorance ceases, mental formations cease; mental formations cease, consciousness ceases; consciousness ceases, name and form cease... until birth ceases, then aging and death cease; sorrow, worries, affliction, suffering, and the massive culmination of suffering cease. It is the accomplishing of the Noble Truth of the Cessation of Suffering, the liberation of *nirvāṇa.* As for the Eightfold Noble Path: right view, right thought, right speech, right action, right livelihood, right effort, right mindfulness, and right concentration; it is the Noble Truth of the Path Leading to the Cessation of Suffering.

Keys for Practice in Humanistic Buddhism

It is evident that the Buddha observed the transmigration and cessation of human existence, so it is Humanistic Buddhism. The Buddha believed that all phenomena and life arise and cease due to limitless causes and conditions; therein exist mutual causes and conditions as well as mutual cause and effect, so it is Humanistic Buddhism. The Buddha instructed us to rely on precepts, meditative concentration, and wisdom to eradicate greed, anger, and ignorance of the body and mind, so it is Humanistic Buddhism. Humanistic Buddhism is what the Buddha taught, what is needed by people, what is pure, and what is wholesome and beautiful; all teachings that help us in making progress for a happy life is Humanistic Buddhism.

The enlightenment of the Buddha is in accordance with contemplating the Noble Truth of Suffering. He ceaselessly progressed in his contemplative reasoning until he realized Dependent Origination wherein "When this arises, that comes up; when this is present, that comes to be;" and dependent arising wherein "when this is conditioned, that will therefore arise." The dependent origination in the gate of cessation is such that without ignorance or wrong thought, there are no mental formations; with no mental formations, there is no consciousness. This is an inevitable principle, which has always been as such, and it is as such everywhere. Dharma nature, Dharma determined to be normal, Dharma realm, and the rules of Dharma are also as such. When the Buddha discovered or realized this Dharma principle and came to refer to it as "Dharma." What is called Dharma means: ignorance ceases, mental formations cease; mental formations cease, consciousness ceases; consciousness ceases, name and form cease... until birth ceases; sorrow, worries, affliction, suffering, and the massive culmination of suffering cease! This is like if a plane flying from Hong Kong to Los Angeles has been delayed for two hours, then the same plane flying back to Hong Kong from Los Angeles will also be delayed for two hours.

Due to thoughts regarding all suffering, knowing that the origin of suffering is dependent origination of phenomena. Dependent Origination is the Noble Truth of the Path Leading to the Cessation of Suffering. Beginning from actualizing the Noble Truth of the Path Leading to the Cessation of Suffering, subdue the origins by eradicating and ceasing them with the Twelve Links of Dependent Origination. Then one enters the Noble Truth of the Cessation of Suffering. Hence, the Four Noble Truths and Dependent Origination have similar content.

When followers of the Buddha propagate the Dharma, the Northern tradition of Buddhism employed many skillful means. However, when it came to benefiting themselves in personal cultivation, they were at a distinct disadvantage. This is especially true with regard to subduing worries and getting rid of habitual tendencies. It is because they tend to neglect contemplation and actualization of the Four Noble Truths, Twelve Links of Dependent Origination, and Three Dharma Seals. As most of them take the empty nature of *prajñā-wisdom* as their main focus, making the best of the present here and now, realizing that all phenomena are empty; with a mind free of worry or obstruction, attaining ease of the body and mind. Although these achievements are truly auspicious and these states are advanced and profound, but it seems to lack some roots!

Cultivating Meditative Concentration and Cultivating Wisdom are Mutually Linked to One Another

When faced with external states that we dislike such as personal disputes, we should know how to use wisdom to reflect on such situations. We should think: "Everything comes to be through causes and conditions. When the causes and conditions are complete, a given thing naturally exists; when causes and conditions are not complete, then no matter how much we seek, it will not be attainable." If we follow causes and conditions as such, then our mind will be calm and serene. Wisdom should be used to cultivate meditative concentration; this is what is called the dual cultivation of cessation and contemplation.

Using the Contemplation on Impurity to Subdue Sexual Lust

The key to begin the practice of cessation and contemplation is the five contemplations. Since I have already mentioned this in the first chapter, I will not repeat here. However, I will make more explanations regarding the contemplation on impurity and the contemplation on counting the breath because these are the two especially important methods of cultivation in Buddhism.

First, I will begin with the contemplation on impurity. I have found a *sutta* wherein it is explained how a young *bhikṣu* contains sexual lust and is able to calm his mind in cultivating the Way.

> Thus have I heard:
> One time the Honorable Piṇḍola was residing in Ghoṣilārāma Garden in Kauśāmbī.
>
> At that time, there was a king from the Matsya Kingdom named Udayana-vatsa. He came to visit the Honorable Piṇḍola, and they both bowed to one another with joined palms. After bowing, King Udayana-vatsa sat to one side and asked the Honorable

Piṇḍola, "There are some questions I wish to ask. Do you have time to answer them now?"

The Honorable Piṇḍola answered, "Great King! Great King please ask now and I will answer in accordance with what I know."

King Udayana-vatsa of the Matsya Kingdom asked the Honorable Piṇḍola, "What are the causes and conditions for young *bhikṣus* to learn the Dharma and Vinaya, having only recently renounced, but they abide within peace, tranquility, and happiness; their faculties are joyful and at ease, their appearances are pure, their complexion is fair and fresh, they delight in quietude and tend toward stillness. They live in a state of non-contrivance, they tame the wildness of their minds, they are capable throughout the entirety of their lives, they cultivate and uphold the pure practices, and they achieve unadulterated purity?"

The Honorable Piṇḍola replied, "This is done in accordance with what has been said by the Buddha, what the Tathāgata, Arhat, and the Supreme Enlightened One has known and seen. He told the young *bhikṣus*, 'All you, *bhikṣus!* If you see an elderly secular person, you should think of her as a mother. If they are middle-aged, think of them as a sister; and if they are young, you should think of them as a daughter.' These are the causes and conditions for young *bhikṣus* to learn the Dharma and Vinaya, having only recently renounced, but they abide within peace, tranquility, and happiness; their faculties are joyful and at ease, their appearances are pure, their complexion is fair and fresh, they delight in quietude and tend toward stillness. They live in a state of non-contrivance, they tame the wildness of their minds, they are capable throughout the entirety of their lives, they cultivate and uphold the pure practices, and they achieve unadulterated purity."

King Udayana-vatsa of the Matsya Kingdom spoke to the Honorable Piṇḍola, "Now all of the worldly greed and desire in your mind is such that if you see an elderly secular person, you should think of her as a mother; if they are middle-aged, you should think of her as a sister; and if they are young, you should think of her as a daughter. When you do this, your mind will arise, burning with greed, burning with anger, and burning with ignorance. Then you will need even better causes and conditions, right?"

The Honorable Piṇḍola told King Udayana-vatsa of the Matsya Kingdom, "There are more causes and conditions. As spoken by the

World Honored One, as seen and known by the Tathāgata, Arhat, the Supreme Enlightened One. He taught these *bhikṣus,* 'This body, from head to toe, a frame of bones filled with muscle and blood and covered with thin skin, it is full of all impurities. If we observe extensively, there are hair, body hair, nails, teeth, dusty dirt, saliva, skin, flesh, white bones, muscle, veins, heart, liver, lungs, spleen, kidneys, intestines, stomach, reticulum, large intestines, womb, tears, sweat, mucus, frothy spittle, fat, lard, phlegm, puss, blood, brains, bile, feces, and urine.' Great King! These are the causes and conditions by which young *bhikṣus* to learn the Dharma and Vinaya, having only recently renounced, but they abide within peace, tranquility, and happiness... and they achieve unadulterated purity."

King Udayana-vatsa of the Matsya Kingdom spoke to the Honorable Piṇḍola, "The mind flutters about wildly. In observing impurities, thoughts of purity will follow. Are there other causes and condition for the young *bhikṣus* to learn the Dharma and Vinaya, having only recently renounced, but they abide within peace, tranquility, and happiness...and they achieve unadulterated purity?"

The Honorable Piṇḍola replied, "Great King! There are causes and conditions. As spoken by the World Honored One, as seen and known by the Tathāgata, Arhat, the Supreme Enlightened One. He taught these *bhikṣus,* 'You all should protect and guard the gates of your senses and concentrate your minds well. When the eyes see form, do not cling to notions of the form; do not cling to the goodness of the object, but should progress in upholding concentration. If the eyes cannot be brought under control, then worldly greed and desires, evil and unwholesome phenomena will defile your minds. That is why you should uphold precepts for your eyes; ears and sound, nose and scent, tongue and taste, body and touch, and mind and dharmas are also as such, till upholding precepts for the consciousness.'

Thereupon, King Udayana-vatsa of the Matsya Kingdom told the Honorable Piṇḍola, "Excellent! You spoke the Dharma well all the way to the point of upholding precepts for the sense bases. Honorable Piṇḍola! I am also as such. Sometimes I do not guard and protect my body, not upholding precepts for all my sense organs, and not focusing the mind. On entering the palace, my mind gives rise to burning greed and burning delusion. Even if I am alone in a quiet room, the three poisons still burn in my mind, and even more so when inside the palace! Yet, there are also times when I guard my body well, focusing on my sense organs and concentrating my mind. Then if I enter the palace, greed, anger, and ignorance do not arise and burn within my mind. Within the palace, my body does not burn nor my mind, and even more so when alone in quietude! Therefore, these are the causes and conditions for young *bhikṣus* to learn the Dharma and Vinaya, having only recently renounced, but they abide within peace, tranquility, and happiness, till they achieve unadulterated purity."

Thereupon, King Udayana-vatsa of the Matsya Kingdom, who had heard the Honorable Piṇḍola's teaching, felt blissful joy and acceptance. He stood up and took his leave.

~ From Fascicle Number 1165 in the *Connected Discourses.*

The Honorable Piṇḍola is also known as the Long-eyebrow Arhat because his long brow sweeps the ground, the head of the eighteen *arhats.* This *sutta* uses the conversation between the Honorable Piṇḍola and King Udayana-vatsa to show the methods for controlling sexual lust, which include the contemplation on friends and family, the contemplation on impurity, and guarding the six sense organs.

The contemplation on friends and family is in accordance with the four immeasurable mindfulness, visualizing all sentient beings are like our own friends, family, brothers, and sisters. The contemplation on impurity involves cultivating meditative concentration and think of impurities, giving rise to aversion, and further cultivating the mind for renunciation in order to have the strength for self-control.

Additionally, in our daily lives it is crucial that we rigorously guard our six sense bases so as to be able to eradicate desire and worries. The meaning of guarding the gates of our sense organs is to carefully guard our eyes, ears, nose, tongue, body, and mind, not allowing them to come into contact with environments of strong temptations.

Use Contemplation of Breath-counting to Counter Distraction

When Śākyamuni Buddha was in the world, there were sixty *bhikṣus* who cultivated the contemplation on impurities who had come to detest their bodies, and they either committed suicide or found someone to kill them. Later on, two schools emerged: one cultivated the contemplation on white bone; progressing from visualizing a "rotting corpse" to visualizing "snowy whiteness of the bones." Once that visualization was stable, then visualize the bones emitting light. This method also had the function of controlling sexual lust. The other school is the cultivation of breath-counting. This is what I mentioned in a few earlier chapters, "*ānāpānasmṛti*."

I. From the Contemplation on Impurity to the Contemplation on Counting the Breath

Thus have I heard:
One time the Buddha was residing in Śāla Grove at the riverbank of Vaggumudā River where the Vṛji dwell.

At that time the Buddha spoke to the *bhikṣus* about the contemplation on impurity. He praised the contemplation on impurity stating, "All *bhikṣus* should cultivate the contemplation on impurity. Those who cultivate and actualize it more will attain great fruits and good benefits." (Attaining the four fruits of practice or *arhatship*.)

Thereupon, the *bhikṣus* cultivated the contemplation on impurity and many came to detest very much their unwholesome bodies. Some committed suicide by stabbing themselves, taking poison, hanging with ropes, jumping to their deaths off of cliffs, or had fellow *bhikṣus* kill them.

A certain *bhikṣu* fell into extreme detest over his unwholesome body's impurities which is subject to foul discharges. He traveled to where Deer Woods Brāhmin lived, and spoke to Deer Woods Brāhmin, "Venerable leader, if you are able to kill me, these robes and alms bowl will be yours."

Thereupon, Deer Woods Brāhmin immediately killed the *bhikṣu*. He carried his knife to the riverbank of Vaggumudā River.

When he began washing his knife, a *māra-deva* appeared in the sky before him and praised Deer Woods Brāhmin: "Excellent! Excellent! Venerable leader! You have attained limitless merits. You are able to deliver the *śramaṇa* disciples of Sakyamuni with virtues in upholding precepts; liberate those who have yet to be liberated; calm those who have yet to be calmed; and bring those into *nirvāṇa* who have yet to attain *nirvāṇa*. All their robes, alms bowls, and miscellaneous possessions will then be yours."

At that time, Deer Woods Brāhmin heard these praises, which exacerbated his wickedness and wrong views, and thought to himself, "Now I truly have gained great blessings and merits. I am able to deliver the *śramaṇa* disciples of Sakyamuni with virtues in upholding precepts; liberate those who have yet to be liberated; calm those who have yet to be calmed; and bring those into *nirvāṇa* who have yet to achieve *nirvāṇa*. All their robes, alms bowls, and miscellaneous possessions will then be mine." So he carried a sharp knife and went to all the *bhikṣu* rooms, walking meditation paths, temple rooms, and meditation halls. Whenever he would see *bhikṣus*, he would say, "Are there any *śramaṇas* with virtues in upholding precepts who have yet to be delivered? I am able to deliver you. Those who have yet to be liberated, can be liberated; those who have yet to be calmed, can be calmed; and those who have yet to attain *nirvāṇa*, can attain *nirvāṇa*."

Thereupon, *bhikṣus* who detest their unwholesome bodies all came out of their rooms and said to Deer Woods Brāhmin, "I have yet to be delivered, you should deliver me; I have yet to be liberated, you should liberate me; I have yet to be calmed, you should calm me; I have yet to attain *nirvāṇa*, you should bring me to *nirvāṇa*."

At that time, Deer Woods Brāhmin killed these *bhikṣus* with his sharp knife. He did this repeatedly until he had killed sixty *bhikṣus*.

Thereupon, when the World-Honored One spoke on the precepts on the fifteenth day of the month, he sat before the *bhikṣus* and asked the Honorable Ānanda, "What are the causes and conditions by which the *bhikṣus* have grown few, decreased, and disappeared?

The Honorable Ānanda told the Buddha, "The World-Honored One spoke to the *bhikṣus* on practicing the contemplation on impurity and you praised the contemplation on impurity. After the *bhikṣus* practiced the contemplation on impurity, they fell into extreme detest of their unwholesome bodies and this resulted in the killing of sixty *bhikṣus*. World-Honored One! These are the causes and conditions by which the *bhikṣus* have grown few, decreased, and disappeared. Our only wish is for the World-Honored One to speak of other teachings for the *bhikṣus* to hear so they may diligently cultivate wisdom, receive the correct Dharma with joy, and abide in the correct Dharma with joy."

The Buddha told the Honorable Ānanda, "As such, I will now sequentially explain how to abide in the subtle abode and following the sequence to be awakened. For deviant and unwholesome phenomena which have already arisen or have yet to arise, put them to rest quickly. It is like a great rain washing away all the dust which has arisen and also the dust which has yet to arise. As such, *bhikṣus*! The cultivation of the subtle abode for all deviant and unwholesome phenomena which have already arisen or have yet to arise can be put to rest. Ānanda ! Which subtle abode when frequently cultivated and following the sequence to be awakened, putting to rest all evil and unwholesome phenomena? It is known as the meditative abode of *ānāpānasmṛti*.

Ānanda asked the Buddha, "How to cultivate the meditative abode of *ānāpānasmṛti* and following the sequence to be wakened, and bringing to rest all deviant and unwholesome phenomena which have already arisen or have yet to arise?"

The Buddha replied to Ānanda, "When *bhikṣus* reside in villages, they do as was explained in detail above…till learning the cessation of inhalation and exhalation."

When the Buddha finished speaking this discourse, the Honorable Ānanda who had heard the Buddha's teaching, was delighted to hear the words of the Buddha and faithfully received this teaching and practice.

~ From Fascicle Number 809 in the *Connected Discourses*.

This *sutta* describes the causes and conditions the Buddha taught the practice of *ānāpānasmṛti* meditation. At that time, many *bhikṣus* cultivated the contemplation on impurity, resulting in detest for their bodies leading to suicide or killing one another. Later on, a shaman named Deer Woods was attracted to massacre them, with sixty *bhikṣus* dead in half a month. After the Buddha came out of his retreat and heard what Ānanda reported, he then taught the sangha the cultivation method of *ānāpānasmṛti* meditation.

Although the Buddha instructed his disciples to control sexual lust, the emphasis switched from the contemplation on impurity to 'abiding in a subtle abode,' which is cultivating the method of *ānāpānasmṛti*. However, for a pure-minded renunciant, the contemplation on impurity or the contemplation of skeletons are still the most effective for reducing the habitual tendencies of sexual lust.

II. The Attitude for Cultivating Contemplation on Counting the Breath

The Buddha taught his disciples who wish to cultivate *ānāpānasmṛti*, they must:

1) Uphold pure precepts.
2) Reduce desires, affairs, and chores.
3) Moderate intake of food and drink.
4) Be diligent and not be slack, do not waste time with sleeping.
5) Find a quiet place far from distractions and noise.

> Thus have I heard:
> One time the Buddha was residing at Anāthapiṇḍada's Park in Jeta's Grove near Śrāvastī.
>
> At that time, the World-Honored One addressed the *bhikṣus*: "There are five methods for cultivating *ānāpānasmṛti* meditation which has many benefits. Which five? Abide in pure precepts *pratimokṣa* complete in etiquette and comportment wherever you are; give rise to fear for even minute transgressions, and uphold the teachings of precepts. This is the first method for cultivating *ānāpānasmṛti* meditation which has many benefits. Furthermore, *bhikṣus!* Decrease desires, affairs, and chores. This is the second method for cultivating *ānāpānasmṛti* meditation which has many benefits. Furthermore, *bhikṣus!* Moderate the intake of food and drink, no more, no less; do not give rise to desirous thoughts over

eating and drinking. Be diligent in contemplation. This is the third method for cultivating *ānāpānasmṛti* meditation which has many benefits. Furthermore, *bhikṣus!* During the first and third of the three divisions of night, do not sleep, but be diligent in contemplation. This is the fourth method for cultivating *ānāpānasmṛti* meditation which has many benefits. Furthermore, *bhikṣus!* Reside in quiet forests, far from confusions and noise. This is the fifth method for cultivating *ānāpānasmṛti* meditation which has many benefits."

After the Buddha had said these words, the *bhiksus* were delighted to hear the words of the Buddha and faithfully received this teaching and practice.

~ From Fascicle Number 801 in the *Connected Discourses.*

III. Five Conditions for Cultivating the Contemplation on Counting the Breath

The following *sutta* describes the five conditions for the cultivating contemplation of counting the breath.

Thus have I heard:
One time the Buddha was residing at Anāthapiṇḍada's Park in Jeta's Grove near Śrāvastī.

At that time, the World-Honored One addressed the *bhikṣus:* "You should cultivate *ānāpānasmṛti!* If *bhikṣus* cultivate *ānāpānasmṛti* frequently, attaining cessation in body and mind, awakening and contemplation, tranquility, pure singularity, and completion in the cultivation of observation and discernment. What is the frequent cultivation *ānāpānasmṛti* for attaining cessation in body and mind, awakening and contemplation, tranquility, pure singularity, and completion in the cultivation of observation and discernment?

1) If *bhikṣus* abide in villages and cities, in the morning they don their robes, carry their alms bowls, and enter nearby villages to beg for food. In doing so, they should protect their bodies well, guard the gates of their sense, and focus the mind well in abidance.

2) After collecting alms food, return to their residence, put away the robes and alms bowls. Then wash your feet and go into the woods, a quiet room, under a tree, or on the open ground. Sit upright

and focus your attention to the present.

3) Sever worldly greed and desire, give up lust for purity; eliminate anger, drowsiness, anxieties, and doubt; be resolute in all wholesome Dharmas. Distance the mind from the defilements of the five hindrances which will weaken wisdom, are obstacles for liberation, not progressing toward *nirvāṇa*.

4) Focus on inhalation, be mindful in learning well; focus on exhalation, be mindful in learning well. Long breath or short breath; be aware of the entire body on inhalation and learn well from the entire body on inhalation. Be aware of the entire body on exhalation and learn well from the entirety body on exhalation.

Be aware of the entirety of inhalation attaining gradual quiescence and ease and learn well from the entirety of inhalation attaining gradual quiescence and ease. Be aware of the entirety of exhalation attaining gradual quiescence and ease, and learn well the entirety of exhalation attaining gradual quiescence and ease.

Be aware of joy, be aware of pleasure, be aware of feelings; be aware of the feelings of calmness on inhalation; learn well from the awareness of the feelings of calmness on inhalation. Be aware of the feelings of calmness on exhalation; learn well from the awareness of the feelings of calmness on exhalation. Be aware of the mind, be aware of joy in the mind, be aware of the mind liberated on inhalation; learn well from the awareness of the mind liberated on inhalation. Be aware of the mind liberated on exhalation; learn well from the awareness of the mind liberated on exhalation.

5) Observe impermanence, observe severing, observe being desireless, and observe inhalations extinguishing, and learn well the extinguishing of inhalations. Observe exhalations extinguishing, and learn well the extinguishing of exhalations; this is called the cultivation of *ānāpānasmṛti*, attaining cessation in body and mind, awakening and contemplation, tranquility, pure singularity, and completion in the cultivation of observation and discernment.

After the Buddha had said these words, the *bhiksus* were delighted to hear the words of the Buddha and faithfully received this teaching and practice.

~ From Fascicle Number 803 in the *Connected Discourses*.

IV. The Merits of Cultivating the Contemplation of Counting the Breath

The following *sutta* explains if contemplation of counting the breath is well cultivated, the final fruit of attainment can be realized.

> Thus have I heard:
> One time the Buddha was residing at Anāthapiṇḍada's Park in Jeta's Grove near Śrāvastī.
>
> At that time, the World-Honored One addressed the *bhikṣus:* "You should cultivate *ānāpānasmṛti.* Those who often cultivate *ānāpānasmṛti* eradicate their thoughts for the senses. How do those who often cultivate *ānāpānasmṛti* eradicate their thoughts for the senses? If *bhikṣus* abide in villages and cities…, as spoken above in detail, till learning well the extinguishing of exhalations; this is called the cultivation of *ānāpānasmṛti*, frequently practiced in eradicating all thoughts for the senses."
>
> After the World-Honored One had spoken the *sutta*, the *bhikṣus* were delighted to hear the words of the Buddha and faithfully received this teaching and practice!
>
> ~ From Fascicle Number 804 in the *Connected Discourses.*

In eradicating thoughts for the senses, if immovable as such, great attainments and great benefits can be realized; like sweet ambrosia, the ultimate sweet ambrosia. One can attain the second fruit, the fourth fruit, and the seventh fruit just as each was spoken of above.

V. Experience of the Buddha

Given that *ānāpānasmṛti* is so beneficial, did the Buddha personally experience it? He certainly did! Please refer to the following *sutta*:

Thus have I heard:
One time the Buddha was residing in a woodland thicket in the village of Icchānaṅgala.

At that time the World-Honored One addressed the *bhikṣus:* "I wish to practice meditation for two months. No *bhikṣus* should come and go except for *bhikṣus* bringing food and for *poṣadha*."

Thereupon, the World-Honored One finished speaking and then immediately began his two-month meditation. Not one *bhikṣu* dared to come and go except for bringing food and for *poṣadha*.

Thereupon, the World-Honored One finished his two months of seated meditation. After exiting his meditation, he sat before the *bhikṣus* and spoke to them: "If shamans from another religion come here and ask you, 'Why did Śramaṇa Gautama spend two months in seated meditation?' Then you should reply, 'The Tathāgata spent two months to contemplate in abidance with *ānāpānasmṛti.'* Why is that so? During my two months of *ānāpānasmṛti* meditation, I abide in reflections; on inhalation, I was mindful of inhalation and knew as such. On exhalation, I was mindful of exhalation and knew as such. Whether the breaths were long or short, my entire body was aware of inhaling and knew as such, my entire body was aware of exhaling and knew as such…till extinguishing of exhalation and knew as such. I was fully aware and thought: 'This reflective abode is still coarse, I now cease on this reflection; I should further cultivate other subtler abodes and abide within.'

"Thereupon, I ceased my contemplation in the abode which was coarse and immediately entered even subtler contemplation, sustaining long in the abidance. At that time, three *deva-putras* of superb physical forms came to my place in the night. The first *deva-putra* exclaimed, "Śramaṇa Gautama has passed away." The second *deva-putra* countered, "This is not passing away yet, it is close to passing away." The third *deva-putra* concluded, "It is neither having passed away nor close to passing away. This is a cultivating abode, the tranquil cessation of an *arhat!*"

The Buddha told the *bhikṣus*, "In explaining correctly, sacred abode, celestial abode, *brāhma* abode, *śaikṣa* abode, *arhat* abodes, and *tathāgata* abode are attainments which practitioners attains by non-attaining; destinations which are arrived upon by non-arriving, and realizations which are realized by non-actualizing. When *arhats* abide in peace and ease in the current life, this is called *ānāpānasmṛti*. This is speaking correctly. Why is that so? It is because *ānāpānasmṛti* is a sacred abode, celestial abode, *brāhma* abode…up to *arhats* abiding in joy in this life"

After the Buddha had said these words, the *bhikṣus* were delighted to hear the words of the Buddha and faithfully received this teaching and practice.

~ From Fascicle Number 807 in the *Connected Discourses*.

The general meaning of this *sutta* is that after having spent two months in meditation, the Buddha told his disciples, "If anyone asks you what method of meditation the Buddha used for the past two months, you should answer that the Buddha used *ānāpānasmṛti* meditation." The Buddha continued by explaining that he mindfully observed all of the processes of his inhalations and exhalations, including how he began in a state of coarse contemplation and arrived at the subtlest state of contemplation. This is how to abide in meditative concentration.

In the end, the Buddha concluded that *ānāpānasmṛti* consists of "sacred abode, celestial abode, and *brāhma* abode." This means that every practitioner including the Buddha should cultivate *ānāpānasmṛti,* which can enable us to reach sacred abode, heavenly abode, and *brāhma* abode, up to *arhatship* and attain ease and joy in the current life.

Chapter Ten
The Buddha's Special Methods in Education

The Buddha was born as a prince of the Kapilavatsu Kingdom in the northern region of ancient India. Upon seeing the suffering in the human world, he resolutely chose to renounce the home-life to seek the way to depart from suffering, attaining joy, and in the end, through meditative concentration, he realized the law of Dependent Origination.

All phenomena develop in accordance with the laws of causes, conditions, and effects. Our bodies and minds are also this way, they are causes and also effects. Through the *Agamas* in the earlier chapters, we have come to recognize our body and mind, understanding that "self" and "objects of self" come into being through the combination of causes and conditions. The world is in constant change; if we are able to understand "non-self," then we will remain unperturbed in facing external states.

I would like to emphasize again: the key to managing emotional states is "adjusting the mind." The reason why humans are susceptible to suffering is their minds are tainted by attachments to greed, anger, and ignorance. Only by clearly recognizing that "the true form of phenomena has no real substance," can we attain more ease and peace in spirit. It is said in the *Diamond Sūtra*, "all conditioned phenomena are like dreams, illusions, bubbles, and shadows, like dew and lightning. One should contemplate them in this way." It explains none of the phenomena in the world will remain unchanged; all phenomena are subject to Dependent Origination and empty in nature. It is because they are not self-becoming, self-arising, or self-existing. If we can truly understand this and always contemplate all conditioned phenomena are like dreams, illusions, bubbles, and shadows, then we will not be calculating nor becoming attached. We will not be happy when we are valued, nor becoming anxious and worried when we are not valued; in the end, we will be able to subdue the mind.

However, with regards to the truths of impermanence,

suffering, emptiness, and non-self, the Buddha faced doubts and questions from outsiders. We can see what transpired as follows.

A Vajrapāṇi with Glaring Eyes! Subduing Agnivesyāyana the Layperson

During the Buddha's time, a considerable number of believers of other paths came to him to request instructions in the Dharma. Some of them came to challenge, but they were all subdued by the Buddha. Among these, there was a layperson, Agnivesyāyana who was so impressed by the Buddha's unimpeded expounding of the Dharma that he was ready to throw himself at the feet of the Buddha in admiration. Since this *sutta* is quite long, I will explain in different sections so as to bring you all through the exciting drama of the debate between the Buddha and the believer of another path.

> Thus have I heard:
> One time the Buddha was residing at Monkey Pond in Vaiśālī.
>
> There was a Nirgranthas in Vaiśālī who was intelligent, wise, and well-versed in philosophy. He had an excellent understanding of treatises and took pride in his intelligence. He had amassed various treatises, understanding their wisdom and subtleties. He had taught the multitudes, and he had bested all the debate masters. He often thought to himself: "All of these *shamans* and *brāhmins* are no match for me; I could even debate with the Tathāgata. On hearing my name, these debate masters will sweat profusely from their foreheads, armpits, and pores. I debate like a strong wind which flattens grasses, breaks down trees, obliterates metal and stone, and subdues elephants and *nāgas*. No debater in this human world is my equal!

The "follower of Nirgranthas" refers to a follower of the Nirgrantha faith, and the Buddha often referred to him as Agnivesyāyana. The above passage is about how the follower of the Nirgranthas boasts that "no one can compare with him." It is evident that he had an attitude of profound arrogance.

> At that time, there was a *bhikṣu* named Aśvajit. In the morning, he donned his robes, took his alms bowl, walked with dignity and

> mindfulness as he entered the town to beg for food. Thereupon, Satyaka, follower of the Nirgranthas, was running some errands and happened to be in the village. As Bhikṣu Aśvajit was exiting the town gates, he was seen by Satyaka who immediately went to him and asked, "How does Śramaṇa Gautama teach the Dharma to his disciples? What Dharmas does he teach to his disciples to cultivate and practice?"

The follower of the Nirgranthas came before the Buddha's disciple, Aśvajit, and asked him, "Your master, Gautama, what specific methods of Dharma does he teach you? How does he have you practice?"

> Aśvajit replied, "Agnivesyāyana! When the World-Honored One instructs his disciples in Dharma and guides us in our cultivation and studies, he says, '*Bhikṣus!* In form you should observe non-self, and likewise in feeling, perception, mental formations, and consciousness you should also observe non-self. With the defilements of the five aggregates, you should be diligent and skillful in observing them as being like a disease, abscess, being stabbed, and being killed. They are impermanent, suffering, empty, and non-self.'"

Aśvajit answered, "Agnivesyāyana, the World-Honored One instructs us to cultivate and study in the following way. The Buddha says, '*Bhikṣus!* In form you should observe that there is not a substantial self, and likewise observe in feeling, perception, mental formations, and consciousness. You should often observe the five aggregates tainted by greed and desire as like suffering from a disease, abscess, being stabbed, and being killed. Form, feeling, perception, mental formations, and consciousness are all impermanent, suffering, empty, and non-self.'"

> Hearing these words, Satyaka, follower of the Nirgranthas, was displeased and remarked, "Aśvajit! You must have misheard him; Śramaṇa Gautama could not have spoken those words. If Śramaṇa Gautama spoke in that manner, then it is wrong view. I should go to him, critique him, and put an end to such teachings."

After hearing this, Satyaka, follower of the Nirgranthas, was really unhappy. He said to Aśvajit, "Surely you misheard him. I don't think your master taught you like that. This is wrong view! I should go debate him, and tell him not to speak like this anymore."

Thereupon, Satyaka, follower of the Nirgranthas, made his way to the village and then to the place where the Licchavis gathered. He spoke to all the Licchavis, who had gathered there, "Earlier today I saw the premier disciple of Śramaṇa Gautama named Aśvajit. We engaged in a brief debate; given what he told me, when I go to debate with Śramaṇa Gautama, everything will unfold however I wish.

Like when a worker goes into a grass field to weed, pulling from the base of the blades, he uproots them into the air and shakes the dirt from them. In the same manner, I will debate with Śramaṇa Gautama and critique him. I will take hold of the essential points, advancing my position and overturning his. It will all unfold just as I wish, and I will eradicate his heretical teachings.

Like how a peddler selling alcohol would firmly grip a filter-sack full of brew and squeeze out a strong, clear distillation while filtering out dredges and sediment. In the same manner, I will debate with Śramaṇa Gautama and critique him. I will take hold of the essential points. I will distill the clear truth and eradicate his heretical teachings.

It is like a master mat-weaver, carrying dirt with the mats, would first have to wash them with water to remove their stench and dirt before being able to sell them in the marketplace. In the same manner, I will debate with Śramaṇa Gautama and critique him. I will take hold of the essential points. I will hold fast to the doctrinal essentials, and eradicate his soiled teachings.

It is like how the king's master elephant trainer leading an intoxicated elephant into deep waters to wash its body, its four legs, ears, and trunk, washing it thoroughly on all sides in order to clean away all dirt and dust. In the same manner, I will go to Śramaṇa Gautama's place of residence. I will debate and critique him. I will take hold of the essential points. I will hold fast to the doctrinal essentials, and eradicate these his soiled teachings. You, Licchavis, should all come along and watch the gains and losses of the debate."

In these paragraphs above, the follower of the Nirgranthas went before a gathering of many from the Licchavi Clan and boasted with great pride as he revealed an exaggerated prediction about how he and Gautama would debate!

One of the Licchavis replied, "It would be impossible for Satyaka, follower of the Nirgranthas, to be able to debate with Śramaṇa Gautama!"

One person among the Licchavis stepped out of the group and remarked, "Satyaka, follower of the Nirgranthas, debating Śramaṇa Gautama is not even a possibility!"

> Another person countered, "Satyaka, follower of the Nirgranthas, is intelligent, wise, and advanced in his faculties. He will be able to debate with Śramaṇa Gautama."
>
> Five hundred Licchavis accompanied Satyaka, follower of the Nirgranthas, as he made his way to the Buddha's place of residence in order to debate with him. At that time, the World-Honored One was sitting below a tree in the forest and set to abide there for the day. Thereupon, many *bhikṣus* had exited their rooms to practice walking meditation. They saw Satyaka, follower of the Nirgranthas, who was gradually approaching them. Arriving, he asked the *bhikṣus,* "Where is Śramaṇa Gautama currently residing?"
>
> One of the *bhikṣus* answered, "He is in the great forest seated under a tree where he is set to abide for the day."

Yet another Licchavi Clansman spoke up, "Satyaka, follower of the Nirgranthas, is intelligent and wise. He is fit to debate with Śramaṇa Gautama." After that, five hundred Licchavis accompanied Satyaka, follower of the Nirgranthas, as he made his way to the Buddha's place of residence, and Satyaka asked the *bhikṣus,* "Where is Śramaṇa Gautama?" One *bhikṣu* answered, "The Buddha is under a tree practicing meditation at the moment."

> Satyaka, follower of the Nirgranthas, made his way to where the Buddha was and respectfully bowed before the Buddha with joined palms. Then he sat to one side. The Licchavi elders likewise came to the Buddha, they were respectful and bowed before the Buddha with joined palms, and then sat to one side.
>
> At that time, Satyaka, follower of the Nirgranthas, spoke to the Buddha, "I have heard that you, Gautama, teach the Dharma and instruct your disciples in the following manner: you teach your disciples that in form they should observe non-self, and likewise in feeling, perception, mental formations, and consciousness they should also observe non-self. They should skillfully observe the five aggregates as like suffering from a disease, abscess, being stabbed, and being killed; they are all impermanent, suffering, empty, and non-self Do you, Gautama, instruct in this manner or did the person who reported this do so to slander Gautama? Was it said this way,

or not said this way? Was it said in accordance with Dharma, or in the correct sequence of Dharma? If it was, then there would not be anyone intolerant of your views to come here, critique you, and lead you into a place of defeat, would there?"

When Satyaka, follower of the Nirgranthas, and five hundred Licchavis saw the Buddha, they first greeted one another. Afterwards, Satyaka, follower of the Nirgranthas, told the Buddha, "Your disciple, Aśvajit, has told me that you instruct your disciples to observe the five aggregates as empty, impermanent, characterized by suffering, and non-self. Did he slander your teachings by not relying on the Dharma you actually taught or their sequence? Should you be wary of provoking someone intolerant of these teachings to come debate you and leave you embarrassed?"

The Buddha replied to Satyaka, follower of the Nirgranthas, "That which you have heard is as I said it. It is the Dharma I spoke and follows the sequence of Dharma as I spoke it. It is neither slanderous nor would its critique lead me into a place of defeat. What is the reason for this? I truly spoke the Dharma to my disciples in that manner. I truly teach my disciples regularly in following the sequence of Dharma. They are led to observe that form is non-self, and likewise in feeling, perception, mental formations, and consciousness they should also observe non-self. They should observe the five aggregates as empty, impermanent, characterized by suffering, and non-self as being like a disease, abscess, being stabbed, and being killed as they are impermanent, suffering, empty, and non-self."

The Buddha said, "He spoke correctly, and this is what I taught them!"

Satyaka, son of the Nirgranthas told the Buddha, "Gautama, now I will speak on an analogy."

The Buddha answered Satyaka, follower of the Nirgranthas, "Know that now is the right time."

"It is like everything in the world relies upon the earth, as such, form is self, a person, from which wholesomeness or unwholesomeness arises. Feeling, perception, mental formations, and consciousness are likewise self, wholesomeness or unwholesomeness arises. In the same token: the human realm, *deva* realm, medicinal herbs, and trees all depend on the earth to grow. In the same manner, form depends on self, and feeling, perception, mental formations, and consciousness also depend on self."

The Buddha told Agnivesyāyana, "You have said that form depends on self, and feeling, perception, mental formations, and consciousness also depend on self?"

He answered, "It is indeed that way, Gautama. Form depends on self, and feeling, perception, mental formations, and consciousness also depend on self. Everyone in the assembly here would also say this."

The follower of the Nirgranthas used herbs, trees and how they depend on the earth to grow as analogy to show how people should depend on form, feelings, perception, mental formations, and consciousness in order to become a "self." He further said that all Licchavis also believed as such.

The Buddha told Agnivesyāyana, "You establish your own perspectives. What is the basis for getting other people in this?"

The Buddha asked further, "I would like you to discuss your own position of debate. Why are you bringing up positions held by others?"

Satyaka, follower of the Nirgranthas, replied to the Buddha, "Form truly is the self."

The follower of the Nirgranthas said, "People depend upon form, feeling, perception, mental formations, and consciousness in order to become a 'self.'"

The Buddha told Agnivesyāyana, "Now I will ask you a question, answer me as you will. If there is a king, and there are criminals in his kingdom. He could have them killed, placed in bondage, banished from the kingdom, caned, or their limbs severed. Conversely, if there are individuals who have performed meritorious deeds, the king could present them with gifts of elephants, horses, vehicles, a metropolis, and riches. Would he be able to do that?"

The Buddha asked him further, "Now I will ask you a question and you should answer however you wish. Can a king of a country order his subjects who have committed crimes to be arrested, flogged, or their limbs severed? For subjects who have acted meritoriously, can he bestow gifts of treasures to them?

He answered, "Yes, Gautama!"

Satyaka, follower of the Nirgranthas, answered, "Yes."

The Buddha told Agnivesyāyana, "Those who are masters, are they in control or not?"

Then the Buddha said, "So those who are masters and in control, they can do as they please with complete freedom?"

He, answered, "As such, Gautama!"

Agnivesyāyana replied, "Yes."

The Buddha told Agnivesyāyana, "You have said that form is self, and that feeling, perception, mental formations, and consciousness are likewise self. They thereby would follow the rule of the self. The self could make them be this way or that way. Is that correct?"

The Buddha then spoke to Agnivesyāyana, "You have said that material phenomena is self, and that feeling, mental phenomena, behavior, consciousness, and other such mental processes are self. Then tell me: can you freely make these things be as you wish or not be what you don't wish?"

At that time, Satyaka, follower of the Nirgranthas, just sat in silence.

The Buddha told Agnivesyāyana, "Hurry up and say it! Hurry up and say it! Why are you silent?"

The Buddha pressed him as such three times, yet Satyaka, follower of the Nirgranthas, remained silent.

Thereupon, the follower of the Nirgranthas was questioned to the point of being dumbstruck and speechless.

Thereupon, Vajrapāṇi appeared in the sky over the head of Satyaka, follower of the Nirgranthas, holding his flaring *vajra*-mallet and spoke, "The World-Honored One has asked you thrice. Why do you not answer? I will take this *vajra*-mallet and smash your head into seven pieces."

At that point, Vajrapāṇi raised his fiery, blazing *vajra*-mallet over Satyaka's head and bellowed, "The World-Honored One asked you a question. Why aren't you answering? If you still don't speak, I will smash your head into seven pieces with this *vajra*-mallet."

Due to the Buddha's supernatural powers, only Satyaka, follower of the Nirgranthas could see Vajrapāṇi and no one else in the assembly. Satyaka, follower of the Nirgranthas, became extremely frightened and answered the Buddha, "No, Gautama!"

The Buddha then told Satyaka, follower of the Nirgranthas, "Gradually contemplate this and then state your conclusion. At first you told everyone that form is self, and feeling, perception, mental formations, and consciousness are likewise self, yet now you say it is not so. What was said before and after are contradictory. You have always stated that form, feeling, perception, mental formations, and consciousness are the self. Agnivesyāyana, now I ask you: is form permanent or impermanent?"

He answered, "Impermanent, Gautama!"

He asked further, "What is impermanent, is it suffering?"

He answered, "Yes, it is suffering, Gautama!"

He asked further, "Given that form is impermanent, it is suffering and is subject to change, should noble disciples who have often heard the Dharma perceive within form a self, separate from self, or mutually existing with self?"

He answered, "No, Gautama!"

"Feeling, perception, mental formations, and consciousness are also that way." The Buddha told Agnivesyāyana, "Think this through before you speak."

He further asked Agnivesyāyana, "If in form one has yet to separate from greed, desire, longing, craving, and thirst, then when form changes or becomes different, will anxiety, sorrow, affliction, and suffering arise or not?"

He answered, "It will, Gautama!"

"Feeling, perception, mental formations, and consciousness are also that way." He asked further, "Agnivesyāyana, if in form one has separated from greed, desire, longing, craving, and thirst, then when form changes or becomes different, then anxiety, sorrow, affliction, and suffering will not arise, right?

He answered, "It is so, Gautama! It is true and not different."

"Feeling, perception, mental formations, and consciousness should also be spoken of this way. Agnivesyāyana! This is like a man whose body bears myriad forms of suffering, being constantly filled with suffering, and the endless suffering is unable to be shed. Would he delight in this?

He answered, "No, Gautama!"

"As such, Agnivesyāyana! The body bears myriad forms of suffering, being constantly filled with suffering, and the endless suffering are unable to be ridden off. There is no delight.

"Agnivesyāyana! It is like a man carrying an axe into to the mountains looking for solid timber. Upon seeing a tall, upright banana tree, he immediately chopped down the tree and cut off its leaves. He stripped away the leaves till there were none, but there is nothing solid within. Agnivesyāyana! You are also as such, establishing your own theory, but when I search for the true meaning within, there is no substance, just like the banana tree. Yet you dare speak amongst the multitude: 'I have yet to see anyone among the *śramaṇas*, *brāhmins* or even the perfectly enlightened Tathāgata, Arhat, the Perfectly Enlightened One himself with the knowledge and vision to debate me without falling into destruction.' You said further, 'I debate like a strong wind which flattens grasses, breaks down trees, obliterates metal and stone, and subdues elephants and *nāgas*. I am able to make my opponent sweat profusely from their foreheads, armpits, and pores.' Now, you have come up short in establishing your theory and yet you first bragged about how you would defeat others. You have now exhausted yourself in this undertaking and failed to make even a single hair of the Tathāgata stand on end."

Thereupon, the World-Honored One revealed his chest from within his *uttarâsaṅga* and declared, "Try to see for yourself, are you able to make even a single hair of the Tathāgata stand on end?"

At that time, Satyaka, follower of the Nirgranthas, silently hung his head in shame and turned pale.

In the previous passages, the Buddha mainly dismissed the arguments posited by the follower of the Nirgranthas by pointing out the internal contradictions. He further compared the theoretical arguments of the follower of the Nirgranthas as being akin to a hollow banana tree which looks impressively tall and upright on the outside, however, when the layers are peeled away, there is nothing to be found inside. Lastly, the Buddha chided the follower of the Nirgranthas saying, "You have told others that whoever debates you will end up profoundly embarrassed... Now you should take a look for yourself. Have you even managed to make a single hair of mine stand on edge?" This brought great shame to the follower of the Nirgranthas.

Thereupon, from within the crowd, one Licchavi named Durmukha stood up, straightened his clothes, joined his palms together, and spoke to the Buddha, "World-Honored One, please listen to me speaking an analogy."

The Buddha told Durmukha, "Now is the right time for it."

Durmukha told the Buddha, "World-Honored One! It is like someone taking a bushel sized container to collect two or three bushels of grain from a large grain silo. Now Satyaka, follower of the Nirgranthas is as such. World-Honored One! It is like a merchant who amassed immense riches but was suddenly found guilty of a crime. Thereby, all of his riches are then confiscated by the king. Satyaka, follower of the Nirgranthas, is also as such; all of his skills in debate have been dissolved by the Tathāgata.

It is like a large pond on the edge of a village or city where men, women, the elderly, and children all enter the water to play. They take a crab from the pond, cut off its legs, and then place it on land. Since it is without legs, it is unable to return to the pond. Satyaka, follower of the Nirgranthas, is also as such. His skills in debate have been cut off by the Tathāgata, and from now on, he will not dare to re-engage the Tathāgata in debate."

At this time, Satyaka, follower of the Nirgranthas, cursed the Licchavi Durmukha, "You rude beast! You make no effort to understand these truths, how is it that you prattle so? I am debating with Śramaṇa Gautama. Is this any of your business?"

After he finished scolding Durmukha, Satyaka, follower of the Nirgranthas, readdressed the Buddha, "Putting an end to ordinary and low-minded speech, I now wish to ask another question."

The Buddha told Satyaka, follower of the Nirgranthas, "Ask as you wish. I will answer in accord with your questions."

"How is it, Gautama, that you teach the Dharma to your disciples to lead them away from doubt?"

The Buddha replied to Agnivesyāyana, "For all my disciples, I instruct that all form which exists whether in the past, present, or future, whether internal or external, whether coarse or fine, whether

> attractive or ugly, whether far or near, all of these should be truthfully observed as non-self, separate from self, or mutually existing with self. Feeling, perception, mental formations, and consciousness are also this way. They study so that they should see the track to not be disrupted or corrupted, worthy to succeed, attain knowledge and views of renunciation, and guard the gates of nectar. Even those who may not gain thorough understanding, they still make progress towards *nirvāṇa*. This is the way I teach Dharma to my disciples to lead them away from doubt."

After the Buddha had destroyed the arguments made by the follower of the Nirgranthas, a Licchavi named Durmukha provided the Buddha with some analogies. He said that the follower of the Nirgranthas is now like a person with one small bowl who entered a large granary to obtain two or three small bowls of grain. He said that now the follower of the Nirgranthas is like a wealthy millionaire who commits a crime and then has all of his wealth confiscated by the king. All of the theories posited by the follower of the Nirgranthas have become points for the Tathāgata to refute his arguments.

He said it was like those who went to a pond on the outskirts of their village to play in the water. There, they fish out a crab, cut off its legs, and let it loose on land. The crab has no means to ever return to the water, and the follower of the Nirgranthas is also like that.

At that time, the follower of the Nirgranthas went from embarrassment to rage and retorted, "It's not like I'm talking to you. I'm debating with Śramaṇa Gautama. What does that have to do with you?" After he finished speaking, he turned to the Buddha and asked another question: "How do you teach your disciples to attain liberation?"

The Buddha answered, "For my disciples, I teach that all feelings, perceptions, and mental formations, whether near or far, can be observed to lack a self. These phenomena likewise lack any sort of unchanging and true existence. Although they are not able to immediately do all that I instruct, if they keep using these methods in cultivation, in the end, they will attain liberation!"

He further asked, "Gautama, how else do you instruct your disciples the Dharma so that they cease all outflows, without outflows, they attain liberation of the mind and the liberation of wisdom; there is self-realization and *nirvāṇa:* I have completed my final birth and established my pure practice; all there that is to be done is now done. I know I will no longer be subject to rebirth?"

The Buddha told Agnivesyāyana, "This is the Dharma: all forms whether in the past, present, or future, whether internal or external, whether coarse or fine, whether attractive or ugly, whether far or near, all of which are not a self, separate from self, or mutually existing with self. Feeling, perception, mental formations, and consciousness are also this way. They will attain three unsurpassed states: unsurpassed wisdom, unsurpassed liberation, and unsurpassed knowledge and view of liberation. Upon attaining these three unsurpassed states, they are respected, venerated, and offered to, like a buddha. The World-Honored One is enlightened to all the Dharma and used this Dharma to subdue disciples so they are at ease and calm, so they attain fearlessness, subdued and tranquil, ultimately attaining *nirvāṇa*. The World-Honored One speaks the Dharma to disciples for attaining *nirvāṇa*. Agnivesyāyana! Within this Dharma, my disciples have ceased all outflows, without outflows, they attain liberation of the mind and the liberation of wisdom; there is self-realization and *nirvāṇa*: I have completed my final birth and established my pure practice; all there that is to be done is now done. I know I will no longer be subject to rebirth.

Satyaka, follower of the Nirgrantha, told the Buddha, "Gautama! One may be able to escape from a strong brute recklessly wielding a sharp blade; it is far more difficult to escape from Gautama in debate. One may be able to escape from a venomous snake, a vast swamp or a raging fire; one may be able to escape from a drunk and fierce elephant or from a lion mad with hunger. Within the hands of Śramaṇa Gautama in debate, it is far more difficult to escape. Someone such as myself who is ordinary, an impulsive lowly man, and ill-equipped for debate should not come to Gautama.

Śramaṇa Gautama! Vaiśālī is a flourishing and joyful kingdom, home to Cāpāla stūpa, Saptāmraka stūpa, Bahuputraka stūpa, Guatama-nyagrodha stūpa, Sālavrata stūpa, Dhurānikṣepaṇa stūpa, and Makuṭabandhana stūpa. World-Honored One! There is peace and joy while you are in Vaiśālī. May the *devas*, *māras*, *brahmās*, *śramaṇas*, *brāhmins*, and all others in the world always venerate you, serve you, and make offering to you. This will lead to the *devas*, *māras*, *brahmās*, *śramaṇas*, *brāhmins*, and all others in the world gain peace and happiness at long last! I just wish that you stay here and accept my offerings of food to you and the multitude tomorrow morning."

Thereupon, the World-Honored One remained silent in his acceptance. Then Satyaka, follower of the Nirgranthas, knew that the Buddha, the World-Honored One's silence meant that he had accepted his invitation. Satyaka, follower of the Nirgranthas felt blissful joy and acceptance, stood up, and took his leave.

The follower of the Nirgranthas asked, "How do you teach your disciples to reach the fruit of *arhatship*?"

The Buddha answered, "It is the method that I described to you. My disciples cultivate in accordance to eliminate worries and suffering, attaining purity and liberation, and even the fruit of *arhatship*."

The follower of the Nirgranthas sighed and reproached himself saying, "Under a blade wielded by a maniac, one might be able to escape unharmed, but when debating Śramaṇa Gautama, there is no way to avoid the inevitable fate of losing." Grateful for the compassionate instructions he had received from the Buddha, the follower of the Nirgranthas vowed to make offerings to the Buddha and all the *bhikṣus*.

At that time, Satyaka, follower of the Nirgrantha, spoke to the Licchavis while they were on the way, "I have invited Śramaṇa Gautama and his multitude of disciples to receive offerings of food. You should all prepare a pot of food which you can deliver to my place."

The Licchavis all returned to their homes, and throughout the night they prepared their offerings. In the morning, they delivered those offerings to the residence of Satyaka, follower of the Nirgranthas. Early in the morning, Satyaka, follower of the Nirgranthas swept and cleaned his place, setting seats and preparing offerings of pure water. He sent a messenger to the Buddha to announce: "The time has come."

Thereupon, the World-Honored One and his assembly donned their robes, took their alms bowls, and made their way towards the residence of Satyaka, follower of the Nirgranthas, seating himself before the assembly. Satyaka, follower of the Nirgranthas, made offerings of pure food and drink with his own hands, satisfying the entire assembly. Upon finishing the meal, they washed their alms bowls. After Satyaka, follower of the Nirgranthas knew the Buddha had finished eating and washed his alms bowl, he carried a small seat in front of the Buddha. Thereupon, the World-Honored One recited a *gāthā* to Satyaka, follower of the Nirgranthas:

"Among the great gatherings, the offering of a fire sacrifice is the greatest;

Among the classical *Chandas*, the *Sāvitrī* is the greatest;

Among humans, kings are the grandest, for all rivers, the ocean is the greatest;

Among all stars, the moon is the grandest, among all that shine, the sun is greatest;

Among *devas* and humans in all ten directions, the supremely enlightened is the greatest!"

Thereupon, the World-Honored One spoke various forms of the Dharma to Satyaka, follower of the Nirgranthas. After he brought him joy by speaking the teachings, the World-Honored One returned to his own residence.

At that time, the *bhikṣus* were debating on their way back, "The five hundred Licchavis each prepared offerings of food and drink which they presented to Satyaka, follower of the Nirgranthas. What merits did these Licchavis gain through this? What merit has Satyaka gained through this?"

Thereupon, after the *bhikṣus* returned to their residence, they put away their robes and alms bowl and washed their feet. They then went to the World-Honored One, prostrated at his feet, sat to one side, and spoke to the Buddha, "World-Honored One, When we were on the way back, we were discussing, 'The five hundred Licchavis each prepared offerings of food and drink for Satyaka, follower of the Nirgranthas to make offerings to the World-Honored One and the assembly. What merit did these Licchavis gain from this? What merit did Satyaka gain from this?'

The Buddha answered the *bhikṣus,* "The Licchavis prepared food and drink for Satyaka, follower of the Nirgranthas, and in accordance with the causes and conditions of Satyaka, follower of the Nigranthas they receive their merits. While Satyaka, follower of the Nirgranthas, receives the merits of making offerings to the Buddha. The Licchavis made their offerings tainted by greed, anger, and ignorance, and they will receive karmic rewards accordingly. Satyaka, follower of the Nirgranthas made his offerings without greed, anger, or ignorance, and he will receive karmic rewards accordingly."

~ From Fascicle Number 110 in the *Connected Discourses.*

On the way home, the follower of the Nirgranthas advised the Licchavis around him that they should respond together in making offerings: "I invited Śramaṇa Gautama and his followers to come to my place for a meal. You should all go back, prepare some food, and then bring it to me!"

After the offerings, some *bhikṣus* asked the Buddha, "What merit was gained by the five hundred Licchavis who prepared that offering for the follower of the Nirgranthas? And what about the follower of the Nirgranthas' merit?"

The Buddha told the *bhikṣus*, "Those Licchavis made their offerings on behalf of the follower of the Nirgranthas, and thereby, the merits they receive will be based on the causes and conditions associated with the follower of the Nirgranthas. The follower of the Nirgranthas would gain the merits from making offerings to the Buddha. The karmic rewards gained by those Licchavis making offerings are still tainted with greed, anger, and ignorance. The follower of the Nirgranthas, on the other hand, the karmic rewards from his making offerings are free from greed, anger, and ignorance."

Patient Persuasion!
The Edification of Foolish Tiṣya

When the Buddha delivered sentient beings, due to the capacity and all the different causes and conditions of sentient beings; he manifested 84,000 skillful means in teaching, universally opening the great gates to receive, guide, and deliver.

Thus have I heard:
One time the Buddha was residing at Anāthapiṇḍada's Park in Jeta's Grove near Śrāvastī.

At that time, there was a *bhikṣu* named Tiṣya who was with a large group of *bhikṣus* in the dining hall. He told the other *bhikṣus*, "Honorable ones! I neither discern the Dharma nor enjoy cultivating pure practices. I enjoy sleeping more and have doubts regarding the Dharma."

Thereupon, one *bhikṣu* from within the group went to visit the Buddha. He prostrated before the Buddha's feet and stood to one side. He reported to the Buddha, "World-Honored One! Bhikṣu Tiṣya who was gathering with a large group of *bhikṣus* in the dining hall and spoke as follows: I neither discern the Dharma nor enjoy cultivating pure practices. I enjoy sleeping more and have doubts regarding the Dharma.'

The Buddha told that *bhikṣu,* "Bhikṣu Tiṣya is a foolish person, not guarding his gates of the senses and has no moderation in eating and drinking. In the first third and final third of night his mind is not awake, slack and lazy. He is not diligent and cannot contemplate or reflect well on the wholesome Dharma. As such, it is impossible for him to discern the Dharma, cultivating pure practices with joy in his mind, depart from sleepiness, or overcome doubts through the Dharma! If *bhikṣus* guard their gates of the senses, have moderation in eating and drinking, are awake during the first third and final third of night, not slack and lazy, mindful and diligent, contemplating and reflecting well on wholesome Dharma, they are able to discern the Dharma and cultivate pure practices with joy, departing from sleepiness and have no doubts about the Dharma. It should be as such"

The Buddha had a cousin named Tisya. One time, while eating, Tiṣya told other *bhikṣus,* "I do not discern the all the various Dharmas nor do I enjoy cultivating pure practices. I love to sleep and I have doubts and no understanding regarding Dharma." The *bhikṣus* reported this to the Buddha, and the Buddha replied, "Tiṣya is a foolish person who does not how to guard his gates of the senses. He has no moderation in eating and drinking, and he lazily slacks off during the first third of night (from 6:00-10:00 pm) and also during the final third of night (2:00-6:00 am). He is not diligent in cultivation nor contemplates well the teachings. It is impossible for him to have joy in cultivating pure practices, depart from sleepiness, and resolve doubts from the Dharma teachings!"

At that time, the World-Honored One told a *bhikṣu*, "You go to Bhikṣu Tiṣya and say, 'Your great master summons you!'"

The *bhikṣu* replied, "Yes, I will do as you have instructed." He bowed before the Buddha's feet and went to where Tiṣya was staying. He said, "Elder Tiṣya! The World-Honored One has summoned you!" Tiṣya heard this order and made his way to where the World-Honored One was. He prostrated before the Buddha's feet and stood to one side.

Thereupon, the World-Honored One spoke to Tiṣya: "You Tiṣya! Is it true that while eating with a large group of *bhikṣus*, you said: 'Elders! I am neither able to discern the Dharma nor do I enjoy cultivating pure practices. I get greater joy from sleeping and have doubts regarding the Dharma'?"

Tiṣya answered the Buddha, "It is true, World-Honored One!"

The Buddha asked Tiṣya, "Now I will ask you a question, answer me as you will. What do think? If in form, one does not free oneself from greed, desire, craving, longing, and thirst; then when that form changes or alters, what do you think? Would anxiety, sorrow, affliction, and suffering arise?"

Tiṣya answered, "It is indeed that way, World-Honored One! If in form, one does not free oneself from greed, desire, craving, longing, and thirst; then when that form changes or alters, then anxiety, sorrow, affliction, and suffering truly do arise. World-Honored One! It is truly so, and not otherwise."

The Buddha said to Tiṣya, "Excellent! Excellent! Tiṣya! This is just as one ought to explain the Dharma of separating oneself from greed and desire. Tiṣya, with regards to feeling, perception, mental formations, and consciousness, if one does not free oneself from greed, desire, craving, longing, and thirst; then when consciousness changes or alters, how will one's mind be? Would anxiety, sorrow, affliction, and suffering come to arise?"

Tiṣya answered the Buddha, "It is indeed that way, World-Honored One. With regards to consciousness, if one does not free oneself from greed, desire, craving, longing, and thirst, then when consciousness changes or alters, anxiety, sorrow, affliction, and suffering truly do arise. World-Honored One, it is exactly so and not otherwise."

The Buddha said to Tiṣya, "Excellent! Excellent! This is just as one ought to explain the Dharma on consciousness not separated from greed and desire."

The Buddha asked Tiṣya, "What do you think: if in form, one frees oneself from greed, desire, craving, longing, and thirst and then that form changes or alters; would anxiety, sorrow, affliction, and suffering come to arise?

Tiṣya answered, "No, World-Honored One!"

"It is so and not otherwise. What do you think? For feeling, perception, mental formations, and consciousness, if one is free from greed, desire, craving, longing, and thirst and if consciousness changes or alters; would anxiety, sorrow, affliction, and suffering arise?

Tiṣya answered, "No, World-Honored One! It is indeed this way and not otherwise."

However, the Buddha asked Tiṣya to come for discussion and guided him with patience, asking him, "If one is unable to give up the material phenomenon of form and the mental phenomena of feeling, perception, mental formation, and consciousness; once form, feeling, perception, mental formation, and consciousness change, would that give rise to worries, sorrow, and suffering?" Tiṣya replied truthfully, "Yes." The Buddha further asked him reversely: if one knows to give up the material phenomenon of form and the mental phenomena of feeling, perception, mental formation, and consciousness, once form, feeling, perception, mental formation, and consciousness change; would that give rise to worries, sorrow, and suffering? Tiṣya answered truthfully, "No."

The Buddha said to Tiṣya, "Excellent! Excellent! Tiṣya! Now I will speak an analogy; those of great wisdom use analogies in understanding.

It is like two people accompanying one another on a path. One of them knows the way well and the other does not. The one who does not know the way asks the knowledgeable person as such: 'I would like to go to such a city, such a village, and such a town. Please show me the way.' Thereupon, the knowledgeable person shows him the way by saying, 'My man! From this path, ahead there will be two separate paths. Abandon the left path and proceed along the right path. You will later encounter some steep precipices and canals, but you should still abandon the left path and proceed along the right path. Later still you will encounter a dense forest, but you should still abandon the left path and proceed along the right path. If you travel in this manner gradually proceeding, you will arrive at such and such a city.'

The Buddha told Tiṣya, "The analogy is such: the person not knowing the path is a metaphor for foolish, unenlightened beings. The knowledgeable person is a metaphor for the Tathāgata, Arhat, and the Perfectly Enlightened One. The two divergent paths are the doubts of sentient beings. The left path represents the three unwholesome states: greed, anger, and harmful cognition. The right path represents the three wholesome realizations: the realization for renunciation and abandoning desire, the realization for no anger, and the realization for no harming. Progressing on the left path is known as wrong view, wrong intention, wrong speech, wrong action, wrong livelihood, wrong skillful means, wrong mindfulness, and wrong meditative concentration. Progressing on the right path is known as right view, right intention, right speech, right action, right livelihood, right skillful means, right mindfulness, and right meditative concentration. The steep precipices and canals represent greed, anger, obstructions, anxiety, sorrow, and affliction. The dense forest represents the five sensual pleasures. The city represents *nirvāṇa*."

The Buddha told Tiṣya, "The Buddha is the great master. I have done all that I can do for the *śrāvakas*. Just as now, I have done all what should be done out of compassion and loving-kindness, by giving meaning of the teachings for their peace and happiness. Today, you all should do what should be done: you should go under a tree, a place in the open, or a cave amid the mountain cliffs and make a seat with grass. Contemplate well with right mindfulness and practice with no slacking. Don't allow your mind to have any regrets in the future. I am teaching this to you now."

After the Buddha had said these words, Tisya was delighted to hear the words of the Buddha and faithfully received this teaching and practice.

~ From Fascicle Number 271 in the *Connected Discourses*.

The Buddha provided an analogy to explain. There are two travelers on a path together, and one of them is familiar with the road situation. The traveler who is unfamiliar with the path asks the traveler with knowledge: "I'm trying to get to such a city, such a village, such a town. Could you show me how to get there?" The traveler who is familiar with the way replies, "Take this path, but after a short while, it will fork into two paths. Remember to stay on the right path. You will encounter steep crags and streams, but you should continue on the right. After a while, you will also encounter a dense forest, but you should still stay to the right. If you keep traveling forward this way, you will be able to reach the city."

The Buddha told Tiṣya, "The traveler unfamiliar with the path is a metaphor for ignorant, ordinary beings, and the one familiar with the path is comparable to an enlightened individual. The two paths that emerge are like doubts that sentient beings face. The left path is the three unwholesome dharmas of greed, anger, and ignorance, whereas the right path represents the three wholesome minds: abandoning greed, abandoning anger, and not harming others."

Traveling down the left path symbolizes wrong view (biased viewpoints), wrong intention (biased thinking), wrong speech (biased remarks), wrong action (improper behavior), wrong livelihood (improper professions), wrong skillful means (diligence towards an incorrect end), wrong mindfulness (biased and ill-intentioned beliefs), and wrong meditative concentration (biased and ill-intentioned meditative practices).

Traveling down the rightward path is known as right view (correct viewpoints), right intention (correct thinking), right speech (correct remarks), right action (proper behaviors), right livelihood (proper professions), right skillful means (diligence directed towards a correct end), right mindfulness (correct beliefs), and right meditative concentration (correct meditative practices). The steep crags and rivers are like greed, anger, obstructions, anxiety, sorrow, and affliction. The dense forest represents the five sensual pleasures of form, sound, scent, taste, and touch. The city symbolizes the tranquil state of *nirvāṇa.*

Lastly, the Buddha said, "As your teacher, I have done everything that should be done for my *śrāvaka* disciples, and have taught you the method to attain peace and happiness. I have told you everything. Today, you should go and do all that you should do. Go sit under a tree, out in an open space, or inside a mountain cave, making a seat with grass. Contemplate well with right mindfulness, cultivate with diligence and do not fall into laziness. As such, so you won't have any regrets in the future."

A Wanderer Stealing the Dharma! Susīma's Sincere Repentance

Thus have I heard:
One time the Buddha was residing in Elder Karaṇḍa's Garden in Rājagṛha.

The Buddha and all his disciples obtained great benefits when various kings, high-ranking ministers, *brāhmins*, village elders, householders, laity, and other people showed them respect and veneration with offerings of clothing, food, bedding, and medicines. None of them showed respect, veneration, or made offerings of clothing, food, bedding, and medicine to the mendicants of other faiths.

At that time, many shamans from other paths assembled in one place, and they discussed, "Prior to now, we had always been shown respect and veneration by various kings, high-ranking ministers, *brāhmins*, village elders, householders, laity, and all others who presented us with offerings of clothing, food, bedding, and medicine. Yet now, all of these have stopped, instead Śramaṇa Gautama and his *śrāvaka* disciples are shown respect and veneration through the presentation of offerings of clothing, food, bedding, and medicine. Now, who here in this assembly is wise and strong, and thereby able to covertly join Śramaṇa Gautama's community as a renunciant, listen to his Dharma, and then return to us to transmit those teachings? So we can reuse them on various kings, high-ranking ministers, *brāhmins*, village elders, householders, laity, and all others, thereby gaining their trust and then receiving offerings from them like before. "

At that time, someone said, "There is a youth named Susīma who is intelligent and learned in worldly wisdom. He would be able to covertly join Śramaṇa Gautama's community of renunciants, listen to his Dharma, and then return to us to transmit those teachings."

At that time, these shamans from other paths went to where Susīma was and said, "Today we assembled in a hall and discussed, 'Previously, we had always been shown respect and veneration by various kings, high-ranking ministers, *brāhmins*, village elders, householders, laity, and all others who made us offerings of clothing, food, bedding, and medicine. Yet now, all of these have stopped and the kings, high-ranking ministers, *brāhmins*, village elders, householders, laity, and all others only made offerings to Śramaṇa Gautama and his *śrāvaka* disciples.

Who here now in this assembly is intelligent and wise and able to covertly join Śramaṇa Gautama's community of renunciants? So as to listen to his Dharma, and then return to us to transmit those teachings for teaching the various kings, high-ranking ministers, brāhmins, village elders, householders, laity, and all others? We can then gain their respect, veneration, and offerings as before.' Someone among us said, 'There is a youth named Susīma who is intelligent and learned in worldly wisdom. He would be able to covertly join Śramaṇa Gautama's community, listen to his Dharma, and then return to us to transmit those teachings.' Therefore, that is the reason we have come to request your consideration, kind sir!"

At that time, a considerable number of shamans gathered and discussed the following together: "In the past, we were respected and venerated by kings, high-ranking ministers, *brāhmins,* village elders, householders, laity, and others who offered us clothing, food, bedding, and medicine, but now, all that is gone. They choose to only make offerings to Śramaṇa Gautama and his *śrāvaka* disciples by providing them with clothing, food, bedding, and medicine. Which one of us is clever, wise, and able to secretly work his way into Śramaṇa Gautama's community to become a monk? After hearing the Dharma, he could return to us, explain it, and then we could use it on the kings, high-ranking ministers, *brāhmins,* village elders, householders, laity, and others to become agreeable and accepting. Then things would be like before when they made offerings to us." Someone suggested that they send the young man, Susīma, to be their spy. Thereupon, a group of them went to visit Susīma, and after hearing their idea, he agreed to take on the task.

Then, Susīma silently accepted their request and made his way to Elder Karaṇḍa's Garden in Rājagṛha.

Thereupon, many *bhikṣus* had exited their living quarters to practice walking meditation. At that time, Susīma approached the group of *bhikṣus* and asked them, "Honorable ones! Would it be possible for me to become a renunciant of the right Dharma, receive precepts for full ordination, and cultivate pure practices?"

Thereupon, that group of *bhikṣus* brought Susīma to the World-Honored One's place. They prostrated before the Buddha's feet and then sat to one side and addressed the Buddha, "World-Honored One! Now this wandering mendicant, Susīma, expressed an aspiration to become a renunciant of the right Dharma, receive precepts for full ordination, and cultivate pure practices."

At that time, the World-Honored One knew what Susīma was thinking and told the *bhikṣus*, "You can ordain this mendicant Susīma to become a renunciant." Thereupon, the *bhikṣus* ordained Susīma.

When Susīma arrived at Elder Karaṇḍa's Garden in Rājagṛha, he saw that many *bhikṣus* were practicing walking meditation in the open. He expressed to them the reason he had come, and the *bhikṣus* took him to pay homage to the Buddha. Actually, the Buddha already understood what Susīma was plotting, but the Buddha did not expose him and still agreed that Susīma could renounce.

After half a month had passed since Susīma renounced, a *bhikṣu* spoke to Susīma, saying, "Susīma, you should know that: we have completed all births and deaths, and established our pure practice; all there that is to be done is now done. We know we will no longer be subject to rebirth."

At that time, Susīma asked the *bhikṣu*, "Honorable one! How is it that you learned to abandon desire and deviant and unwholesome states, achieved awareness and contemplation, departed from birth with joy, attained the first *dhyāna* and no longer give rise to any outflows and bring your mind to wholesomeness and liberation?"

The *bhikṣu* replied, "No, Susīma!"

He asked further, "How is it that you abandoned awareness and contemplation, purified within for single-mindedness, achieved no awareness or contemplation, given rise to joy through concentration, attained the second *dhyāna*, no longer giving rise to any outflows and brought your mind to wholesomeness and liberation?

The *bhikṣu* replied, "No, Susīma!"

He asked further, "How is it, honorable one, to have abandoned joy and equanimity, abided in right mindfulness and right wisdom, achieved joy in body and mind, given up such states as taught by sacred sages, attained the third *dhyāna*, no longer giving rise to any outflows and brought your mind to wholesomeness and liberation?

The *bhikṣu* replied, "No, Susīma!"

He asked further, "How is it, honorable one, to have abandoned suffering and extinguished joy, first severing sorrow and joy, and then abandoned states of neither suffering nor joy, purified within for single-mindedness, attained the forth *dhyāna*, no longer giving rise to any outflows and brought your mind unto wholesomeness and liberation?"

The *bhikṣu* replied, "No, Susīma!"

He asked further, "Is it that on cessation and liberation, you have realized abidance in transcending form and formlessness, no longer giving rise to any outflows and brought your mind unto wholesomeness and liberation?"

Replied, "No, Susīma!"

Susīma asked further, "Why, honorable one, your words lack consistency in that what was said that previously contradicts later statements? How is it that you have not achieved any states of *dhyāna* and yet said so?"

The *bhikṣu* replied, "I am of wisdom liberation."

He spoke as such and then the many *bhikṣus* each stood up and left.

After half a month since Susīma had become a renunciant, a *bhikṣu* came to Susīma and said, "You should know: we have all already abandoned the transmigration within the Three Realms. Our physical, verbal, and mental karma have all been completely purified and fulfilled, and all the worries that should be eliminated are eliminated. From now onward, we are no longer subject to any wholesome or unwholesome karmic effects."

Hence, Susīma asked the *bhikṣu* to instruct him how to enter into first *dhyāna*, second *dhyāna*, third *dhyāna*, and fourth *dhyāna*. However, the bhikṣu said that he could not even do it himself, and only responded by saying, "I am an *arhat* of wisdom liberation."

At that time, Susīma, knowing all the *bhikṣus* had left, thought to himself: What these honorable ones say lack consistency in that what they have said previously contradicts later statements. They say they lack the attainment, yet they said they know they already have realizations. Having thought as such, he went to visit the Buddha. He prostrated before the Buddha's feet, sat to one side, and then addressed the Buddha, "World-Honored One! A group of *bhikṣus* came before me and made the following declaration: 'We have completed all births and deaths, and established our pure practice; all there that is to be done is now done. We know we will no longer be subject to rebirth.' I asked those honorable ones, 'Have you learned to abandon desire and deviant and unwholesome states… and no longer giving rise to any outflows and bringing your mind to wholesomeness and liberation?' They answered me by saying, 'No, Susīma.' Then I asked, 'Your words lack consistency in that what was said previously contradicts later statements. How is it that you have not attained any states and yet you say you have realizations?' They answered me saying, 'We have wisdom liberation.' After finished saying this, they each stood up and left. Now, I ask you, World-Honored One, "Why their words lack consistency in that what was said previously contradicts later statements. How is it that they have not attained any states yet they said they have realization?"

The Buddha told Susīma, "First, they came to know the Dharma abode, and later, they came to know *nirvāṇa.* All these good men have been alone in a place of quietude, focused in their mindfulness, not slacking, having abandoned self-view, not giving rise to any outflows and bringing their minds unto wholesomeness and liberation."

Susīma addressed the Buddha, "Now, I do not know how 'First, they came to know the Dharma abode, and later, they came to know *nirvāṇa.* All these good men have been alone in a place of quietude, focused in their mindfulness, not slacking and abandoned self-view, not giving rise to any outflows and bringing their minds unto wholesomeness and liberation.'"

The Buddha told Susīma, "Regardless of your knowing or not knowing, it is still that they first came to know the Dharma abode, and later, they came to know *nirvāṇa.* All these good men have been alone in a place of quietude, focused in their mindfulness, not slacking, having abandoned self-view, not giving rise to any outflows and bringing their minds unto wholesomeness and liberation."

Susīma addressed the Buddha, "My only wish is that the World-Honored One speak the Dharma to me to enable me to know wisdom of the Dharma abode, and see wisdom of the Dharma abode."

Filled with doubt, Susīma went to ask the Buddha for an explanation. The Buddha responded to him saying, "That *bhikṣu* 'first, came to know the Dharma abode, and later, he came to know *nirvāṇa.*'" Susīma heard this, but was still puzzled. The Buddha then said, "It does not matter if you know or do not know the meaning of 'first, coming to know the Dharma abode, and later, coming to know *nirvāṇa,*' but you should at least know the sequential order of 'first, coming to know the Dharma abode, and later, coming to know *nirvāṇa.*'" At that point, Susīma asked the Buddha to explain how to gain the ability to "first, come to know the Dharma abode, and later, come to know *nirvāṇa.*"

The Buddha told Susīma, "Now I will ask you a question, answer me as you will. Susīma! What do you think? With birth, so there are aging and death; not abandoning birth, will there be aging and death?"

Susīma replied, "It is so, World-Honored One."

The Buddha continued, "With birth, there are aging and death; so not abandoning birth, there will be aging and death. As such, birth, becoming, clinging, craving, feeling, contact, six sense organs, name and form, consciousness, mental formations, and ignorance; with ignorance, there are mental formations; so not abandoning ignorance, will there be mental formations?"

Susīma addressed the Buddha, "It is so, World-Honored One! With ignorance, there are mental formations; not abandoning ignorance, so there will be mental formations."

The Buddha told Susīma, "With no birth, there will be no aging and death; so with birth ceased, aging and death would be ceased?"

Susīma addressed the Buddha, "It is so, World-Honored One! With no birth, there will be no aging and death; so with birth ceased, aging and death would be ceased."

"As such… even to no ignorance, there would be no mental formations; so if ignorance ceased, mental formations would be ceased?"

Susīma addressed the Buddha, "It is so, World-Honored One. With no ignorance, there would be no mental formations; so if ignorance ceased, mental formations would be ceased."

The Buddha told Susīma, "Those who have known as such and seen as such, abandon desire, unwholesome and wholesome states… up to having realizations and upheld them or not?"

Susīma answered the Buddha, "No, World-Honored One!"

The Buddha told Susīma, "This is known as first to know the Dharma abode and later know *nirvāṇa*. All these good men have been alone in a place of quietude, focused in their mindfulness, not slacking, having abandoned self-view, not giving rise to any outflows and bringing their minds unto wholesomeness and liberation."

Susīma asked the Buddha for an explanation on how to know the wisdom of the Dharma abode and how to see the wisdom of the Dharma abode. The Buddha explained with the Twelve Links of Dependent Origination to show that causes result in effects and without a given cause there will not be a corresponding effect. For example, because of "birth," there will be "aging and death;" because of "clinging," there will be "becoming;" and because of "ignorance," there will be "mental formations." Furthermore, he used the gates of *nirvāṇa* to explain to Susīma: "When this is absent, that does not come to be; when this ceases, that is extinct." If there was no "ignorance," there would be no mental formations and no consciousness; to if there was no birth, there would be no aging and death. Thereby, Susīma came to know the wisdom of Dharma abode and to see the wisdom of Dharma abode.

The Buddha used questions and answers to explain to Susīma the transmigration of life and *nirvāṇa* through the Twelve Links of Dependent Origination. Furthermore, he stressed that we must first build a correct view of Dependent Origination in the world. Then we are able to concentrate the mind, abandon self-view, not giving rise to defilements and arriving upon liberation.

> When the Buddha finished speaking this discourse, the Honorable Susīma abandoned dusts and defilement far behind, attaining the purity of the Dharma eye.
>
> At that time, Susīma saw the Dharma and attained the Dharma, and awakened to the Dharma as he overcame his doubts. It was not due to others that he believed, nor due to others that he was delivered, and it was from within the right Dharma that his mind attained fearlessness. He prostrated before the Buddha's feet and addressed the Buddha, "World-Honored One! I now repent! From within the right Dharma, I have acted as a thief by renouncing. Therefore, I repent for my transgression."
>
> The Buddha said to Susīma, "Why is it that from within the right Dharma, you acted as a thief by renouncing?"
>
> Susīma addressed the Buddha, "World-Honored One! A group of shamans came to where I was and told me: 'Susīma, you should know that: previously, we had always been shown respect and veneration by various kings, high-ranking ministers, *brāhmins*, village elders, householders, laity, and all others who presented us with offerings of clothing, food, bedding, and medicine. Yet now, that has ended and instead they make offerings to Śramaṇa Gautama and his *śrāvaka* disciples. Now you should go to Śramaṇa Gautama and his *śrāvaka* disciples to become a renunciant, attain the Dharma, return here to teach to us; then we will edify the people of the world, and they will show us respect and veneration and make offerings to us, just like before.' That is why, the World-Honored One, from within the right Dharma and *vinaya*, I have acted as a thief by renouncing. Today, I repent for that transgression. My only wish is

that the World-Honored One hear me repent for that transgression out of empathy for me."

The Buddha told Susīma, "I accept your repentance of that transgression. You should say: 'In the past, I was foolish, ignorant, unwholesome, unwise, and from within the right Dharma and *vinaya*, I acted as a thief by renouncing. Today I repent for this transgression, see my transgression, know my transgression, and in the future, I will accomplish in *vinaya* and liturgy, my merit and virtues will increase, and I will never digress.' Why is this? All who commit transgressions, see what they have done, know what they have done, and repent their transgression, in the future will come to accomplish in *vinaya* and liturgy, their merits virtues increase, and never digress."

The Buddha told Susīma, "Now I will speak an analogy. Those who are wise can understand through analogies. It is like a king who had patrolling officers and they have caught a thief, bound him, and brought him before the king. They reported to the king, "Great king! This person committed a robbery. We seek your punishment for him." The king said, "Take this criminal outside, bind his hands behind him, and proclaim his wickedness throughout the kingdom. Afterwards, bring him to the ground where criminals are punished outside the city, and throughout his body and four limbs, stab him with one hundred spears." The executioners received the orders instructed by the king, carried off the criminal, bound his hands behind his back, and proclaimed his wickedness throughout the town. Then he was taken to the ground where criminals are punished outside of the city, and all throughout his body and four limbs, he was stabbed with one hundred spears. At midday, the king asked, "Is the criminal still alive?" The minister replied, "Alive." The king re-issued the edict saying, "Stab him again with one hundred spears." That evening, he was stabbed again with one hundred spears yet still did not die."

The Buddha told Susīma, "As punishment, that king ordered the criminal to be stabbed by three hundred spears. Is there any part of his body as large as palm left intact?"

Susīma answered the Buddha, "No, he would not, World-Honored One!"

He further asked Susīma, "The criminal at that time, given the causes and conditions of being stabbed by three hundred spears, is that excruciating pain and suffering or not?"

Susīma answered the Buddha, "It is excruciating pain and suffering, World-Honored One! Even being stabbed by one spear causes unbearable pain. With three hundred spears, how could anyone endure?"

The Buddha told Susīma, "Even this would be more endurable than the fate of one acting as a thief and renouncing within the right Dharma and *vinaya*, stealing the Dharma, and teaching it to others; the pain and suffering of that would be many times worse."

When the Buddha spoke this Dharma, shaman Susīma ended all outflows and gained understanding. After the Buddha spoke this Dharma, the Honorable Susīma was delighted to hear the words of the Buddha and faithfully received this teaching and practice.

~ From Fascicle Number 347 in the *Connected Discourses.*

After Susīma heard the teachings of the Buddha, he immediately attained purity of the Dharma eye. Thereby, Susīma, who was suddenly enlightened, confessed before the Buddha. The Buddha accepted Susīma's repentance, and reminded him that if someone becomes a renunciant with a desire to steal the Dharma, then the pain and suffering will be many times greater than that of a thief who is punished by a king.

Wisdom of the Dharma Abode is Knowing Transmigration, Wisdom of Nirvāṇa is Knowing Cessation

This previous *sutta* explains how, shaman Susīma attempted to steal the Dharma, yet was able to succeed in gaining wisdom of the Dharma abode from the Buddha's teachings. Susīma further attained purity of the Dharma eye and left behind the dusts and defilements of the world. The sequence of the *sutta* is truly a treasure that all students of Buddhism, and especially monastics, should contemplate deeply. In addition, this *sutta* also mentions an important concept: "first wisdom of Dharma abode, later wisdom of *nirvāṇa*." I will explain separately as follows:

1. Wisdom of the Dharma Abode: All of sentient beings' living and dying rely on causes and conditions in order to arise. If there is craving, there will be clinging; and if there is clinging, then there

will be becoming; if there is becoming, then there will be birth, and with birth, there will be aging, sickness, and death.

The arising of craving is from incorrect thought (ignorance). Having this cause, there will be a corresponding result. If the past was a certain way, the present will be a certain way, and the future will be a certain way. There is no way for a cause and effect to be unrelated to one another. Without coffee beans, there could not be coffee grounds, and without coffee grounds, you could not have a cup of coffee, and so on and so forth. Everything, all matters and objects, must have certain causes that ripen into certain effects: When this arises, that comes up; when this is present, that comes to be. Having firm faith in causes resulting in related effects within Dependent Origination is the insight known as the wisdom of the Dharma abode. When equipped with wisdom of the Dharma abode, then we can realize the wisdom of *nirvāṇa.*

2. The Wisdom of *Nirvāṇa*: Relying upon wisdom of the Dharma abode, the right view of Dependent Origination, we contemplate consciousness, name and form, and body and mind rely on conditions to arise and likewise rely on conditions to be extinguished. It is always through reliance on conditions that phenomena arise, and in the end, they will be extinguished. By observing the exhaustion, decay, separation, and cessation of all phenomena, there is realization of *nirvāṇa.* This is the wisdom of *nirvāṇa.*

In other words, in seeking realization and enlightenment, we first need to cultivate the right view of wisdom of Dharma abode and then cultivate for realization of the wisdom of *nirvāṇa.* It is because we need to first attain the firm foundation of wisdom of Dharma abode, firmly understanding that all conditioned dharmas are impermanent, all dharmas are without self, when faced with setbacks, we can resolve them with the strength of our thoughts: "Oh, all conditioned dharmas are impermanent, so let it go! Oh, all dharmas are without self, there is not self-mastery, there is no substance; all are empty, what is there to bicker over?" When there is no enlightenment in daily living, it will be difficult to resolve in the face of setbacks. When we are awakened and understand the reality of the world, we can be carefree and at ease in the here and now. This called "contemplation in ease and peace."

On page 319 of Master Yin Shun's book, *The Path to Buddhahood*, there is a clear explanation regarding the order and importance of wisdom of the Dharma abode and the wisdom of *nirvāṇa*:

> *"Wisdom of the Dharma abode is knowing transmigration and knowing the inevitability of cause and effect. The wisdom of nirvāṇa is knowing cessation and knowing the empty nature of cause and effect. Through the wisdom of the Dharma abode, one comes to know arising and cessation. Through the wisdom of nirvāṇa, one comes to know that there is no arising and cessation. The wisdom of the Dharma abode is conditioned, mundane truth; the wisdom of nirvāṇa is unconditioned, ultimate Truth. Rely on the mundane truth of cause and effect of Dependent Origination for entering into the ultimate truth of arising and cessation of Dependent Origination. This is the correct observation of phenomena, an essential process on the path to liberation. It has to be so with absolutely no exception."*

Chapter Eleven
Less Worries, More Happiness

People have worries because of the six sense bases of their eyes, ears, nose, tongue, body, and mind that are often in pursuit of external states. These further give rise to possessive desires which are tainted and unrelinquishable attachments to greed, anger, and ignorance. As their emotions go through the ebb and flow of such, happiness, suffering, anxieties, and other comparable states follow.

Throughout the previous chapters, I kept stressing that as long as the six sense bases interact with the six sense objects and then differentiate through the six consciousnesses, then physical, verbal, and mental karma will arise endlessly. For the last chapter of this book, I will analyze our thinking and behaviors using the Twelve Links of Dependent Origination to explain the process by which the past life evolve into the current life and then further on to the future life. The goal of this is to enable everyone to appreciate: cultivation must start from upholding precepts, cultivating concentration, and contemplating wisdom. Only then will we be able to sever the transmigration in living and dying, and be able to truly abandon worries and attain true happiness.

Equation for Worries: The Twelve Links of Dependent Origination

Within the Twelve Links of Dependent Origination, ignorance and mental formations are the mistakes made in our previous life in thinking and behavior. The consciousness, name and form, six sense organs, contact, are the feelings of our current life. From feeling various behavior continuously arise, and hence, craving, clinging, and becoming are sustained in our current life; then in the future life, there will be birth, aging, and death.

In other words, ignorance and mental formations are causes planted in the previous life. Consciousness, name and form, six sense organs, contact, and feeling are effects coming to fruition in the current life. Craving, clinging, becoming are the causes created in our current life, and birth, and aging and death are effects that will come to fruition in the future life. Among these links, contact, feeling, craving, and clinging are those we should counter with cultivation. If we can counter them effectively, then we have the cool, dispassionate serenity to transform worries and to bravely face any challenges.

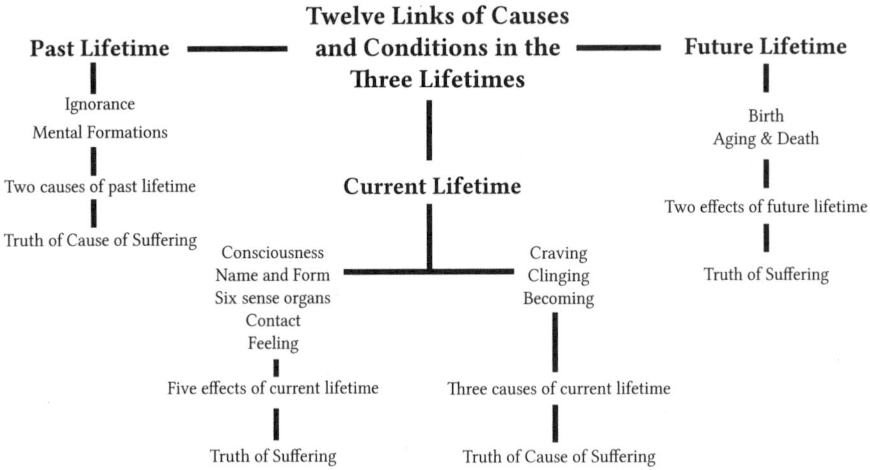

Contact

When the six sense organs encounter the six sense objects, contact takes place. This contact includes two types: agreeable contact (that contact that is in accord to what we wish) and disagreeable contact (contact that is not in accord to what we wish). Both these forms of contact are responses to ignorance, meaning our mind has latent thoughts of a self and attachment to the self. As long as the mind is thinking, "That's how I want it, that's what I think, and I believe it should be as such…;" then it is responding to self-attachment.

Feeling

Once contact has occurred, what is in accordance with our wishes are perceived as pleasant feelings; feelings of happiness. Coming across pleasant feelings, there will be tainted hopes to possess or occupy this given object, person, or environment. On the other hand, when feelings of suffering are met with, then there will be hopes to avoid, attack, destroy, or extinguish these matters. Overall, feelings will arise on contact; upon having feelings, ideas and impressions deepen. These will strengthen the power of thinking within the mind, then naturally will give rise to behaviors of the body and of that of speech.

Clinging and Craving

If intention is strengthened unceasingly, we will not forget these pleasant sensory conditions (favorable states) and keep thinking of them again and again, this stage is known as craving. This is mental karma; a very strong form of mental karma. Tainted attachments arise within the mind for these favorable states (people, matters, and objects), they have become stuck and unable to let go. Thinking all day, thinking when the mind is unoccupied, and thinking of this matter or this person when whatever should be done is completed. This state is called craving. Craving endlessly feeds the power of these thoughts, allowing these thoughts to give rise to intensely tainted attachments. These further give rise to physical karma and verbal karma behaviors; in the Consciousness-Only School, these are known as functions. This is called clinging.

Becoming

After acting upon clinging, a momentum for the next birth is left behind. According to the Twelve Links of Dependent Origination, this momentum is known as becoming. In karma principles, this is known as unmanifested karma. According to the Consciousness-Only School, these permeate into the *ālaya-vijñāna* to become habitual tendencies. In modern terms, we could call them memories. The various types of memory differ in strength and will direct us to our future rebirths, but they cannot escape the Desire Realm, Form Realm, or Formless Realm.

Within the Three Realms, craving, clinging, and becoming, belonging to the three states of existence: desire existence, form existence, and formless existence, the momentum which lead to birth into the Desire Realm, Form Realm, and Formless Realm. In other words, the karma we create are all within the Three Realms, including positive and negative behavioral karma as well as neutral karma. When we practice meditation and enter into concentration, it is called unmanifested karma because our body, speech, and mind do not give rise to thoughts or behavior within meditative concentration. This unmanifested karma allows future rebirth into the heavens, including heavens in the Desire Realm, Form Realm, or Formless Realm. Overall, it is still transmigrating within the realms of ordinary unenlightened beings.

Due to the way in which contact, feeling, craving, and clinging react with ignorance, none of them can transcend the cycle of transmigration within the Three Realms. So with craving, clinging, and becoming, birth, aging, and death will certainly follow. In future lives, we continue in the same way: consciousness, name and form, and the six sense organs give rise to contact and feeling, which then brings about craving and clinging. From craving and clinging, intensely strong manifested activities are again created, and at the same time, the force of unmanifested activities are instantly formed. This force of memory again will carry over into another rebirth, leading us to take up another form. People are like this from the past to the future; endlessly transmigrating in *saṃsāra*.

The Four Kinds of Clinging

The clinging in Buddhism is another name for worries, clinging has four kinds as follows:

1. Clinging to Desire

The five desires of form, sound, scent, taste, and touch are also often known as wealth, sex, fame, food, and sleep. The greed, tainted attachments, and pursuit of these desires are called, clinging to desire. Clinging to desire will give rise to a powerful momentum. For example, within the family, there are tainted attachments of love and emotions; among siblings, there is fighting over inheritance; and in society, there is the pursuit of fame and power etc.

2. Clinging to Wrong Views

Clinging to a given system of thought or viewpoint is called clinging to wrong views, including attachment to a philosophy or a view of life. For example, in Taiwanese politics, there is the Democratic Progressive Party and the Nationalist Party; in philosophy, there is monism, dualism, and pluralism, and these different political and philosophical systems of thought amass a great deal of power. Sometimes conflicts arising from different perspectives even bring about terrible consequences. For example, Christianity and Islam have been battling one another for centuries, and democratic nations and communist nations have likewise triggered global proximity wars over their conflicts. This is all due to clinging to different views.

3. Clinging to the Idea of a Self

With regards to a person's love of their own form, self-love; and love of sensory states, love for the people, matters, and objects to which they have a relationship, will give rise to strong tainted attachments so that we always remember and never forget the self. We are very protective of it, and firmly sustaining the existence of this self through many past lives into the current life. Once we die, it will certainly continue to be born again in another life. This is clinging to the idea of a self; what is called *pudgala* in the Consciousness-Only School, is the self that sentient beings are attached to. The intensely tainted attachment to the self is able to form a very powerful strength.

4. Clinging to Misunderstanding of Precepts

Some people believe that method A can bring about liberation from living and dying, whereas others believe method B can bring about liberation from living and dying... To most people, they may be considered pointless and a waste of time, but certain practitioners believe that their particular way is the one and only Dharma method to liberation. If a person's opinionated method of cultivation is wrong, it is called, clinging to misunderstandings regarding one's practice. Clinging to misunderstandings regarding one's practice can also form a powerful force that leads to be born into future lives.

In short, with regards to clinging, there are many types of grasping and pursuing. It can be divided into four categories: clinging to desires for the five desires; clinging to viewpoints in abstract thoughts and philosophies; clinging to an idea of self which affects transmigration in living and dying; and clinging to misunderstanding of precepts regarding the way of cultivation. Each category has a sufficiently powerful force that leads to being reborn again in another life.

All of these have been processed through our minds with the belief that for what is considered right we keep craving and loving it endlessly, including for what is mine as self-love and what we possess as the love for external states as well as our philosophical thoughts and viewpoints.

From craving we move to clinging. When clinging is manifested through our behaviors, we need to control it with upholding precepts. For example, whether our thoughts or methods of cultivation is correct or not, we still need to adopt the spirit of compassion, respect, and non-violation for others. It does not matter how we cultivate on our own, do not affect other people's lives. However, there are some doctrines or philosophy that naturally transgress on other people when actualized, and this point warrants our attention and caution.

Must Uphold Precepts and Cultivate Concentration to Eradicate Worries

Continuing on the topic of upholding the precepts, we should discuss the following two methods for abandoning worries.

Method 1: Uphold Precepts ~
Control of Language and Behavior

Craving and clinging are the links more likely to manifest in our behavior. They are comparatively coarse worries, and therefore, we must use the five precepts and the ten wholesome deeds to control ourselves.

Craving is the joyful feelings that we have already developed towards various people, matters, and objects. We feel they are very much in accordance with our intentions, and so craving is formed. Since they are in accordance with our intentions, they will always be thought about; upon thinking about them, the power of our thoughts increase so that our memories keep deepening. When our impressions keep deepening and the power of our thoughts keep strengthening, action will certainly be taken in the end.

If craving and clinging form mental activity, this is called mental karma; when they form physical activity, it is called physical karma; and when they form verbal activity, it is called speech karma or oral karma. These are the three karmas of body, speech, and mind. Once behaviors are formed, they become the past and belong to the links of ignorance and mental formations. If the mental formations formed in this lifetime can be felt by one another in the present, they are called manifested karma. If such karma is stored to become a memory and has to wait for a future lifetime to manifest as a function, it is unmanifested karma and comes after craving and clinging, as becoming.

Therefore, what is becoming in this current life is the ignorance and mental formations of previous lives. This craving and clinging need contact in order to come into being; it is only when there is contact, there will be feeling. The reason for us to uphold precepts is to prevent craving from giving rise to mental formations through our behavior and manifesting as behavior. Because behavior brews in the mind for a long period of time before it truly comes to fruition, we must be able to control it during the brewing process. To take that next step, we must cultivate meditative concentration.

Remember: the core spirit of upholding precepts is so that in our physical behaviors we refrain from killing, refrain from stealing, and refrain from sexual misconduct; in our speech we refrain from harsh speech, refrain from duplicitous speech, refrain from nonsensical speech, and refrain from lying. If we can uphold these principles, then no matter what philosophies or viewpoints we may have, we are able to avoid creating negative karma.

Method 2: Meditative Concentration ~ Control of Thoughts

Cultivating meditative concentration is actually for preventing subtle points and ending gradual attrition. When our six sense organs come into contact with the six sense objects, if at the point of contact, concentration is present then the mind can always maintain its clarity. We will be able to know with great certainty in the here and now whether this thought is pure, or is tainted.

Seeing with our eyes, we know what we can see and what we should not see. We know that we should not look at this anymore because if we keep looking, it will cause trouble. Listening with our ears to others talking; we may be better off not listening because on listening we may take things out of context. We might think others were speaking ill of us. So if we had not listened, there would be no problems; but having listened to a few random sentences and assumed others were slandering us behind our back, it will only lead to worries and suffering. So by not listening, then there would not be any problems, would there?

If we are able to maintain the clarity of our minds at the moment when the six sense organs come into contact with the six sense objects, then we will be able to control our impulses. This ability can only be cultivated with meditative concentration. When our craving and clinging have yet to develop, if we can subdue them with the strength of concentration in the contact and feeling stages, then they will not be able to develop into craving and clinging.

Perhaps some people might ask, "In cultivation, why must we practice meditative concentration?" Cultivating meditative concentration is cultivating our mind. Cultivate our mind so that when our mind comes into contact with various states, it will not be confused. Because once there is confusion, we will become tainted by external states and have greed and longing for these external states, then the mind cannot let go.

In the contemplation of breath-counting, we need to be realistically and honestly counting the breaths. The reason for us to have scattered and delusional thoughts is because we are caught up in either favorable states or detestable states and keep on differentiating endlessly in our imagination. Our impression of these deluded thoughts grows deeper and deeper and the mental force grows stronger and stronger. In the end, behaviors and activities manifest.

We need to look after our breaths realistically and honestly, following our habit whether in preference of inhaling or exhaling, as long as we keep it up without switching back and forth. Within a session, if it is counting inhalations from beginning to end, then keep counting inhalations; if it is counting exhalations, then keep counting exhalation.

If we are truly committed and focused on counting our breaths attentively, there will definitely not be any delusional thoughts. After practicing for a day or two, or if we are especially diligent, try sitting through multiple sessions throughout the day. Train the originally scattered thoughts to be no longer swirling ceaselessly and not arising anymore. After practicing for a long time, we will naturally be skillful. When the ability to concentrate deepens, due to the constant permeation and training of the mind on the point of focus, when other thoughts and other states arise, we will be able to detect them. At this point, we have reached the stage of cultivating the mind.

If we have reached this stage in cultivating the mind, concentration is attained and the mind is very clear in understanding. When faced with any arising states, we will immediately understand what we are thinking, and not be confused the way we were before. With regards to any given activity, whether it is getting dressed, walking, eating, or going to the bathroom, our mind will maintain their clarity at all moments and in all places.

Cultivating meditative concentration allows us to maintain our clarity when we come into contact with external states. It enables us to prevent the development of stray thoughts. This is why meditative concentration is used to counter the two stages of craving and clinging.

Ignorance is the Origin of Transmigration within Living and Dying

Due to beginningless habitual tendencies carried over from previous lives into the current life, we are being led involuntarily by such habitual tendencies. Sometimes, we realize that certain thoughts should not be sustained any longer; sometimes, we may also know that we should no longer be tainted with attachments. However, when our sensory organs respond to sense objects we are unwilling to let go. We should just let it go, but there is no way to let go; and we still like to look, like to listen, like to eat, and like to do. These habitual tendencies are deep-rooted and extremely difficult to control.

When thinking of people we detest, the more we think, the more we hate and the angrier we get. We know very well that continuing to think about them serves no purpose and will only harm our health. These are some of our aversive habitual tendencies. When we think instead of favorable states or people we like, our thoughts will likewise keep thinking of them and we cannot control ourselves. Consequently, when practicing meditative cultivation, sometimes we are defeated by our habitual tendencies and ignorance. In the end, we still erupt angrily perhaps by shouting abuse at others or acting in a rude manner.

We must further understand the key factor for such ignorance and habitual tendencies to cause trouble. That is our egos are too strong and our self-attachments are too powerful. In other words, eradicating ignorance is the first key in countering worries. Due to ignorance in the past, including mistakes in thinking and understanding, we keep believing that every matter in the world is real, and the self is also real, so giving rise to greed and craving or anger and hate.

Habitual Tendencies in the Current Life were Brought from Previous Lives

The wrongful behavior of our body, speech, and mind were created by ignorance and mental formations. Such powerful karmic energy can build lifeforms, and also bring about consciousness for the current life. This consciousness needs to depend on a material form: name and form, meaning spiritual and material form; so with the condition of consciousness, there is name and form. The conditional material substance of name and form must at the same time have this consciousness in order to continue existing. So consciousness and name and form come together for the lifeform of this current life. After that, in order to develop the future life, eyes, ears, nose, tongue, body, and mind, the six sense organs, came into existence. After the six sense organs have exited the womb, they come into contact with external states. Once contact occurs, feelings will also occur. However, their origins are all in ignorance.

What is called ignorance is the clinging of the ego; whatever the situation may be, we just think that everyone else is wrong. In this world, there are these kinds of people who are quite pitiful; their conduct has transgressed on others and they are unaware of it. They do not understand that such actions have transgressed on others, and that such language has transgressed on others because their habitual tendencies are just as such.

If the habitual tendencies in their previous lives were as such, then the habitual tendencies in this current life will be as such. In terms of education, the ignorance brought about by education inside the family is already quite serious; adding on the habitual tendencies sustained from previous lifetimes, these will become patterned behaviors that cannot be controlled. What we do and say, we consider they are a matter of course. So when we see people who have already transgressed on others and still believe that they are right and are unable to monitor themselves, these are called ignorance.

Think of Ways to Eradicate Contact, Feeling, Craving, and Clinging

Perhaps, people may consider "ignorance, mental formations, consciousness, name and form, six sense organs, contact, feeling, craving, clinging, becoming, birth, and aging and death," the Twelve Links of Dependent Origination, to be just Buddhist terminology that are learned for the sake of academic research. Maybe they misunderstand the concepts to be just a process: "Whatever the previous life was like, it will be as such in the current life; whatever we do in this lifetime, then it will be as such in a future life." But as a practitioner of the Dharma who truly seeks liberation from living and dying, then we need to understand our wrong behavior from within and to know what is needed to counter them.

The craving and clinging we have created in this current life should be countered with upholding precepts. With regards to craving and clinging, if we wish to prevent them from developing into actual behaviors, then we need to be clearly aware here and now of the subtle moments of contact and feelings. So we must cultivate concentration to counter contact and feeling; once contact and feeling are resolved, then craving and clinging will not arise.

With the condition of ignorance, there is mental formation; with the condition of mental formation, there is consciousness; with the condition of consciousness, there is name and form; with the condition of name and form, there is the six sense organs; with the conditions of the six sense organs, there is feeling; and with the condition of feeling, there is craving. This is the gate of transmigration. Inversely, when contact is ceased, then feeling ceases; when feeling is ceased, craving ceases; when craving is ceased, clinging ceases; when clinging is ceased, becoming ceases; when becoming is ceased, birth ceases; when birth is ceased, aging and death cease; when aging and death cease, then all the purely great suffering ceases. This is the gate of cessation.

Our ultimate goal in learning Buddhism is to enter into *nirvāṇa* and attain Buddhahood. *Nirvāṇa* is liberation; it is what the Buddha told us, "I vow to lead all sentient beings into *nirvāṇa* without remainder and to cessation." However, if contact, feeling, craving, and clinging are not ceased, then how can we achieve this goal? We should all work hard to cultivate concentration, then it would be easy to uphold precepts in the future. In addition to cultivating concentration well, we also need to be able to see through matters, and to be able to let go; this is when we need the gate of wisdom.

Understanding Causes, Conditions, and Effects, then it is Easy to Let Go

Each of us should have this perspective: the world is changing at every moment. Whether it is biological or technical, the external environment or inside our body and mind; all phenomena are changing all the time. Even though we may not be able to change the world, we can change our own body and mind. What affects the body and mind the most is emotions. Knowing how to think from another perspective can help improve our immunity. Just by being angry regardless, it will only allow our body to secrete toxins and we are just harming ourselves.

Understanding causes, conditions, and effects allows us to let go of grudges. After all, brooding about what has passed is useless. The past has already passed, and the future has yet to arrive. People suffer because they cannot let go just over a few words. Once we cannot let go, it is ourselves who suffer!

Glossary

Āgama. In *Sanskrit* and *Pāli,* "text" or "scripture"; a general term for received scriptural tradition.

ānāpānasmṛti. *Smṛti* or mindfulness of inhalations and the exhalations of breathing; *āna* being inhalation, *apāna* being exhalations.

arhat. An *arhat* is the highest of the four grades of a Buddhist "enlightened person."

arhatship. The enlightened state of an *arhat.*

Arrow Analogy Sutta. This *sutta* uses the arrow as an analogy to describe the process of the mind and its relationship to pain.

bhikṣuṇī. The female members of the Buddhist sangha who have renounced household life and received full ordination.

bhikṣus. The male members of the Buddhist sangha, who have renounced household life and received full ordination

Brahmā. An Indian god who was adopted into the pantheon of Buddhism as a protector of the teachings.

brāhmin. In ancient India, Brāhmins are the highest caste, usually the priests in temples and perform rituals, rites, prayers and other socio-religious ceremonies.

chanda. Zeal or the desire to act.

Connected Discourses. A division of the *Āgamas* that was collected between 200 and 400 CE.

dantien. Sometimes referred to as the energy center and is located just below the navel and often mentioned as a point of focus for meditative purposes.

deva. A type of non-human celestial being.

deva-putras. A more filial form of deva, as a son of.

dharma. A general term that refers to a myriad of phenomena.

dhyāna. Specific meditation practices where the mind is temporarily withdrawn from external sensory awareness and is in a state of internal awareness.

dvādaśâyatana. The twelve sense bases comprised of six sensory organs and six sense fields.

gāthā. "Odes" or "religious verse," usually recorded as the fourth of *Pāli* ninefold and Sanskrit twelvefold divisions of Buddhist literature.

kāṣāya. Dyed robes worn by ordained monks and nuns, patched together by discarded cloth and typically colored reddish brown, saffron or ochre.

Māra. The personification of evil who is the demon that tempted Prince Siddhartha (Buddha) with his daughters. Most times depicted as forces opposed to enlightenment.

Māra-pāpīyān. An evil king of the five desires with great skill in battle and detested the enlightenment of sentient beings.

nāgas. *Pāli,* "Serpent" or "dragon" ancient beings said to inhabit bodies of water and the roots of great trees, often guarding hidden treasures.

nirvāṇa. Regarded as the extinguishing of the "three poisons" or primary afflictions of greed, anger, and delusion.

oṃ maṇi padme hūṃ. A very well known six syllable mantra often interpreted as "Homage to the Jewel-Lotus One."

poṣadha. The semi-monthly recitation of precepts and vows for the purpose of purifying misdeeds and to renew commitments of principled conduct. The ceremonies are typically held on the new moon and full moon days.

Prajñā. Referring to wisdom in English. Prajna-wisdom is the highest form of wisdom. It is the wisdom of insight into the true nature of all phenomena.

pratimokṣa. Refers to a code of conduct within the Buddhist vinayas.

pratyekabuddhas. Refers to those who awaken to the Truth through their own efforts when they live in the time without a Buddha's presence.

śaikṣa. Refers to a novice or newly ordained nun or monk, and in certain contexts refers to a nun or monk just becoming a stream enterer.

samādhi. A foundational term referring to concentration and the practice of maintaining a one-pointedness of mind.

saṃsāra. In *Sankrit* and *Pāli* it literally means "wandering" the "cycles of rebirth." The wheel of samsara refers to the returning again and again to existences subject to birth and death.

satkāyadṛṣṭi. Known as, view of the body and view of the self, wrong views of having substantial existence. Fundamental view of all: 1) Due to all in the past lifetime, 2) Due to all in the future lifetime, 3) Due to all in the past and future lifetimes.

shamans. Ritual specialist that serve the folk beliefs of certain areas.

śramaṇa. In *Sanskrit*, generally refers to a mendicant, renunciant or recluse. In Buddhism, it is used to describe all monks including the Buddha.

śrāvaka. In *Sanskrit* it means "listener;" a direct disciple of the Buddha.

śṛgāla. Sanskrit word for jackal or cave dwelling canine.

Śūnyatā Samādhi. Emptiness or voidness and combined with *samādhi* refers to the one-pointed concentration of such.

Sūtra. Refers to the discourses of the Buddha or teachings.

Tathāgata. Thus-Come One. Along with Bhagavat is of the most common epithets associated with the Buddha.

upāsakas. A lay Buddhist male that takes the three refuges and the five precepts.

upāsikās. A lay Buddhist female that takes the three refuges and the five precepts.

uttarâsaṅga. An upper part of a robe.

vajra-mallet. Referring to an extremely forceful weapon that is similar to a scepter.

vīṇā. A lute that was commonly used in ancient India.

vinaya. Commonly understood as the code of discipline or basket of discipline that make up the second of the three baskets of the Buddhist Tripiṭaka.

About Buddha's Light Publications

Ever since he became a Buddhist monk, Venerable Master Hsing Yun has strongly believed that books and other documentation of the Buddha's teachings unite us spiritually, allowing us to reach a higher level of Buddhist practice, and continuously challenge our definition of our lives.

In 1996, the Fo Guang Shan International Translation Ceneter was established to fulfill this purpose. This marked the beginning of a string of publications translated into various languages from the Master's original writings in Chinese. In 2001, Buddha's Light Publishing was founded to further facilitate this progress. Presently, several translation centers have been set up worldwide. Centers located in Los Angeles, USA; Sydney, Australia; Berlin, Germany; Argentina; South Africa; and Japan coordinate to complete and distribute translation or publication projects across the globe. In 2015, the publishing house was reorganized as Buddha's Light Publications, USA Corp.; continuing the Fo Guang Shan International Translation Center mission of publishing translated Buddhist books and other valuable works. Buddha's Light Publications is committed to building bridges between East and West, Buddhist communities, and cultures. All proceeds from our book sales support Buddhist propogation efforts.

About the Author

Venerable Hsin Ting was born in Yunlin County. He was born into a family of farmers and grew up in the country. In 1968, he became a monastic under Master Hsing Yun and took full ordination the following year in Keelung. Hsin Ting graduated from the Eastern Buddhist College and the India Research Institute of the Chinese Cultural University. He further received an honorary doctorate degree from the Fo Guang Shan affiliated University of the West in Rosemead, California in 1998.

He is the current abbot of Tai Hua Temple in Bangkok, Thailand. In addition to leading meditation retreats around the world, Venerable Hsin Ting has spent his life as a monastic promoting humanitarian work and the popularization of Buddhist music and chanting.